George Sigerson

Bards of the Gael and Gall

Examples of the Poetic Literature of Erinn

George Sigerson

Bards of the Gael and Gall
Examples of the Poetic Literature of Erinn

ISBN/EAN: 9783337208769

Printed in Europe, USA, Canada, Australia, Japan

Cover: Foto ©Thomas Meinert / pixelio.de

More available books at **www.hansebooks.com**

BARDS

OF THE

GAEL AND GALL

EXAMPLES OF THE

POETIC LITERATURE OF ERINN

❧✺❧

DONE INTO ENGLISH AFTER THE METRES AND
MODES OF THE GAEL

BY

GEORGE SIGERSON, M.D., F.R.U.I.

PRESIDENT OF THE NATIONAL LITERARY SOCIETY OF IRELAND, CORRESPONDING
MEMBER OF LA SOCIÉTÉ D'ANTHROPOLOGIE, LA SOCIÉTÉ
CLINIQUE, AND LA SOCIÉTÉ DE PSYCHOLOGIE
PHYSIOLOGIQUE DE PARIS, ETC.

LONDON

T. FISHER UNWIN

PATERNOSTER SQUARE

1897

The portrait of O'Carolan, the minstrel-bard, is taken from a print engraved and published by John Martyn, Dublin, in 1822.

TO

SIR CHARLES GAVAN DUFFY,

PRESIDENT OF THE IRISH LITERARY SOCIETY OF LONDON,
A REPRESENTATIVE OF THE GAEL,

AND TO

DR. DOUGLAS HYDE,

PRESIDENT OF THE GAELIC LEAGUE OF DUBLIN,
A DESCENDANT OF THE GALL,

this book is dedicated

BY

ONE OF THE GALL-GAEL,

PRESIDENT OF THE NATIONAL LITERARY

SOCIETY OF IRELAND.

Eudoxus. But tell me (I pray you) have they any art in their compositions? or bee they anything wittie or well savoured, as poemes should be?

Irenæus. Yea truely, I have caused divers of them to be translated unto me, that I might understand them, and surely they savoured of sweet wit and good invention, . . . sprinkled with some pretty flowers of their naturall device, which gave good grace and comelinesse unto them.—EDMUND SPENSER, *A View of the State of Ireland,* 1596.

Will no one tell me what she sings
   Perhaps her plaintive numbers flow
For old, unhappy, far-off things,
   And battles long ago. —WORDSWORTH.

If thou, as I, but knew the tale
  It sings to all the Ancient Isle,
Thy tears would rise, and thou wouldst fail
  To mind thy God, a while.—OISIN *to a Critic.*

CONTENTS.

BARDS OF THE GAEL
AND GALL.

INTRODUCTION.

MAY not a buried literature have claims upon our attention? If it be of interest to delve and discover a statue or a city, long concealed, should it not be more attractive to come upon a kingdom, where long-forgotten peoples live, love, and act?

What a stir there would be, could some delver declare that he had, in his researches underground, discovered a lost literature of Gaul or of Germany, and in it the song, story, and music of nations speaking for themselves, whom now we know but by the description of alien foes. Such a treasure-trove is beyond hope. The Romans went over the regions they subjugated, like the sands of Sahara over meadows, destroying all that was of native growth. Of the Bards they preserved nothing but the name. From the Gauls they adopted articles of attire, their sculptors depicted the native warriors with torques and truis, but their men of letters saved nothing from the wreck of mental work. The term "barbarians" sufficed then as now to sway opinion. Let us, who are

B

of their descendants, call them instead the "Free Nations," and remember that, however simple their customs, they never committed deeds like those which deluged Rome with blood. Nor did they annihilate its literature.

It is impossible to suppose that these Free Nations had no lays or legends which could have been preserved, and it is equally impossible to believe that there was no diffusion of knowledge between the classic and the non-classic worlds. Their frontiers were not rigid and impassable. Six centuries before the Christian era, the Greeks founded a colony at what is now Marseilles, and were in contact with the Celts. A century later, Herodotus described their territory; later still, Aristotle told of their manners and customs, and Pytheas made his voyage to Britain. They often went over the borders in war. Five times in the fourth century B.C. the Gauls invaded Italy. They conquered Rome, and settled in Liguria, Istria, etc., founding Milan and other civic centres. Manlius got his name "Torquatus" because he captured a torque or collar of gold from "a proud invader." The unresting Celts marched into Greece in the third century; menaced Delphi, and made a settlement in Phrygian Galatia.[1] Then came the Roman outflow, when the *tumultus gallicus* was proclaimed, and Cisalpine Gaul conquered. The legions advanced against the transalpine Celts, and some fifty years before our era, Cæsar had formed the young Celtic chieftains

[1] The Galatians still spoke Celtic in St. Jerome's time.

into the Legion of the Lark, made them citizens of Rome, and admitted their magnates to the Senate.

Under such a policy there was hope that something of Celtic knowledge and culture might be saved, more especially as attention was given to the position and influence of the druids and bards. And now I come through a region of facts to a supposition which may seem bold, though it is simply that some of the bardic work was noted and preserved. We know with what interest Cæsar's fortunes in Gaul were followed by Cicero. Philosopher as well as orator, Cicero studied the religious rites of the Celtic druids. This he could do at first hand, for he was personally acquainted in Rome with the Chief Druid of the Aedui, Divitiacus, whom he esteemed. Now as Cicero the philosopher studied druid rites, is it not probable that Cicero the poet studied bardic methods? His opportunity was at hand, in the person of an intelligent expert;[1] and his inquiring mind was not likely to stop short when there was question of exploring a new system of verse-structure. Why should not he, anticipating Spenser, have caused divers Celtic poems to be translated for him? Lastly, I venture to suggest, temerarious though the suggestion be, that Cicero not only studied a specimen of Celtic verse, but imitated it. The evidence which I adduce in support of

[1] Cicero (after the forum) and young Cæsar studied under the Gaul Gnipho, a grammarian and rhetor (B.C. 88); they heard the great actor Roscius, a Gaul, and Cicero regretted that he had been too young to hear the Gaul L. Plotius, the earliest teacher of rhetoric in Rome.

this view may be found in those much-abused lines which pained Quintilian and scandalize Cicero's admirers :

> " Cedant arma togæ, concedat laurea linguæ,
> O fortunatam natam me consule Romam."

These verses, in the eyes of some critics, brand Cicero as a poetaster. But they should have remembered that a man of his genius, and a true poet, might compose such lines as an experiment in verse-structure. Let us suppose, for a moment, that they were written in imitation of Celtic verse, and that this verse was identical in form with an ancient Irish quatrain. Then we arrange the lines thus :

> " Cedant arma toga
> Concedat laurea linguæ :
> O fortunatam natam
> Me consule Romam."

Now, if we test this by the strict laws of an ancient Gaelic quatrain, it amazes one to find that the Latin lines fulfil certain requirements. (1.) It is composed of a leading and of a closing couplet (the sense, which may be complete in each couplet, must be complete in the quatrain). (2.) The end-words rime by their vowels ; the rime being monosyllabic in the first couplet, and dissyllabic in the second. [If we adopt the reading "laudi " instead of " linguæ," then the rime becomes dissyllabic in the first couplet also ; as " laudi " is in true asonance with " togæ."] (3.) Two words in some lines should begin by vowels, or by the same consonant. This alliteration is perfect in the second line, and is

secured in the third, by the repetition of the letter
" n." Its apparent (but permissible) absence in the first
and last lines makes the matter more curious still, be-
cause we get class-correspondence in its stead; for the
initials c and t in the first line, and m and r (rr), in the
last, obey the Gaelic law of correspondence.

Are these remarkable similarities of structure noth ng
but a chance coincidence? If so, my theory that Cicero
made an experiment in verse-structure on a Celtic
model vanishes,—leaving in its place, however, the
greater difficulty of explaining how so complex a coincid-
ence could occur, and how so skilled a word-workman,
and so eminent a poet, could prove so inexpert. His
lines have provoked ridicule; they would command
interest, perhaps admiration, if his purpose were as the
theory suggests it may have been. As in the fossiliferous
rock we find moulded the delicate form of a plant, whose
substance has long disappeared, we should then discover
the graces of a verse of vanished Gallic, petrified in a
lasting Latin mould.

Whatever hope, if any, there was of a development
amongst the Romans of an intellectual interest in Celtic
life and literature was extinguished by the policy of
Augustus; Rome, dominating men and minds, latinized
Gaul, advanced her eagles into Britain, and confronted
the Celts in their last strongholds. Ireland, then in her
heroic age, fomented, fostered, and kept up immortal
hostility against the common foe; and, in alliance with
the Caledonians and independent Britons, shook the

invader's power. Claudian, in his praise of Stilicho, declares the fact. Possibly Roman persistence and discipline would have at last prevailed, had not the outburst of the turbulent Teuton tribes saved the Celts!

It was fortunate, indeed, that one island on the western verge of Europe escaped the Roman eagles. Agricola, while in Britain, often thought of crossing the Irish Sea with his forces, so that Rome might dominate all, and liberty be put quite out of sight. Had he gone, Ireland also would have seen her mental independence and all its fruits submerged. As it is, we have, in her ancient literature, the noblest monument which witnesses to the intellect of the Ultra-Roman world. Ireland is thus in letters, as once in arms, the champion of the Free Nations.

Hence, the interest which attaches to the literature of Ireland is manifold. It does not only reveal the inner natures of the inhabitants of the island at different epochs, before the coming of the Christian faith, during its progress, and since, but it also enables us to gain some glimpse into the homes of other nations—Teutons as well as Celts—whose lamps were extinguished.

Unhappily for history, that literature was long buried in neglect. Then, for a time, it lay locked in an archaic language, like some splendid missal, claspt in covers of wrought silver which could not be opened. For years, however, the keen and capable minds of scholars, in Germany, France, Italy, and Ireland, have been at work, and have rendered into the modern languages the con-

tents of many most ancient and interesting documents.
Now, at last, these are accessible—though sometimes not
readily, for they must often be sought for in the pages of
foreign periodicals.

One department of Irish literature possesses special
and singular interest. This is the section of poetry.

The creation of a system of verse-structure, absolutely
independent of that of Greece and Rome, was an
achievement which must command increasing attention
as it becomes more known. It is indeed difficult to
become familiar with it, so elaborate did that system
become. The introduction and use of rime as an art-
method constitute an epoch in the history of European
literature. The importance of the innovation becomes
greater the more we consider the mastery exhibited, and
the very subtle and refined modes invented for producing
desired effects. It is impossible here to do more than to
make allusion to this subject, for it would require a
treatise to deal with it in an adequate manner.

We know the ingenuity that the ancient Irish dis-
played in their ornaments of gold and silver, which
command the admiration of all workers in the precious
metals, as well as of all artists. Those who have seen
the illuminated initials of the " Book of Kells," know the
wonderful grace of form shown in the interwoven lines,
and the exquisite taste displayed in the tints which still
freshly adorn them. A similar ingenuity, grace, artistic
power, delicacy, and taste, were employed in the service
of poetry.

No translator can hope to reproduce, in English, the finer traits of this art, because these demand a language of open vowels, and other aids. This fact must be remembered, for it gave the advantage of subtle and elusive rime, without tiring the ear. But though such refined graces must be sought for in the originals, something may be done to represent the form, style, and methods of the bards, whilst keeping faithful to the spirit and substance of their lays.

With this view the accompanying collection has been made. It does not, of course, represent all diversities of verse-forms, but it does reproduce some which will be novel. Those who are wont to associate Irish poetry with effusiveness of thought and luxuriance of language will be surprised to find that bardic poetry was characterized by classic reserve in thought, form, and expression. This, perhaps, is not the least message of the ancient bards to their successors.

The poems have been placed in chronological order so far as may be. This is done tentatively in the case of the earlier lays, for their date is uncertain, though ancient.

I. The series begins by the strange incantation attributed to Amergin, the poet-druid of those southern invaders of Ireland known as Milesians. In structure the verse is peculiar, the most striking feature being the riming of the last word of each line with the first word of the succeeding line. This rime is often complete: sometimes only the vowels rime. There is alliteration, also; two words

in each line begin either by vowels or by the same con-
sonants. Conaclon is the name given to this form of
verse, which has been occasionally imitated in later days.
Usually, however, later bards chose rather to make the
last word of the stanza rime with the first of a succeeding
stanza. It was very usual to unite the first and last word
of an entire poem by a link of rime.

Conaclon rime, such as Amergin's, would necessarily
be rare in literature. In modern times we have the poem
of Marc de Papillon, Sieur de Lasphrise (A.D. 1597),
who vaunts it as his own invention. He wrote:

> "Fallait-il que le ciel me rendit amoureux
> Amoureux, jouissant d'une beauté craintive,
> Craintive à recevoir la douceur excessive
> Excessive," etc.

In this case, indeed, the rime is obtained by repeating
the word in a somewhat different sense; but, curiously
enough, in this he caught the method sometimes used by
Amergin. Samuel Lover, in his "Fairy Child," makes
interrupted use of this iteration. In mediæval Latin
verse, which must have been largely manipulated by
Irish monks, we find some forms which recall conaclon.
Thus, in *versus immediati*, the last syllables of one line
rime with the first of the next:

> "Si fugias obsc*oenas*   po*enas* ternas barat*orum*
> Qu*orum* press*urae*   d*urae* fuerunt mihi curae."

If we divide the verses, as indicated, the resemblance
becomes still greater.

The "Triumph Song of Amergin" is remarkable in that,

for the most part, it appears not only to dispense with rime, but to reject it. This is the "Rosg," which consists of short impetuous sentences, rhythmical though unrimed, designed to express or to stir up vehement enthusiasm. It was not seldom used, in the elder epoch, in framing war-odes.

This is, in fact, the earliest example of blank verse— which is supposed to be a modern invention. It is exceedingly remarkable that blank verse should have been invented by a people to whom the introduction of rime is peculiarly due.

Still, though the short lines end as blank verse ends, there is, I believe, rime of a kind here intended by the bard, though it has escaped notice. The first words of the short verses are identical: in the translation "I," in the original "Am" (I am). This constitutes what I would call "Entrance-rime" to distinguish it from "End-rime." That it is intended to impress the ear I infer from the fact that where it is absent, in the longer lines, alliterative-rime is often introduced. This entrance-rime has been used by moderns without special rime-intention, as a rhetoric mode. Thus, in Sabine's apostrophe to her native town :

> "Albe, où j'ai commencé de respirer le jour,
> Albe, mon cher pays et mon premier amour," etc.

Again, in Camille's striking invective :

> "Rome, unique objet de mon ressentiment,
> Rome, à qui vient ton bras d'immoler mon amant,

Rome, qui t'a vu naître et que ton cœur adore,
Rome, enfin que je hais parcequ'elle t'honore."—

The first Elegy ascribed to the nephew of Miled (or Milesius), archaic in form, possesses alliteration and rime, both asonant and consonant, in an elaborated manner.

II. We come next, over a wide time-chasm, to the Cuchulainn[1] Period. From intrinsic evidence its literature must be relegated to the pre-Christian ages; its spirit is as pagan as that of the Iliad, and pervades it so entirely that no scribe thought of altering it, save, perhaps, by the addition of a Christian tag. It is, indeed, one of the highest honours of Irish monasticism that, though ascetic and zealous in the extreme, it had a liberal large-minded respect for the literature of the ancients, and preserved it.

The Cuchulainn Age is represented here by poems taken from some memorable historic tales or romances. The first is "The Sick-bed of Cuchulainn and the only Jealousy of Emer." Here the hero is shown in commerce and communion with the spirit world. The second is the famous "Táin Bo Cuailgné," or "Cattle-Spoil of Cuailgné," where untoward Fate (in the person of Queen Mave) compels him, as Champion of Ulster, to fight and slay his friend Ferdiad. With this is given, from the Battle of Ros-na-ree, a dialogue-poem between Queen Mave and her Envoys. Lastly come three lays from "The Fate of the Children of Usnach," in order to show the metric form of the originals.

[1] Pr. Cuhulainn.

The perfection and diversity of the verse-forms, in this period, come on us with sudden surprise, as if the Gaelic muse had sprung into new being, fully equipped; but this seems due to the fact that an intermediate developmental period has irrevocably disappeared. Fand's "Welcome to Cuchulainn" supplies examples of alliteration and of end-rimes:

> " Stately stands the charioteer
> Beardless, young, who hasteth here ;
> Splendid o'er the plain he speeds
> His careering chariot-steeds."

Lest it should grow monotonous, double rimes are introduced, though sparingly:

> " At sight of those steeds, fleeing,
> I stand there, silent, seeing :
> Never hoofs like these shall ring
> Rapid as the winds of Spring."

The concluding stanza presents another change, displaying internal or inlaid rime:

> " Blood drips from his lofty lance.
> In his glance gleams battle fire ;
> Haughty, high, the victor goes,
> Woe to those who wake his ire."

Then follows Liban's irregular "Rosg," which, in its burthen, or short wheel followed by a longer burthen, anticipates forms which made no appearance in English until the thirteenth or fourteenth century.

There is also onomatopeia in the Gaelic lines, describing how Cuchulainn's wheels are more resonant than the entire chariot of another.

The "internal rime," shown in the last verse, was introduced afterwards into Norse by the Irish-Icelandic poets. It is the progenitor, also, of the so-called "inverse rime" in English ; this becomes clear if we make a couplet of the line in which it appears :

> " Gave him great *aid*
> And *made* him more inclined."—Spenser, " Faërie Queene."

Again :

> " She must lie *here*
> On *mere* necessity."—Shakespeare, " Love's Labour's Lost."

Fand's " Farewell to Cuchulainn," coming from one who rejoiced to see him red with the blood of battle, surprises one by its great tenderness and refinement, as well as by its nobility of thought.

It is the first Love-Song of Erinn, and touches chords that will vibrate in the human heart till mankind is no more. Deirdré's plaints are more objective, Fand's more subjective ; her grief is implied and suggested more than directly expressed.

Cuchulainn's lament for the friend who had proved false to their friendship is a noticeable poem in a noble episode. Each stanza begins with the same two lines, so that the burthen (of late date in English) was invented and used very early by the Irish bards. Cuchulainn declared his combats with previous champions had been play and pleasure to him until Ferdiad came. The poem ends thus :

> "*Play was each, pleasure each,*
> *Till Ferdiad faced the beach ;*
> Loved Ferdiad, dear to *me*
> I shall *dree* his death for aye ;
> Yesterday, a Mountain he,
> But a Shade to-day."

The iteration and return displayed in this poem came into other literatures at a late period. In some respects it appears to anticipate the "broken stave" of Marot, and of English poets of the sixteenth century.

To another form of verse-structure, found, not in one but in several of the poems which intersperse the "Táin Bo," a special interest belongs. A specimen is given in "The Queen's Envoys," taken from the "Battle of Ros-na-ree." It consists of two or of three lines ending in dissyllabic rimes, followed by a shorter line with single rime.[1] In the first case, it anticipates the structure of Moore's "Go where Glory waits thee," in the second of the "Groves of Blarney" and "The Bells of Shandon." The latter is the more usual form, and is found in the following :

> "Here, if come King Connor
> Back shall turn his banner
> Low shall lie his honour,
> Vanquished shall he be."

Guest, observing on the difficulty of ascertaining the origin of English metres belonging to triple measure, says he has seen none of earlier date than the fifteenth century. He gives some verses which Gawin Douglas mentioned as popular amongst the people in 1512.

---

[1] These forms were imitated in mediæval hymns, *e.g.*, by Adam of St. Victor, a "Briton."

These I quote in order to show that they are identical in rime-arrangement with the ancient Irish verses ; and (what should set the origin of their structure beyond all cavil) they also present alliteration, according to the strict rule of the Gaelic bards. This, which escaped Guest's notice, I have marked :

> " Hay, now the day dawis
> The jollie cock crawis,
> Now shroud is the shauis
>   Throw nature anone ;
> The thrissel cok cryis
> On lovers wha lyis,
> Now skail is the skyis,
>   The night is neir gone."

This must have been framed on a Gaelic model, as every peculiarity is reproduced. It is even more exact in observing the rule of alliteration than some Gaelic verses. Anyone can verify this identity of structure by glancing at the following verses from a dialogue poem in the " Táin : "

> " Ni ragsa gan rata
> Do cluci na h-ata
> Meraid colla m-brata
>   Go m-brut is co m-brig.
> Noco geb ge esti
> Ge ra bet dom resci [1]
> Gan grein ocas esci [1]
>   La muir ocas tir."

The Irish presents consonant as well as asonant rime in this very ancient poem.

King James V. of Scotland, a critic of poetry, gave the

---

[1] C (hard) corresponds in class with t. I have omitted dots over certain letters.

name of "cuttit or broken" to all staves containing lines
of unequal length. Guest, who quotes this, says the
"broken stave," as he defines it, made its appearance in
English about the middle of the sixteenth century, having
been borrowed from the continent. Frenchmen, Italians,
and Spaniards, in this century, varied the monotony of
their chansons and ballades by shortening certain lines.
The finished culture of the ancient Irish is shown by
their invention of this, as well as of other metres, a
thousand years previously.

Some examples are before the reader. Another will be
found in Deirdré's touching "Farewell to Alba," and
several others follow. The old historic romance of which
she is the heroine contains a number of lays, and these
differ in structure. Besides the specimens given in this
volume, we have her "Lament for the Sons of Usnach,"
the spirit of which has been so admirably transfused in
Sir Samuel Ferguson's version. The original, however,
is peculiarly elaborate. Each line ends with a double
rime. The double end-rime of the first line chimes with
an internal double-rime within the second : the same
system holds good for the third and fourth lines. Then
the double end-rime of the second line is answered by
the double end-rime of the fourth.

This will be more readily understood by an example in
verse :

> " Long is my day of sorrow—
> A morrow brings them never :
> Comrades of golden glory
> Whose story lives for ever."

It would be impossible to give a metrical version exactly faithful to the poet's metre, sense, and rime-system. But, later on, the reader will find an exact translation of Cailté's "Isle of Arann," in alternate double rime; and here, another Lament for the Sons of Usnach, which Deirdré is supposed to sing, "Wail for the Warriors." It is specially remarkable, since, with alliteration, single and double rimes, and the broken stave, it presents an example of those sudden transitions from one measure to another, to suit the sense, which were especially effective and dramatic. This variation was a favourite with the ancient Irish, though it came but lately into the literature of other European nations.

III. Following the epoch of Cuchulainn comes the epoch of Fionn,[1] which is usually known as the Ossianic Period. For convenience I subdivide the latter into (a) the period of Fionn, when the Leader yet lived and the Great Companionship of the Fianna stood together, and (b) the Ossianic period, or the Age of Lamentation, when Ossian[2] sings their departed glory.

It is believed that the Fianna, a disciplined standing army, was organized in imitation and in defiance of the Roman legions. Considering with what valour and success the ancient Irish fought the latter in Caledonia and Britain, we must credit them with skill in arms. The references to battles with the Romans which appear in the Ossianic lays represent a core of old tradition or old verse, for unfortunately the lays have been often

---

[1] Find or Finn is the archaic form. [2] Oisin is the correct form.

retouched by later bards.   This they did for the dramatic
purpose of setting Paganism and Christianity face to face,
confronting them in the persons of Ossian and Patrick.
With this view, they interpolated passages.   Yet, if the
names were omitted, the idea would not depart far from
historic truth, for some knowledge of the new Faith had
certainly reached the restless Gael, from Britain and
Gaul, before the days of Patrick or of Palladius.   And
some of the poems, judged by their archaic tone of
thought, loftier atmosphere, and classic reserve, appear to
have remained untouched.

The poetic era of Fionn opens by a strange little lay,
given in a prose narrative of undoubted antiquity, entitled
" The Boyish Exploits of Finn, Son of Cumal."   The
verses are cited as the first lay of the Chief, whilst yet a
youth, and they are consistently simple in structure, with
occasional alliteration and rime.   In their subject, as in
its treatment, they remind one of the early English verses
(A.D. 1250-1260) on the approach of summer.   To the
student of literature, and not less to students of history
and of biology, it must be interesting to compare two
poems on the same topic, composed in these islands at a
distance in time of possibly a thousand years.   Here, there-
fore, I give the early English verses, not inquiring whether
or not they were suggested by the more ancient Irish poem :

> " Sumer is i-cumen in
>   Llude sing cuccu :
> Groweth sed and bloweth med
>   And springth the wde nu,
>   Sing cuccu, cuccu.

> Awe bleteth after lomb
>   Llouth after calve cu ;
> Bullock sterteth, bucke verteth,
>   Murie sing cuccu.
> Wel singes thu cuccu,
> Ne swik thou nauer nu
>   Sing cuccu, cuccu."

Archaic also in thought and expression, but more matured in form is Fionn's staccato description of the approach of winter. Could any poet in eight lines condense a more complete description, or produce a more chilling effect?

In " A Warrior's Duty " we have one of several ancient poems, in which the ethics of the ancient pagan Irish were set forth. Others are Cormac Mac Art's " Institutes of a King," and Cuchulainn's instructions to a prince. They teach the same lesson of loyalty, faithful companionship, knightly courtesy, sobriety of bearing, and kindness to the weak.

The intense appreciation of Nature, revealed in Amergin's Chant extends, like a woof of gold, from the earliest to the latest Irish poem. Nowhere else is found a love so tender, so passionate at times, so constant, and so enduring. It is more than an affection, in some cases it almost seems a fusion.

In this period the larger and deeper human note is sounded, with increasing intensity. First struck in Lugai's Elegy, it becomes clearer and fuller as the ages pass. The chord of noble friendship vibrates. In no place nor time was loyal companionship more highly honoured, or its cleavage more keenly felt. This powerful sentiment gives their graver interest and pathos to the heroic and romantic tales—with which the Irish bards were the first to endow Europe. This is the tragic element in the "Táin Bo." It does not stand alone, but underlies other tales such as the "Fate of the Children of Usnach" and the "Pursuit of Diarmad." There woman's love appears in the persons of Deirdré and of Grainné,—in the former guarding, in the latter breaking, the beloved companionship, which forms in both cases the dramatic background.

Such loyal comradeship was known among other nations, such as the Greeks, but the ancient Irish possessed in addition what the Greeks did not possess, a high chivalrous love of woman. For woman with the Irish was man's equal in position, in estate, in power, and in friendship.

To the ancient Irish Europe owes its earliest love songs, and its first prose romances. Examples of the former have been given, for the Cuchulainn Period, in the songs of Fand and of Deirdré. Here may be found the poem of a lover to his lady, Crédé—a chieftainess whose favour was sought by many, but whose coquetry was great as her beauty was admirable. Her suitor, Cael, approaches her with a poem of praise. In structure the poem is seven-syllabled (even when the rime is double) with end-rimes and alliteration. I quote the last stanza given, when, having eulogized her mansion and herself, her suitor says :

" If she grant me grace at all,—
She, for whom the cuckoos call—
Then I, for thanks, will give her
More lays to live for ever."

Is it not surprising how the thought, in this verse of an ancient Irish Bard whose words are exactly rendered, anticipates that so nobly expressed by the Marquis of Montrose, in the seventeenth century?

" But if thou wilt prove faithful then
And constant of thy word,
I'll make thee glorious by my pen,
And famous by my sword."

But there is a line in the Irish which incloses a subtle and exquisite compliment. Who is she for whom the cuckoos call? Is it not the youthful Summer? So, when Crédé appears, the cuckoos call at her coming as at the coming of young Summer. This is surely one of the most beautiful compliments ever paid to woman.

Successful in his suit, Cael fell in desperate combat on the sea-shore with an invader, and the billows broke over them. In this case we have the earliest European expression of reciprocal love. Cael declared his devotion for Crédé, in her splendid mansion; Crédé reveals the intensity of her affection, beside the incarnadined sea. In structural form her Lament recalls that of some verses of Deirdré's " Farewell to Alba." Whilst the remaining lines of the stanza are of seven syllables, the first line is short, having but three. Later copyists, not understanding this metre, eked out the line, in both cases, by repeating the words with an exclamation between. But though this may have adapted the stanzas to music, they lose the higher grace of classic firmness. They possess alliteration usually, with internal and end-rimes.

> " Woe is me !
> Dead my Cael is, fair and free ;
> Oft my arms would ward his *sleep*,
> Now it is the *deep*, dark sea."

Sometimes variety is produced by dissyllabic rimes :

> " Ever *raining*
> Fall the *plaining* waves above ;
> I have hope of joy no *more*
> Since 'tis *o'er*, our bond of love."

Crédé associates nature with her grief. She hears not only the wailing waves, but notes the heron defending its young, the stag sobbing for the slain hind, the thrush and blackbird's lament, and the swan mourning her dead mate. Then, with a sudden, and highly poetic reflection, she gauges the force of that grief which makes her (a chieftainess, once so given to the joy of life) take share of sorrow with a dying swan.

Another lay, whose subject refers it to this epoch is "The Cold Night of Innisfail."

> " Cold, cold,
> Chill this night is Lurc's wide wold
> Foodless now the gaunt deer *goes*,
> High o'er hills the *snows* are rolled."

Keats has told us that " the owl for all its feathers was a-cold." But this fine image is surpassed, if not by that which shows the wren unable to shelter in its close nest, at least by the picture of the old eagle shivering in expectation that the bitter wind will freeze its beak in ice.

Of a different character, bright, buoyant, and witty is the poem: "Where is sweetest music?" Here the individual characteristics of the chiefs of the great Companionship of the Fianna are reproduced.

IV. The death of Finn, and the disruption of the Great Companionship, so pathetically told in the "Discourse of the Ancients"[1] brings us to the second section of this period, with which the name of Ossian must be associated. This is the Age of Lamentation. The Hebrews felt not more keenly the fall of Jerusalem, than the ancient bards the fall of Finn and the disbandment of the Fianna. In modern days there is nothing to parallel the sentiment save that which racked the Scottish Jacobites after Culloden, or rather that which wrung the hearts of his Old Guard on the downfall and death of Napoleon. National sorrow refines and induces national song. But neither the Jacobite Laments nor Béranger's strains can be taken as surpassing those ascribed to Ossian, in nobility of thought, refinement of feeling, or pathetic suggestiveness.

Look on that picture of "Ossian after the Fianna," a phrase which became the synonym of all survivors'

[1] "Silva Gadelica."

sorrow. The days and nights drag wearily, hopelessly
on, whilst he recalls the splendid fellowship of the past.
Now, blinded by tears, broken by age, he has no fellow-
ship but with grief:

> "No hero now where heroes hurled,—
> Long this night the clouds delay—
> No man like me, in all the world,
>   Alone with grief, and gray.

> "Long this night the clouds delay—
> I raise their grave-carn, stone on stone,
> For Finn and Fianna passed away—
>   I, Ossian, left alone."

What poetry, also, in that conception of the Blackbird
whose voice was still singing from its nest in the oak tree
of Darricarn, long after the mighty hand of Finn, who
placed it there, had turned to dust. Every note recalled
the days of old to Ossian, and to the Ancient Isle. What
dignity also, and what reserve in the classic poem on the
"House of Finn." *Vidi tantum !*

With these may be taken his warrior-comrade, Cailté's
poem on winter. He strikes a bold chord, and brings
us amongst the snowy mountains, where wolves are
heard. The stag leaps up and bells aloud to warn its
kindred. Then another stag, "arousing, Hears wail of
wolves carousing." Cailté had "heard the chimes at
midnight," with other mind than Falstaff. With Oscar
and Diarmid, he heard "the rousing wolves a-wailing."
In the winter of the year, and in the winter of his life,
the memory of his deeds gives him cheer:

> " I am aged now and gray,
> Few of Men I meet this day :
> But I hurled the javelin bold,
> Of a morning, icy cold.

> "Thanks unto the King of Heaven,
> And the Virgin's son be given :
> Many men have I made still
> Who this night are very chill."

The baptismal sprinkle given to the last quatrain adds force by contrast with the cause of the thanksgiving. One might imagine that a pagan divinity had been displaced from the first two lines : yet, as it stands, Cailté only anticipated some modern monarchs.

Cailté's poem on Arann isle displays the characteristic love of nature, whilst the verse-structure, having alternate dissyllabic rimes, is remarkable :

> "Arann, in deer delighting !
> Ocean smiles on her shoulders ;
> Men have feasts there and fighting
> Blue darts redden mid boulders."

V. It has not been observed that a great catastrophe may influence the character and disposition of a nation. Yet, I would attribute the pathetic strain in Scottish poetry largely to the cruel consequences of the Jacobite defeat. Burns drew in new life from the fresh enthusiasms of the French Revolution, and so his poetry is more buoyant. There can be no doubt, I believe, that the sad dirges of Ossian—continued as the note was by other bards and generally spread—did influence the character and sentiment of the Gael, and probably infused that tone of melancholy, which, renewed from time to time by recurring disasters, is supposed to be an essentially Celtic peculiarity.

Fortunately, there was a burst of sunshine when the Christian faith came forth upon the waters. Otherwise the refinement which sorrow produces might have been carried to enervation. Fortunately, also, St. Patrick chose the Irish, and not the Latin, as the language of his famous hymn "The Guardsman's Cry." This was a fruitful fact; for whilst the Latin hymns by Irishmen (with the illustrious exception of the works of Sedulius) are of secondary, the Irish hymns are of primary, interest and importance. They are the children of "The Guardsman's Cry."

St. Patrick gave his Confession in Latin, and might perhaps have given us rimed Latin verse.[1] He composed some lines in Irish regular verse. But for "The Guardsman's Cry," which is his authentic work, he chose that peculiar impetuous form known as the "Rosg," so often used as an incitement to warfare. No choice could have been more admirable. He pours through it all the ardent passion of his vehement spirit, and we see it swell and fall, pulsating with the life of faith, appealing, imploring, defiant and confident. Clarence Mangan has paraphrased the original in a beautiful and eloquent ode.

---

[1] See hymn ascribed to him (but falsely, I think) in Cotton MSS.:

"Constet quantus honos humanæ conditionis
Scire volens, hujus serie videat rationis,
Non hominem verbo solo Deus effugiavit
Quem facturus erat, sic quomodo cuncta creavit," etc.

Here an effort is made to represent the original exactly in English, as what it is, an intense impassioned prayer.

As it was the first hymn composed in a European language, beyond the classic world, the Hymn of St. Patrick makes an era in literature.

This was the Dawn-light of Christianity. There are many pieces in prose and verse which reflect the condition of things then prevailing. They present the elder beliefs in all their plenitude, and yet are given a Christian touch or colour. Some of them may have been composed before Christianity came, and been subsequently revised, as the Ancient Laws were revised ; but it must be said that the Irish Christians respected the pagan classics. They may, indeed, have been composed in two lights. As a pale wan moon is sometimes seen in the sky when the sun is shining, so the dim light of paganism lingered long after Christianity sent its rays over the island. Even Christians retained belief in the activity of Powers which they no longer worshipped.

These Twilight-pieces have many attractions. One is " The Fate of the Children of Lir." Transformed by the maleficence of their stepmother, the Swan-Children were doomed to suffer until Christianity should come to set them free. There is tender pathos in this tale, displayed in many of the poems. An antithetical treatment will be noticed in Fionnuala's " Lamentation on the Moyle," which style is also observable in Bran's " Voyage to the Isle of Delight." As regards structure, the most remarkable thing is the appearance of trisyllabic rimes—which

make a very late appearance in English and other litera-
tures. These triple rimes are sometimes secured by single
words, sometimes by more words than one.

One quatrain may be cited where triple alternate with
double rimes :

> " Dark our doom and tragical—
> Condemned the waves to wander ;
> Ne'er such ill-fate magical
> Did mortal yet fall under."

The " Isle of Delight " follows.   Here, again, we seem
to have the new Christian belief grafted on the elder
heathen : and the beauties and delights of the ancient
pagan paradise combined with Christian hopes.   Christi-
anity came, as in Greece and Italy, to a civilized and
cultured people. This poem bears witness to the Ariel
imagination of the ancients, which flew so easily from the
visible to the invisible.   Next to the episode of Fand, it is
probably the earliest of those visionary pieces which the
Irish precursors of Dante produced in successive ages,
usually in prose, and which, when translated, became
universally popular over Europe.

Some passages have a special charm, and offer a certain
modernity of thought and expression :

> "'Tis the beauty of things bright,—
> Loveliness is in its sight."

And again :

> " They have music in the night,
> Through this Isle of all Delight—
> Flash of Beauty's diadem !"

Lovers of sports will find a novel suggestion in the mention of races between chariots and barques. These, however, took place in a region where time could be accurately kept as the boats sailed along the surface of the sea, whilst the chariots ran on the invisible isle beneath them. Bran went forth over the sea to discover the delectable island, and was met by Manannan, the Ocean-Spirit, in his chariot. The bard, by a fine conception, makes Manannan the author of a lay which, antithetically, contrasts the faculties of the Mortal with those of the Immortal:

> "The sea is clear,—
> So thinks Bran, when sailing here;
> I, in car, with purer powers
> Know the happy Plain of Flowers."

The bard changes his metre occasionally to prevent monotony, and to arouse attention.

VI. For three centuries, from the fifth to the ninth, the Civilization of Europe belonged to Ireland, says a German historian. This evidence of intellectual culture and supremacy, the greatest glory of the country, is strangely ignored in its schools. The influence of the ancient Irish on the Continent began in the works of Sedulius, whose "Carmen Paschale," published in the fifth century, is the first great Christian Epic, worthy of the name. Though he adopted the Latin forms of verse, he infused into them certain characters which reveal the Gael. One of these is the vowel end-rime, another systematic alliteration. These, of course, could not be continuously employed; but, on the other hand, they could not accidentally occur. A few examples may suffice for our present purpose. Consider these lines:

> " Neve quis ignoret speciem crucis esse colendam,
> Quæ Dominum portavit ovans, ratione potenti,
> Quatuor inde plagas quadrati colligit orbis,
> Splendidus auctoris de vertice fulget Eoüs,
> Occiduo sacræ lambuntur sidere plantæ
> Arcton dextra tenet, medium læva erigit axem."

The rime in the end-words of the first two lines is "en," where the slender vowel "e" serves; in the second two lines the broad vowel "o," and in the last two the broad vowel "a" give the Gaelic asonance. The systematic alliteration is obvious, and correctly complies with the Irish rule which, requiring the same consonants, permitted broad and slender vowels to alliterate.

In his shorter compositions, the Irish features are equally distinct. We find them in his celebrated Hymn:

> " A solis ortus cardine
> Ad usque terræ limitem,
> Christum canamus principem
> Natum Maria virgine.
>
> " Beatus auctor seculi
> Seruile corpus induit,
> Ut carne carnem liberans
> Ne perderet quos condidit."

There are what one may call stolen alliterations, in the first couplet of the second stanza, where the last letters of "beatus" and "corpus," coming before vowels serve as initials. Sometimes, as in "detulit" and "sustulit," both vowel and consonants rime, as occasionally in ancient Irish verses.

In this way, I have tested and discovered the presence of ancient Irish characteristic in the Sedulian verses. In addition, I have found a counter-test, which affirms our position in most satisfactory manner. This, with other hymns, came under the Revisers of the Roman Breviary, in the days of Urban VIII. These erudite Latinists took in hand the lines:

> " Parvoque lacte past*us est*
> Per quem nec ales es*urit.* "

They are perfect, judged by the bardic standard. The Latinists, demurring to the adjective, altered the first line thus:

> " Et lacte modico pastus est."

By so doing, they destroyed the careful Celtic alliteration, which had escaped their ears. The Parisian Latinists made a yet greater change:

> " Et indiget lactis cibo."

This annihilates not only the alliteration, but the end-rime. Again, let us take another instance. The hymn is abecedarian—each stanza begins with a different letter, in due succession. In that beginning with " h," Sedulius wrote:

> " Hostis Herodes imp*ie*
> Christum venire quid t*imes,*
> Non eripit mortal*ia*
> Qui regna dat cœlest*ia.* "

Erasmus first, and the Revisers afterwards, protested

that "hostis," followed by "Herodes," was a trochæus and should not be found in iambic metre. Arevalus noted, later, that the "h" of the proper name being aspirated had the force of a consonant, and left "hostis" a spondee, which is allowable. The Irishman aspirated the "h;" the Romans occasionally dropped it. However, the revising Latinists thought to set things right by a few touches. They accomplished this:

> " Crudelis Herodes deum
> Regem venire quid times."

With what marvellous rapidity the Irish characteristics have disappeared! The alliterative structure of both lines is destroyed, and the perfect end-rime rendered imperfect. The subtle sound-echoes which charmed the bardic ear are expunged, in order to satisfy the metrical Latin ear. It is as if an artist, imbued with a perfect sense of form, but colour-blind, proceeded to revise the drawing in another artist's picture, and, whilst correcting its lines, painted out its more delicate tints.

The presence of characteristics, so readily recognized by those conversant with Gaelic verse, and their erasure by the unwitting Latin Revisers, supply the test and the counter-test. By these, we demonstrate that the characteristics in question were Irish, not accidental peculiarities natural to a Latin poet, and from these we can deduce the bard's nationality. Huemer, who doubts that Sedulius was an Irishman, as Trithemius stated, was not aware of the intrinsic evidence here indicated.

The question of the transfusion into Latin verse of Irish peculiarities is one of such curious interest that a few examples may be added. They passed chiefly into the Latin hymns, and, through the hymns, influenced the verse-forms of European literatures when these became articulate.

The fifth century, which gave Sedulius and St. Patrick to letters, gave also St. Secundinus, a nephew and co-temporary of the latter. His verses in praise of St. Patrick betray the influence of the bardic schools. Zeuss drew attention to some rimes sprinkled through the verses (as " omn*es* amant*es* "), but I would point to other and yet more remarkable signs, such as alliteration and internal rime : these are so characteristically Gaelic that they readily escape general notice. Take the opening lines :

> " Audite omnes ama*ntes*
> Deum sa*nct*a merita
> Uiri in Christi be*ati*
> P*atr*icii episcopi.

> " Quomodo bonum ob a*ctum*
> Simula*tur* angelis
> Perfectamque propter u*itam*
> Æ*qua*tur apostolis "

In the first couplet, "ant" and "anct" rime; in the second, "ati" and "atri." In the third couplet "actum" and "atur" have the same vowels, and in the fourth, "vitam" and "æqua" have similar vowels. Some consonants, too, reappear. The last syllables of the last two words in the first four lines rime. In the second

D

quatrain there is alternate monosyllabic end-rime. The bards varied the metre, occasionally, in Irish.

"Sancti, Venite" the celebrated post-communion hymn, attributed to the same bard,—angels are said to have sung it in his church at Bangor,—is constructed on a Gaelic model. Here, however, five-syllabled lines alternate with those of seven syllables. To the ordinary eye or ear, there must seem little or most imperfect rime in the following stanza. Once, however, it is tested by the standard of Irish verse-structure, the perfection of the riming is made clear:

> " Sancti ven*ite*
> Chr*isti* corpus SUMITE :
> Sanctum *bibente*s
> Quo r*edempti* SANGUINEM."

There is perfect rime in the first couplet, between the two "slender" vowel-sounds (i e and i i); and in the second between the three similar sounds (i e e and e e i). The last words of the second and fourth lines rime with equal completeness—each having one "broad" and two "slender" vowels (u i e and a i e). Here is another stanza where, at first glance, there appears to be no rime, except in the letter "m" of the second and last lines. It unfolds its perfection to the Gaelic test:

> " Lucis ind*ultor*
> Et salu*ator* OMNIUM,
> Præclaram s*ancti*s
> L*argi*tus est gr*ATIAM*."

It is only necessary to point out that, in the last words of the second and fourth lines there is perfect vowel-rime, according to the Gaelic rule, between o i u and a i a. The bard was not always so successful, sometimes he ekes out his rime, and sometimes foregoes it ; but it is so elaborate that its presence proves purpose.

In the sixth century, St. Columbcille, a bilingual bard, contributed Gaelic and Latin verse. His "Altus," a famous hymn of old, was composed in trochaic tetrameter, as Bede notes. A writer in*the ancient "Lebor Breac," distinguishing between "artificialis" rhythm, with feet of equal times, equal divisions, and equal weight, "arsis" and "thesis," and "vulgaris" rhythm, where there is correspondence of syllables in quatrains and half-quatrains, says the hymn is composed in this popular rhythm. It is noteworthy that these characters are those of the Gaelic stanza. St. Columbcille uses trisyllabic rime, well known to the Gael, and occasionally obtains internal chimes :

> "Altus prositor u*etustus*
> Dierum et ing*enitus*,
> Erat absque or*igine*
> Primordii et crep*idine*."

In another octosyllabic hymn he also employs foursyllabled rime, where consonants sometimes chime :

> "Noli pater ind*ulgere*[1]
> Tonitrua cum f*ulgure*
> Ac frangamur form*idine*
> Hujus atque *uridine*."

Twenty years later St. Columbanus flourished, a fine classic scholar, to whose efforts and example the revival

---

[1] G is pronounced hard in Irish.

of classical literature on the continent was largely due. Though Columbanus composed in classic metres, he did not fail to introduce Irish alliterative and final rimes, *e.g.* :

> " Dilexerunt tenebras tetras magis quam l*ucem,*
> Imitari contemnunt vitæ Domini d*ucem.*"

His charming poem to Fedolius, so praised for its pure latinity, I show, in Appendix, to possess also vowel rime throughout.

In the seventh century flourished the poet-saints Ultan, Cummain, and Colman.

The structure of the hymn of St. Ultan, in honour of St. Brigit, is exceedingly curious and interesting. The riming has escaped attention because of its very profusion. The editor of the "Liber Hymnorum" saw only "asonances" in the middle and end of each line, with possibly alliteration. Take the first two lines :

> " Christus in nostra insol*a* quæ vocatur hiberni*a*
> Ostensus est hominib*us* maximis mirabilib*us.*"

This gives but a meagre monosyllabic rime. Rime, though concealed, is amazingly abundant. In the first line, for instance, there are three trisyllabic internal rimes, as here shown :

> "*in-nostra insola quæ-voca.*"

In the second line there are also three :

> "*ostensus* [1] *homini maximis.*

---

[1] The last syllable preceding a vowel is short, and the vowel is regarded apparently as sufficiently slender.

In the first line the rimes run on one " slender " and two " broad " vowels : in the second this is ingeniously reversed, and the rimes are formed of one " broad " and two " slender " vowels. In addition, I would point out that the lines terminate in trisyllabic vowel rime, for " bernia " and " bilibus " correspond in sound. Curiously enough, they supply a third combination, having two " slender " vowels first and one " broad " vowel. And there is an extra four-syllabled rime, for " hominibus " is in full asonance with " abilibus." The third line reads thus :

"Que perfecit per felicem celestis uite uirginem."

The trisyllabic rimes are four ; but here all are yielded by the slender vowels :

"*perfecit per-feli cem-cele uirginem.*"

St. Ultan's hymn may be the source of the popularity of the verses known as " Tripudiantes."

St. Cummain Fota's hymn is noticeable by its alliteration and trisyllabic rimes :

"Celebra iuda festa Christi g*audia*
Apostulorum exultans mem*oria.*"

In the eighth century, St. Cucuimne (who died A.D. 742) employed both vowel and consonant rime, with alliteration, in a manner most dear to the Gaelic bards of Munster a thousand years later. It is not necessary to italicize the rimes in such verses as these :

" Bis per chorum hinc et inde collaudemus Mariam
Ut vox pulset omnem aurem per laudem uicariam,
Maria de tribu iudæ summi mater domini
Oportunam dedit curam egrotanti homini."

These are even more obvious :

> " Maria mater miranda patrem suum edidit
> Per quem aqua late lotus totus mundus credidit.
> Tonicam per totum textam Christi mater fecerat
> Quæ peracta Christi morte sorte statim steterat."

If we arrange the lines in the form of the Irish quatrain, it will be seen how completely they conform to its rules :

> " Maria miranda *mater*
> *Patrem* suum edidit,
> Per quem aqua late *lotus*
> *Totus* mundus credidit."

His cotemporary, St. Œngus, son of Tipraite, makes use of woven rime with like liberality in his hymn to St. Martin.   As written the lines are :

> " Martinus mirus more ore laudavit deum,
> Puro corde cantavit atque amavit eum."

Here we see the rimes, but not the system, until we arrange the lines as a Gaelic quatrain :

> " Martinus mirus m*ore*
> *Ore* l*audavit* deum,
> Puro corde c*antavit*
> Atque *amavit* eum.

In the ninth century another Sedulius (" Scottus ") was esteemed a distinguished poet.   His poem " The Contest of the Rose and the Lily " might, for conception and treatment, be one of Moore's, it is so light, graceful, and harmonious.   It leads the way of the lighter poetic

literature of Europe. Mingled with the measured tread
of its hexameters, one hears the musical Irish chimes:

> "Ciclica quadri*fidis* currebant tempora m*etis*
> Uernabat uari*o* tellus decorataque peplo,
> Lactea cum ros*eis* certabant lilia s*ertis*,
> Cum rosa sic c*roc*eo sermones prompserat *ore*."

Not the least interesting of the bardic Latin poems
is one which belonged to the monastery of St. Gall.
Dating from the middle of the ninth century, it conforms
to the Latin rules in externals, but its substance is essen-
tially Irish. In slumber the bard suddenly beholds the
radiant vision of a golden-haired maiden, beautiful
beyond the daughters of the earth, with brow brighter
than the sun of the heavens. She calms his fears, and
tells her name. It is Wisdom. Nine hundred years
later almost every bard sang of a similar vision, but the
celestial maid was Erinn.

Through their Latin poetry, and especially through
their hymns, carried abroad over Europe, taught and
chanted in many schools and monasteries, the Irish
influenced the germinating literatures of Europe. The
languages developing from the Latin were naturally
directly affected. This was clearly the case in Spain,
though it has been strangely overlooked until now. A
few words will make this manifest.

The old Spanish *redondellas* were quatrains, with rimes
between first and fourth, or second and fourth lines.
"Their prominent peculiarity," writes Ticknor, "and one
which they have succeeded in impressing upon a very

large portion of all the national poetry, is one which—being found to prevail in no other literature—may be claimed to have its origin in Spain, and becomes therefore an important circumstance in Spanish poetical culture." With this preamble, note the fact : "The peculiarity to which we refer," he adds, "is the *asonante*, an imperfect rhyme confined to the vowels, and beginning with the last accented one in the line, it embraces sometimes only the very last syllable, and sometimes goes back to the penultimate, or even the antepenultimate." He cites as examples the riming of (1) "feróz" with "furor ; " of (2) "cása" with "abárca ; " of (3) "infamia" with "contrária."

Now the slightest knowledge of Irish prosody would have prevented an error such as this, and shown that, far from being a Spanish peculiarity, *asonante* was known and cultivated in Ireland centuries before a line of Spanish was written. It is pitiable to see Bello tracing its origin to the "Vita Mathildis," and Ticknor (whilst rejecting this theory, for the poem was unknown in Spain), declaring that the poem "was singular in this attempt," in presence of so many hymns, and of the works of Sedulius, who was exceedingly popular in Spain.

There is another characteristic of Spanish rime which emphatically proclaims its origin. Ticknor describes it as "a great poetic licence," by which different words were allowed to rime: "Thus 'u' and 'o' were held to be *asonante*, as in 'Venus' and 'minos,' 'i' and 'e' as in 'Paris' and 'males.'"

Now here we have stated, with a start of surprise at the audacity of the licence, a rule of vowel-rime which has been known in Ireland from of old until the present day, the rule, namely, of correspondence between the broad vowels "o" and "u" (and "a"), and between the slender vowels "i" and "e"! There could not well be a more complete evidence of filiation.

VII. In the three centuries after St. Patrick, Erinn became an Island of Learning—the University of Europe. Strangers flocked thither for instruction from all nations, and from none more fervently than from the Anglo-Saxon. They were hailed with a hospitality which has never been equalled. Venerable Bede gratefully testifies that the Irish received all comers with a liberal welcome, hospitably entertained them, gave them books to read, instruction in the arts and sciences, food and shelter, and all gratuitously. From their great schools and monasteries men went forth over Scotland, England, and the Continent, forming centres of teaching everywhere, developing the literary instinct or culture of other nations, and infusing into its poetical forms the characteristics of Gaelic verse.

In Gaelic, many hymns and poems relating to religious subjects made their appearance subsequent to the "Guardsman's Cry." They show originality and independence of thought and expression. Perhaps the earliest is the hymn of St. Ita (who was born A.D. 480); it is classic in form and bold in conception. The absolute faith of the ancient Irish inspired them with the love which casts

out fear, and their poems show no trace of servile dread.
They prefixed the pronoun "mo," "my," to the names
of their saints, which they modified by fond diminutives.
St. Ita, in this way, uses an endearing diminutive with
the name of the Redeemer. "Isa," the ancient Irish form
of Jesus (which is now "Iosa"), became "Isucan"—
Jesukin—in her poem. It was applied to the infant
Saviour who, it was believed, abode with her at night, in
her lone cell in the desert.

> "Jesukin.
> Lives my little cell within :
> What were wealth of cleric *high*
> All is *lie* but Jesukin."

Three lines end in monosyllablic rime, whilst there is
rime (sometimes dissyllabic) between the end word of
the third, and an internal word in the fourth lines.

Next may come the poems of Cellach. He was a
student under St. Kiaran, who died A.D. 540, in the famous
School of Clonmicnóis, whose ruins declare its former
greatness. His father, King Eogan of Connacht, when
dying, induced him to leave his studies, and to rule the
kingdom. Then a powerful rival arose, who expelled
him. The first poem, in regular metre, in which he
regrets his student life, was composed when a fugitive in
the forests, with a band of outlaws. The other is more
tragic, and gives us a remarkable example of how the
bard could adapt his metre to the dramatic requirements
of his subject. The usurper bribed Cellach's four pupils,
chief of whom was Melcron, to murder him. They laid

violent hands upon him in the wood; but spared his life
for one night, keeping him imprisoned in a hollow tree.
When the night had passed, he opened the door of his
prison, but as the first ray of dawn fell upon him, he
closed it suddenly against the fatal light.   Then, after a
moment's thought, he threw wide the door, and welcomed
the morn which brings him death :

> " 'Tis my Love the Morning fair,
> Floating, flame-like, through the air !
> 'Tis my Love who sends her too
> Victor-Morning, ever new.
>
> " O Morning, fair and tender !
> O Sister of Sun's Splendour !
> Welcome thou, O Morning fair !
> Shining on my booklet there."

By a sudden transition of thought and dramatically
abrupt change of metre, he apostrophizes the scall-crow,
which sat watching for his death.   Other birds and
beasts of prey there are, and the verse is varied :

> " O constant croaking *Raven!*
> Is thy hunger-*craving* fresh ?
> Rise not from this rath-topt *hill*—
> Thou shalt have thy *fill* of flesh."

The kite shall come, to bear off his talons' full, and the

> " Fox in forest lurking low
> He shall hear and hail the blow ;
> He will bear my flesh and blood
> Through the wild, dark, dreary wood."

The red wolf will rush thither, ruler of the robbers.

Again the measure is changed, whilst he recalls the
foreboding visions; and yet again whilst he pathetically
reproaches Melcron for his treason.   Not for the world's
wealth would Cellach have betrayed Melcron; he would
have sacrificed all to save him from being a traitor.   But
the voice of the Redeemer comes to Cellach, giving him
a celestial welcome.

This lay, with its strong ideas and rapid changes,
proves the dramatic capacity of its author.   It is note-
worthy for another reason.   Cellach foresees the rending
of his body, and the redemption of his soul.   Compare
this passage with the verses written by the Marquis of
Montrose (1650) after the death sentence which doomed
him to the barbarous penalties of high treason, and
observe how closely they correspond in spirit:

> "Let them bestow on every airt a limb,
> Then open all my veins that I may swim
> To thee, my Maker, in that crimson lake :
> Then place my parboiled head upon a stake,
> Scatter my ashes, strew them in the air ;
> Lord, since thou knowest where all those atoms are,
> I am hopefull Thou'lt recover once my dust
> And confident Thou'lt raise me with the Just."

The poems of St. Columba, or St. Columbcille, have the
singular merit of being the first poems,[1] in non-classic

---

[1] Love of Country is expressed, in prose, in "The Fate of the
Children of Usnach."   To the Envoy sent to invite them to return,
Deirdré urged that their lordship in Alba (Scotland) was greater
than Concobar's in Erinn.   " Better the native land than anything,"
replied Fergus, "for displeasing it is to one, however great his

letters, which display and proclaim Love of Country. They are, similarly, the first poems of exile.

> "There 's an eye of gray
> Looks back to Erinn, far away :
> While life lasts, 'twill see no more
> Man nor maid on Erinn's shore."

Even yet the emigrant peasant, before leaving Donegal, goes to pass a night on the flag-stone which marks St. Columba's birthplace in the hope of obtaining strength to bear the sorrow of exile.

Intense love of nature, sincerity, and simplicity, characterize the verses of St. Columba. He was a natural poet who sang of the welcome of the white-winged sea-gulls, the cuckoo's call at "the brink of summer," the swooning breeze in the elm, the beauty of Benn Edar above its breakers, and the bright-bosomed sea.

There is a marked contrast between this style and that of his eulogist Eocaid—surnamed Dallan—because he became blind from over-study. The latter was one of the great Bardic Corporation, whose training had gone so far that natural expression seemed too common. Preference for a poetic diction has often led to artificiality such as that against which Wordsworth revolted, but who would expect to find that this was the case, more than twelve hundred years ago, in Ireland? Men and nations pass through evolutionary cycles, and even poets do not escape. It is, however, a singular fate that Irish poetry

prosperity and power, if he sees not his own country each day.' " It is true," said Naisi, "for dearer to me is Erinn than Alba though I should obtain more in Alba than in Erinn."

should seem to some to be in the primary stage of evolution, because it completed its cycle so long ago, in an ancient language.

Dallan, a cotemporary of St. Columba, wrote an Eulogy on him, and would have recited it, had he not been restrained, as the saint held that no man should be praised until his death. This Eulogy is extant. It was written in a style so archaic that few could comprehend it. Hence, as Colgan says, the more learned antiquaries illustrated his writings with commentaries. In Colgan's day it was still customary to lecture on, and expound them, in the schools, as rare monuments of the ancient language. Spenser, we know, wrote a comparatively archaic language, Ronsard went far in latinizing French, and Euphues manipulated the English of his time. The strange thing is that these and others were anticipated by Dallan many centuries before. For instance, he did not hesitate to add a syllable, as "Culu" for "Cul," or to retrench a letter as "ru," "ra," for "run," "ran," or to add a letter, as "tenn" for "ten," or to change an initial as "sencas" for "Fencas." These instances of poets' licence were duly noted and classified by his commentators.

It is even more interesting to discover that many centuries ago these learned critics analyzed, grouped, and classified various rhetorical devices, which poets of the present use, unaware of the fact, and without comment. Byron may exclaim: "Roll on, thou dark and deep blue ocean, roll," and Tennyson: "Break, break, break, On thy cold grey stones O Sea;" we hear and admire.

The ancient Irish lecturers did more: they analyzed and classified. Thus, when Dallan repeated "Dia, Dia" (God, God), they explained that he redoubled the first word to show the quickness and eagerness of his praise. They point out, also (as O'B. Crowe translates it), that this device is known to the Gael as "a return to a wonted sound." This happens when Columba speaks of "the pale, pale sea." Then it is noted that there are three species of repetition. First, the doubling of one word in the cycle, without further repetition. Second, re-narration, or the repetition of one word, with others between, as in the verse:

> " Rushed the sea up the strand,
> Rushed the ox thro' the band,
> Rushed, as gallant and grand,
> Brave Cu Dinisk the brown."

This anticipates such turns as Sir Walter Scott loved, *e.g.* "Pibroch of Donuil Dhu; Pibroch of Donuil," and which Burns also used: "Scots, wha hae wi' Wallace bled; Scots wham Bruce has often led."

The third kind was more artificial, and was scarcely employed: it could only be used in scenes of passionate emotion. It was termed re-folding or re-duplication, and may be represented thus:

> " Away, away, O flee, flee,
> This dark, dark day, o'er the wide, wide sea ! "

These remarks from the Commentaries on the Eulogy will suffice to show with what analytical faculty the elder writers entered on their work, and how far advanced they were in culture. Where such attention was given by minds so keen and subtle to verse-structure, it is little wonder that they anticipated many of the modern methods.

Next in order of date is the Dirge for Conall Claen, by his wife (A.D. 634). Original in idea and perfect in form, it is clearly an outburst of the heart. We see the desolate woman, standing by her slain husband, recalling all his looks and all his warrior prowess. Then, at last, she sees the Clay his Fortress, forever—

> "Och !—and here his Fort for aye,—
> The strong cold clay, for all the years !
> Conall's Fort !—where I deplore
> Whose tale is o'er—the House of Tears."

Another example of the daring imagination of the ancient Irish is the ascription of the authorship of a poem to the Devil. The "Sorrows of Satan" may seem new to this generation, but the theme was treated over twelve hundred years ago in Gaelic verse. The date is fixed, so far as may be, from the mention of the name of St. Moling in connection with the cause of Satan's Song, as the saint became bishop A.D. 632. It is amusing to notice that the "Hill-top Novels" of another cotemporary were partially anticipated (in name) by the "Hill-top Satires" of the ancient Irish.

Perhaps we may assign to this period another exceedingly striking poem, the "Lamentations of the Mothers of Bethlehem." No author's name is given. The terrible grief of the distraught mothers of murdered babes is represented in terms of reckless fidelity. The verse-form chosen is the irregular passionate "Rosg," and here, though there is some trace of entrance-rime (as I hold), the poem seems otherwise devoid of rime, and is another example of Irish blank verse.

From the construction of this and similar pieces, I am tempted to infer that there were some forms of dramatic presentation—miracle plays and dramas—amongst the ancient Gael.[1]

We come now upon a literary curiosity. St. Colman (the second), Lecturer in the Theological School of Cork, died in the year 661. Now of the twenty-three stanzas which constitute the original hymn, six are remarkable for the manner in which the author mingles Latin lines or rimes with the vernacular Gaelic. As this is the earliest specimen of this kind of Macaronic poetry in European literature, it should have been noticed before now. Three stanzas may be quoted :

> " Regem regum rogamus in nostris sermonibus
> Anacht Noe a luchtlach diluuii temporibus.
>
> " Melchisedech rex Salem incerto de semine
> Ron soerat a airnighe ab omni formidine.
>
> " Abram de Ur na galdai snaidsium ruri ronsnada
> Soersum soerus in popul limpa fontis ingaba."

Another example of this blending of Latin and Irish will be found in the hymn of Maelisu, at the beginning of the eleventh century. Irish bards have consequently

---

[1] See, in Appendix, the "Fate of Usnach's Sons," a Drama.

been the first to set the fashion of bilingual song, traces of which still linger in the student songs of France and Germany.

This period may close with an excerpt from the Calendar of Œngus the Cele De, composed in the eighth century. The passage quoted is a triumph-lay, and comes as a flash of invigorating sunshine.

The ascetic old anchoret had the spirit of a revolutionist of a pure type. No doubt he had heard bards lamenting bygone glories, and extolling the state and splendour of warrior-kings. With uplifted head, he strikes a new and resonant chord. Our Palaces have fallen, he exclaims, but behold how our Universities flourish! The pomp of paganism has gone, but behold how Christian love advances! Mighty despots, gory warriors disappear, but the scholar, the sage, and the saint arise and are glorified in their stead. For the first time the triumph of Mind was celebrated in song in Europe.

The metre is intricate. Each line is of six syllables, ending in a dissyllable. Those which conclude the second and fourth lines rime, and there may also be internal rime. In the first couplets, two, three, or four words alliterate, and each stanza is often linked to its successor by an echo of its last initial or last word, or even of its last line. Dr. Whitley Stokes dwells upon the peculiarities of this metre in his Introduction, partly because Ezzardi regards it as the model of the Skalldic *dróttvætt*, especially the *hattlausa*.

There are also some stanzas with alternate double rimes, such as this :

" Brog emna rotetha
Acht mairit a clocha
Isruam iarthair betha
Glend dalach da locha."

It will be noticed that there is complete bisonant [1] alternate rime. I have taken this form for a model, as I sought the line of least resistance, and omitted the "fidrad" which is not constant, for the same reason. The variation of metre, desirable in a long poem, is not so needful in a short extract.

" Ruins strew the regions
Once Emania's palace,—
Rome revives its legions
In Glenlocha's valleys."

VIII. Another period of nearly four centuries may be taken. This comprises the space between the establishment of the great Hiberno-Norse empire at the beginning of the ninth, to the arrival of the Normans from England at the close of the twelfth century.

The literature of this period could be simply and succinctly disposed of, if one were to adopt the current view, expressed in all modern pseudo-histories, which declares that the "Danes" ravaged the country, burned the cities, murdered the monks, and made a particular point of "drowning" and destroying all books; this continued until their power was annihilated at Clontarf, and Christendom achieved its final triumph over militant Paganism. Those who repeat the tale have not examined

---

[1] *I.e.*, vowel and consonant.

the testimony borne by the literatures of the Gael and
the Norse.

The Irish annals declare that the wars in Erinn were
more frequent and sanguinary, in the centuries which
preceded the establishment of that empire, than in those
which followed. The Norse sagas show that the power
of the Hiberno-Norse kings immediately after Clontarf
was greater than before it. In the Catalogue of Irish
Writers, nine are named for the century preceding the
empire; seven of more distinction flourished in the
century following; in the next eight, and in the next
eighteen. The Annals of the Four Masters mention
forty bishops in the eighth century, and eighty in the
tenth; they mention thirty learned men of distinction in
the eighth, and sixty-three in the tenth. These statistics
are fully borne out by the fact that important manu-
scripts, such as the "Book of Leinster" and the "Lebar
na huidre," date from this period, and by the evidence of
many works. It was a period of great intellectual
activity, when minds were quickened.

The Norsemen were no new comers in the ninth
century. Gaelic writers state that the fair race of the
Tuata Dé Dananns came to Erinn from Norway, where
they had settled. If we consider them as early Norse,
which I think probable, these were in constant touch
with the island before and after the coming of the
southern Milesians. The Annals of Ireland record
several intermarriages in ancient times. Thus, in the
second century King Tuatal the Legitimate married a

Norse princess, Scal's daughter, and their son also espoused a Norland princess. King Cormac Mac Art, in the third century, the first Christian king, was grandson of a Norsewoman. There were two Norse ancestresses in the lineage of Ossian, the last great pagan bard—whilst Secundinus, the first Irish hymn-writer in Erinn, was the son of one of the Longobards who are supposed to have then recently left Norway.

These statements prove, at least, that the Irish believed in close connections between Gael and Norse, in ancient times. They tend to confirm the statement in the "Book of Rights" that St. Patrick found a Norse colony at Dublin. Over a century and a half before the alleged first coming of the Northmen, the bard Rumann—"The Virgil of Erinn," according to an ancient vellum MS. in the Bodleian Library "composed a great poem for the Galls" of Ath-Cliath" (*i.e.*, the foreigners of Hurdle-ford, or Dublin). They declined to pay his price. Then he made an epigram, whereupon they bade him make his own award. He awarded himself two pinginns (coins) from every noble Gall, and one from every mean Gall. All gave him two.[1] "And the Galls then told him to praise the sea, that they might know whether his was original poetry or not." Then he spoke :

"A great tempest on the plain of Lir" (*i.e.*, the sea).

The bard retired with his wealth to Cell Belaigh (near Rahen, King's Co.), which was a university town.

---

[1] Among the Gaels, the prince gave the guerdon.

"At this time Cell Belaigh had seven streets of Galls (*i.e.*, Norsemen) in it; and Rumann gave the third of his wealth to it because of its extent, and a third part to the schools, and he took a third part to Rahen."[1] O'Curry candidly confesses that "There is no doubt but that there were foreigners settled in Dublin and in other parts of the east and south-east in the peaceful pursuits of trade and commerce long before the fierce invaders of the ninth century."

In Rumann's time one-third of the university city of Armagh was set apart for foreign students, chiefly, but not exclusively, Saxons. Many of the nobility and of the lower ranks of the English nation, says Bede, were in Ireland at that period, studying under Irish professors.

Even the warrior-invaders of the ninth century showed a higher respect for civilization and letters than partisan historians declare. Judge by this entry in the annals for the year 919. "The spoyle of Armagh, by Godfrith O h-Ivar with his men who saved the houses of prayer, with the people of God and lepers, and the whole churche towne, except some houses that were burnt by neglect." Later on, in 1020, an exception is made of "the houses of manuscripts."

The Norse relate that when Heriulf sailed to Greenland (about 986) he took with him a South Island Christian— apparently an Irish monk from Iona. Expert in Norse, he composed the "Halgerdingar," or "Sea-Walls" song,

---

[1] O'Curry, "Manners and Customs," Vol. II., Lecture xx.

in memory of great earthquake waves. It was composed on a Gaelic model, and may be thus rendered :

> " All around should bear the chalice
> That was found in Dwarfs' dim palace ;[1]
> May the Friend of Monks, the purest,
> Make my faring safe and surest
> Let the Lord of earth's high ceiling
> Lift his hand o'er me appealing."

Pseudo-historians confound Vikingr raids with Sea-kings' expeditions. They falsify the balance of judgment by denouncing all warlike advances of the Norse, whilst they suppress or glorify the forays against them. Above all, they ignore the secular plunder of Leinster, for the Borumean tribute, by the other Irish kingdoms—a cruel persecution which made Leinster welcome the Norse as allies and deliverers. The ancient Irish authors bore honorable testimony. They told of wars, but they told also of intimate alliances, of many intermarriages between the ruling families of the Norse and Irish, and relate the fosterage of letters by the Hibérno-Norse. Thus, at the beginning of the eleventh century, the chief bards of the Monarch of Erinn, and of King Brian Boruma, enjoyed the hospitality of King Olaf in Dublin for an entire year. For twelve months they left their own courts without chief poets, whilst they gave their finest efforts to the Irish-Norse. "Time for us to return homeward," at last

---

[1] The Dwarfs' Cup is a Kenning or synonym for poetry. Obscure allusions and synonyms of this kind, used and abused by the ancient Irish bards, were transfused into Norse verse.

wrote Mac Liag in a farewell ode to Erard, "we have been here a year, though short to thee and me seem our sojourn in Dublin."

This is the same Mac Liag whose "Wars of the Gael and Gall," which relate the battle of Clontarf, A.D. 1014, have passages of rhetorical invective against the Norse. So much was allowable in a poet laureate. But his work candidly declares the cause of war, and justifies them; they fought at the urgent invitation of King Brian's queen. From his impassioned descriptions all readers infer a fierce hostility between the races. Yet, immediately after the battle, Mac Liag again received the hospitality of Dublin, where he went to see a dead chief, his patron, whom the Norse-Irish were about to inter honorably. He eulogized them in verse, which O'Curry thus translates:

> "Heavily yet lightly have I come to Dublin,
> To the court of Olaf of the golden shields;
> From Dublin of the swords and the graves
> Swift yet slow shall be my departure.
> O men of Dublin of the bells,
> Including abbots and bishops;
> Raise not the earth over Tadg
> Till I have bestowed on him a last look."

Those he writes of, in these terms, are the same whom the pseudo-historians vilify as "pagan Danes," though their erection and liberal endowment of Christ Church are on record. It is a significant thing that, when Mac Liag composed his lament in exile for his King Brian, the bard's place of refuge was in the Hebrides, the "Isles of the Gall," among the generous Norse-Irish. Their esteem for letters, and their tolerance, must have been great when the bard of their enemy sought them, and sang amongst them the praise of their fallen foe.

Cuan O'Lochain was one of the Duumvirate of Sages to whom the government of the country was intrusted after Clontarf. He was the author of the "Book of Rights," in which are the words of St. Benenn relating how St. Patrick blessed the foreigners of Dublin, and endowed them with seven gifts. If this be not of St. Benenn, it must be the work of Cuan, and the prophecy becomes a testimony borne by the Legislator of Erinn to the high qualities of the Norse-Irish.

Some ninety years later King Magnus sang in Dublin of his Irish Love, and in his verse revealed the influence of the bards :

" Hvatt skal heim-faor kvitta hugr er min í Dyflinni,
Enn til kaupangs kvenna kem-ek eigi austr í hausti.
Unik því at eigi synjar Injan gaman-þinga ;
Oerskan velar því er Irskom ann-ek betr an mer svanna." [1]

A hundred years later, at the close of the twelfth century, a Gaelic bard addressed an impassioned poem to Randal, Lord of Arann (Scotland), grandson of Godfrey, Norse-Irish King of Dublin, urging him to vindicate his claim to the sovereignty of Erinn. He promised him that, if he

[1] " Why should we think of going home? My heart is in Dublin, and I shall not go back in the autumn to Chipping (Nidaros). I am glad that the darling does not deny me her favour. Youth makes me love the Irish girl better than myself."—*Corpus Poeticum Boreale:* Vigfusson and York Powell.

went, the Hill of Tara would ring with music for Randal,
" the best of the world's kings."[1]

The influence of Irish verse-structure on the Norse
may be illustrated briefly by comparing the production
of an Irish bard with that of King Magnus. St. Mura
wrote in the metre called "Rinnard," with three allitera-
tions, as follows :

> Fland tendalach temrach
> tendrig fotla feraind."

King Magnus wrote :

> " Enn til kaupangs kvenna
> kem-ek eigi austr í hausti."

It will be noticed at once that the system of alliteration
is alike in both. In both, also, there appears an imperfect
rime between the last word of the first, and the first word
of the second line. Systematic letter-stress or alliteration
was an essential in Norse and in Anglo-Saxon verse. It
is seen in this specimen from Beowulf, usually written as
one line—

> " rice to rune
> rædes eahtedon."

Another and a most remarkable characteristic of Gaelic
verse is the rule which, requiring the repetition of the
same consonant for alliteration, permits different vowels
to alliterate. Both this law and this exception are found
in Norse and in Anglo-Saxon verse-structure. We must

---

[1] O'Curry, "Manners and Customs of the Ancient Irish," Vol.
III., Lecture xxxv.

conclude, I believe, that they were transferred into these literatures from the Irish, because this was the most ancient, the most cultivated, the most copious in metrical methods, and because both Norsemen and Anglo-Saxons had opportunities for learning ancient Irish, and made great use of these opportunities. The Anglo-Saxons, who thronged the university city of Armagh, and those who studied under the Irish teachers of Northumbria, would have been dull indeed had they not gleaned so much of Irish prosody. The occasional profusion of unaccented words, or "slurs," in both Norse and Anglo-Saxon, which seem a distinguishing mark, may be an imitation of the seemingly irregular Gaelic " Rosg."

Vigfusson recognized the influence of Irish versification on the Norse : " Bragi's innovation of the line-rhyme," he wrote, " and the more regular stressing we should certainly ascribe to foreign influence, probably Keltic : we can account for it in no other way." Bragi's line, he adds, was " the fountain-head of various court-metres." End-rimes occurred in the west, under Irish influence, for they are "alien to old Teutonic poetry."

Burthens, which Bragi introduced, must likewise have been borrowed from the Irish, and the "kennings " or synonyms, often so obscure and so complex, are clearly an imitation of the fashion of some ancient Irish bards.

In the middle of the ninth century Queen Aud, widow of White Olaf, King of Dublin, retired to Iceland on the death of her son. Many of her Irish connections by marriage and their followers accompanied her, and from this Norse-Irish colony sprang the authors of the Sagas. " The bulk of the settlers," wrote Vigfusson, " were men who, at least for one generation, had dwelt among a Keltic population and undergone an influence which an old and strongly marked civilization invariably exercises." Again, " we find among the emigrants of all ranks men and women of pure Irish and Scottish blood, as also many sprung from mixed marriages, and traces of this crossing survive in the Irish names borne by some of the foremost characters of the Heroic Age of Iceland, especially the poets, of whom it is also recorded that they were dark men." And Professor York Powell, writing of the Eddas, which bear traces of southern knowledge, said: " It is well to remark that among the first poets we have any knowledge of the majority are of mixed blood, with an Irish ancestress not far back in the family tree. . . . Their physical characteristics, dark hair and black eyes, like Sighvat and Kormack (Cormac), their reckless passion and wonderful fluency are also non-Teutonic and speak of their alien descent."

The filiation of the Norse literature to that of ancient Ireland has been amply acknowledged : the debt of the Anglo-Saxon insufficiently. Guest, however, showed goodwill but had not data at hand. Stopford Brooke has demonstrated how plentiful were the opportunities in Northumbria, where Gaelic was a court language. Caedmon lived and sang in an Irish intellectual atmosphere. Aldhelm, the first Anglo-Saxon to write rimed Latin verse in the eighth century, was a pupil of the Irish abbot, Mailduff. So Otfried, who in the ninth century introduced rime into High German, was a pupil of the Irish monks of St. Gall. Later, the asonant rime found in Anglo-Norman poems, and common in the Romance of Oc and related dialects "is clearly the Irish *Comharda*" (correspondence), wrote Guest, "though not submitted in the Romance dialects to the nice rules which regulate its assonances in the Gaelic."

St. Donatus, Bishop of Fiesole in 816, a Latin poet, describes his native country at the beginning of this period:

> " Insula dives opum, gemmarum, uestis et auri :
> Commoda corporibus, ære sole solo.
>
> " In qua Scotorum gentes habitare merentur
> Inclyta gens hominum, milite, pace, fide."

To this time belong many historical romances in prose, such as the "Battle of Moyléana," where the "seven sons of Sigir" (Sigurd) are mentioned as allies. The Norse are named in many historical tales, but these may, as I have shown, belong to previous ages. Here, however, may possibly be placed the last of the "Three Sorrows of Story," the "Fate of the Children of Tuireann," from which a poem is quoted. In connection with this tale I came upon a very curious coincidence. Thirty years ago John Bright produced a wide effect by a phrase in his speech at Limerick. He said:

" I believe that if the majority of the people of Ireland had their will, and if they had the power, they would unmoor the island from its fastenings in the deep and move it at least 2,000 miles further westward."

Now, in this ancient Irish story, where Balor one of the chiefs of the Fomorian Norse is mentioned, the following passage is found :

" And Balor followed them to the port and he said : ' Give battle to the Ioldanach, and cut off his head : and tie that island which is called Erinn to the sterns of your ships and your good barques, and let the dense verging waters take its place, and place it upon the north side of Norway, and not one of the Tuata Dé Danann will ever follow it there."[1]

Perhaps, considering how remote is the idea from the possible, a more strange coincidence does not exist in literature.   Here the ancient Gaelic bard anticipated a statesman.   A little later, an ancient Irish statesman, Cormac, King-Bishop of Cashel, anticipated the central thought of an English poet—Tennyson, expressed in " Crossing the Bar."

Most notable and most interesting, from an historical standpoint, is the Gaelic poem which tells so triumphantly of a Norse expedition—which yet gave " glad good news to Innisfail."   There is nothing in Norse literature, prose or poetry, which so vividly yet so accurately describes a vessel and its equipage.   All are Norse and nobles.   It is the expedition of a Sea-King and the ships are adorned with silks and coloured cloths, as the Sagas

[1] O'Curry, " Atlantis," Vol. IV., p. 169. O'Curry gravely adds : " this was an empty boast, as the sequel shows."

tell us sometimes happened. Though the poem has been only preserved phonetically, its structure indicates the skilled bard, who kept the laws, and knew how to vary his metre:

> "Purple wings our ships expand
> O'er the fleckt and flowing wave;
> Mid the masts the champions stand
> Fit for foray, mild and brave.

> "Blue are the seas surrounding,
> Prows o'er the billows bounding;
> Swords in their sheaths are glowing,
> The lances thrill for throwing.

> "Fair are the forms reclining
> On the cushioned couches high,
> Wives in their beauty shining
> 'Neath the chequered canopy.

> "Silks in varied fold on fold
> Clothe our King-ship sailing fast:
> Silks of purple splendour hold
> Wells of wind at every mast."

Though descriptive of a visit by an Irish prince to his comrade-friend, a prince of Norway, the Voyage of Ruad is totally different. Here the voyager finds his ship suddenly stop in mid-sea; after many vain efforts, he dives and discovers that it is held by nine fair straight-limbed women. Descending with them to their quiet under-sea abode, he stays for a time, then suddenly departs, pledged to return. Having paid a seven years' visit to Norway he goes back to his native land, breaking his promise. When he has passed the sea-maidens' abode, a murmur is heard following his ship: it is the sound of their pursuing bark of bronze. As his ship touches land the dead body of his son is flung up against the beach from the sea, where their child had been killed by the mother.

This is a much more dramatic story than that of the Lorelei—which may, however, have been an Irish tale carried to the Rhine by the Irish Saint Goar.[1]

There is a story concerning a little poem of this period which gives it special human interest. Cavaliére Nigra, whilst examining the old scholarly manuscripts of St. Gall's, noticed a few lines written on the margin. This was a little lay addressed to a blackbird, which had begun singing when the monk had written so far on the page. That blackbird's song was sung in the year 850, among the Swiss mountains, where the Irish Saint Gall had planted his famous Monastic School. "Whilst translating these verses," wrote Signor Nigra, "I love to imagine the poor monk who, more than a thousand years ago, was copying the manuscript and, taken off for a moment by the song of the blackbird, saw through the casement of his cell the green crown of woods which surrounded his monastery, in Ulster, or in Connaught; and having heard the quick trilling of the bird he wrote these verses and returned more lightly to his interrupted labours."

The Irish monks loved nature, and all things animate and inanimate. Two centuries before, King Guaire be-

---

[1] *Recté*, Guaire.

sought his hermit brother to return, and repose in a couch, not with uneasy head in a fir tree. Marban replied by giving a glowing picture of his little hermitage in the forest, "and the natural beauties of water, shrub, tree, beast, and insect that surround him and yield him food and consolation of body and mind. Among his musicians he enumerates the redbreast, the cuckoo, and the 'Ciaran' or beautiful large mottled wild bee"—the cry of wild geese at approach of winter, and the call of the merle-hen.[1]

Here we may place the poem on a "Ruined Nest," by some unknown, half-Christian bard, swayed by the storms of love and grief.

Perhaps the most classic poem of this period is Queen Gormlai's noble "Lament for Niall," who was slain in an attack upon the Norse-Irish of Dublin in the year 919. It is original, sincere, passionate, yet restrained. We see her standing beside the open grave, which a monk is filling, whilst a priest stands near to intone the "De Profundis," she exclaims:

> " Move, O monk, thy foot away,
> Lift it now from Niall's side—
> Over much thou'st cast the clay
> Where I would, with him, abide."

There are few stories in history or romance, so tragic as that of Queen Gormlai, which is told in the Appendix.

Some of the hymns composed in this period will surely attract attention. Of these is the bright little hymn, in

---

[1] O'Curry, "Manners and Customs," Vol. III., p. 357.

six-syllabled verse, of Maelisu, "Holy Spirit of Love."
More curious, though not less devotional, is that entitled
"Deus Meus," in which he intermingles Latin with Irish
lines, as had been done two centuries before by St. Colman,
professor at Cork.   But I believe that the hymns of one
of the distinguished bardic O'Dalys will most appeal to
and nearly touch the human heart to-day.   They are
correct in structure, but far removed from formalism :
they are simple, natural, and loving.   This is the first
verse of one hymn :

> "That in Jesu's heart should *be*
> One like *me* is marvellous ;
> Sin has made my life a *loss*
> But his *Cross* shall speak for us."

This of another :

> "Teach thou me, O Trinity !
> O Lord who speech is sweet,
> Teach my tongue, O Trinity !
> Bless it, with blessings meet."

There is a spirit of love in these hymns which must
keep them ever new.

The poem of the Four Men over the grave of Alexander
the Great is, I think, unique.   It displays surprising vigour
of conception and boldness of expression, all the more
remarkable when we remember that the Gael loved rather
to admire than to criticise their hero—and the heroes of
Greece and Rome had long been heroes in Erinn.   Hear
the bard speak :

" Yesterday he hurl'd
Royal edicts o'er the world,
Rode the earth from rim to rim—
Now earth rideth over him ! "

The epoch closes with a very singular poem, extracted
from a most extraordinary work, entitled "The Vision of
Mac Conglinne." One cannot examine the structure of
this curious narrative, without noting its identity, in many
respects, with the structure of Rabelais' work. It seems
imperative to suppose that Rabelais had this Irish tale
before him, in a Latin or French version. Such versions
of Irish tales were not uncommon : many enjoyed a wide
popularity. There is another thing noteworthy, for the
poem entitled " A Vision of Viands " (given in the original
metre, with trisyllabic rimes), manifestly gave origin to
some passages in the " Land of Cokaygne." The Abbey,
whose walls were pasties, flesh and fish, whose shingles
were of flour cake, was originally a Castle. After sailing
a sea of milk, the bard came to it :

" Ramparts rose of custard all,
Where a Castle muster'd all
    Forces o'er the lake :
Butter was the bridge of it,
Wheaten meal the ridge of it,
    Bacon every stake."

It is the earliest example of the mock-heroic poem in
(non-classic) European literature.

IX. Four centuries, from the year 1200 to the year 1600,
would almost cover the period between the arrival of the

Normans from England and the death of Queen Eliza-
beth.   It was a strange invasion, for the newcomers who
besieged the Norse-Celt capital, Dublin, were themselves
descendants of the Norse-Celts of Normandy.   The time
is full of interest.   Again the literature of Erinn was
brought, now forcibly, into contact with that of Britain.
French literature was greatly evolving, and the Anglo-
Normans had their trouvères, ménestrels, seggers, and
disours, but they discovered a new world of beauty in
Erinn which put all these in the shade.   Gerald de Barri,
who accompanied Henry II. to Erinn, declared that the
Irish were incomparably superior to every other nation
in instrumental music.   His countrymen made a similar
discovery with respect to Irish letters.   For a little time
there seemed some chance of a Hiberno-Norman literature
arising; some poems in Norman-French were composed,
relating to the sieges of Dublin and Ross, for instance ;
but the glamour of Erinn's ancient civilization was as
potent over the Normans as over the Norse.   The great
nobles soon acquired the language, became Irish Chieftains
in practice, with brehons, bards, romancists, and harpers.
It was the impassioned lay of his bard which, in the
sixteenth century, decided the revolt of "Silken" Thomas,
Henry VIII.'s Lord Deputy of Ireland.

Celtic literature was not alien to their tastes.   Many
legends had passed from Ireland, Wales, Brittany, and
Cornwall into Latin and Norman-French.   Only twenty
years before Henry landed, Bérou had composed, in
England, the Norman-French lay of Tristan and Iseult,

which of itself would make them familiar with Dublin, where the heroine dwelt. Here her name long abode in " Isolde's Tower," and still abides in Chapel-isod. Morhoult, her brother, was the Norman form of Murcad, now pronounced Murha.

There had been nothing till then in English literature to attract them. It gives one a shock to remember that the Anglo-Normans had been thirty-four years in Dublin when Layamon's "Brut" was completed, and that this represented poetry :

> " An preost wes on leoden,
> Layamon wes ihoten :
> He was Leuonadhes sone
> lidhe him beo drihten."

Even in 1300, Robert of Gloucester wrote explaining that the Normans spoke French, and only the " low men hold to English " :

"Thus come, lo ! Engelond into Normannes honde
And the Normans ne couthe speke tho bote her owe speche,
And speke French as dude atom, and here children dude al so teche,
So that heymen of thys lond, that of her blode come,
Holdeth alle thulke speche that hii of them nome,
Vor bote a man couthe French metolth of him wel lute,
Ac lowe men holdeth to Englyss and to her kunde speche yute."

The Augustinian hermit, Richard Rolle, who died in 1349, wrote in Northumbrian dialect, and appears to have got some of his ideas directly from the Irish—a loan the more probable because Irish influence had greatly influenced northern England. His description of heaven in "The Pricke of Conscience" seems a free translation of passages in Bran's "Isle of Delight":

> "Ther is lyf without ony deth,
> And ther is youthe without ony elde;
> And ther is alle manner welthe to welde;
> And ther is rest without ony travaille,
> And theer is pees without ony strife,
> And ther is alle manner lykinge of lyf:
> And ther is bright somer ever to se,
> And ther is never wynter in that countrie."

Parallel passages are given, in footnotes, between Michel of Kildare's "Land of Cokaygne" and their Irish originals. Langland, who died at the close of the fourteenth century, revived alliteration in "Piers the Plowman," but without the rule of ancient art. Chaucer did not arise, and with him English literature, until the latter half of the fourteenth century. Then the spirit of the Norman, the Celt, and the Saxon breathed into the English language, and its true poetry began.

This period is represented in the following collection by poems composed by the Gael in Erinn and in Alba. The first in date, the "Lay of the Harp of Ransom," is by an Irish bard delegated to Scotland to seek the restoration of a prince's harp, given as ransom for the return of another poet. This harp is supposed to be the original of that which was assigned to the Irish escutcheon. The bard personifies it as a maiden:

> "Sweet thy full melodious voice,
> Maid who wast a Monarch's choice."

A singular poem is that of Gerald, fourth Earl of Desmond. It is the production of a Norman, Fitzmaurice, now become an Irish bard, and there are several more from his pen which have been sedulously preserved in Scotland. It is a satire against women, which was unusual amongst Gaelic bards; and finally, it is in the metre of the song on Rosalind. Indeed, it reminds one of Touchstone's travesty of her lover's verse:

> "Sweetest nut has sourest rind,
> Such a nut is Rosalind;
> He that sweetest rose will find,
> Must find love's prick and Rosalind."

There could be no question of Earl Gerald borrowing from Shakespeare, for the rule of the Desmonds was ended by Elizabeth's confiscation.

Another anticipatory poem is that of a Lennox bard, who antedates Balzac and Kipling by four centuries in his description of the failing power of an artist.

The first Countess of Argyll, Isabel Stuart, a contemporary of Lydgate, contributes a delicate bardic song, "Love Untold." In "A King's Lesson," the reader can observe with what respectful manliness an Irish bard could admonish his monarch, and set forth the principles of sovereign rule amongst the Irish Gael. It will enable us also to make a comparison between this independence and these principles, and the adulation offered to the contemporary English sovereign and the servility desired by her successor. The bard, though his prince had sub-

mitted to Elizabeth, was still a power in Clare, and owned,
by virtue of his hereditary office, the castle of Dunogan
and its appurtenance.   His poem was composed just one
year before Edmund Spenser made his pitiful plaint:

> "Full little knowest thou that hast not tried,
> What hell it is in suing long to bide:
>
>   *   *   *   *   *   *
>
> To speed to-day, to be put back to-morrow,
> To feed on hope, and pine on fear and sorrow:
>
>   *   *   *   *   *   *
>
> To fawn, to crouch, to wait, to ride, to run,
> To spend, to give, to want, to be undone."

Had Spenser been an Irish bard, in even a small
principality, he would not have died of starvation, but
have lived in high honour, with wealth sufficient to tempt
confiscation.   He records his admiration of the gallantry
of the Irish soldier, the chivalric bearing of the Irish
knight—like Sir Thopas—and the poetry of the Irish
bard, though he could have little known its curious
beauties in a mere prose translation.   He made Irish
southern scenery famous in his "Faerie Queene," and
introduced the Gaelic "puca" into English fairydom,
as the "powke," which Shakespeare presented as
"Puck."

Queen Elizabeth, according to the Venetian Am-
bassadors, had learned Irish; she had Irish airs in her
"Virginal Book" and, according to the Talbot papers,
Irish music was all the fashion.   It has been pointed out
that Shakespeare introduces Irish words in the following
passage from "Henry V." Act IV., Sc. 4.

"*French Soldier.* 'Je pense que vous estes le gentilhomme de bonne qualité.'

"*Pistol.* 'Quality! Callino, custure me. Art thou a gentleman?'"

This was recognized as the title of an Irish song, by Malone; Lover made the phrase to be "Cáilin og a stór," Dr. Whitley Stokes, "Cáilin og a's truagh." It might be "Cáilin óg a stuaire." There is another passage in Shakespeare which has puzzled commentators and which I think can be easily explained, in a similar way. In "As You Like It," Act II. Sc. 5, Amiens invites those who love the greenwood to "come hither," and again:

> "Who doth ambition shun,
> And love to live i' the sun,
> Seeking the food he eats,
> And pleas'd with what he gets
> Come hither, come hither, come hither;
> Here shall he see
> No enemy
> But winter and rough weather."

Jaques, in derision, says "I'll give you a verse to this note. . . ."

> "If it do come to pass
> That any man turn ass,
> Leaving his wealth and ease,
> A stubborn will to please
> Ducdàme, ducdàme, ducdàme;
> Here shall he see
> Gross fools as he
> An if he will come to me."

"What is that ducdàme?" asked Amiens, and Jaques mockingly replied, "'Tis a Greek invocation to call fools into a circle."

Amiens' question still remains unanswered. One suggests it comes from the Latin "duc ad me;" another, from the French "douce dame;" another, from the Romany; another, the call of a dame to her ducks! It is agreed that it must correspond, in some way, to the invitation given by Amiens to "come hither."

Now, there was an Irish ballad current at that time, with a romantic history. Eivlin Cavanagh, the secret Love of a forbidden suitor, was about to be married. Her lover, Carrol O'Daly, disguised as a harper, came to her mansion, and with impassioned song besought her to come with him. "Diuca tu" is the phonetic form of the question, "Wilt thou come?" Her reply, given in a succeeding verse is "Tiucame" (which she repeats) " I will come." Now here we have the invitation and the answer, "a verse to this note." As to calling "fools into a circle," which has been made a mystery, it plainly refers to the circle of hearers who assemble round the wandering minstrel. It may be added that another line of this poem has had a world-wide popularity. It is that in which the bard pours out his delight: "Cead milé fáilté romat"—"a hundred thousand welcomes to thee."

X. It seems a strange paradox to say that the Irish suffered most under the sway of kindred rulers. They had been ever a most friendly nation ("natio amicissima") in the eyes of the Anglo-Saxons, who helped to fill their great schools, and whose college in Mayo caused that place to be called Mayo of the Saxons. It was to Dublin Earl Godwin's sons fled for refuge. Of the relations of the Gael with Norsemen and Normans sufficient has been said. The Norman kings of England left their national life practically as it had been. Their days of disaster began when the kindred Cymric Tudors assumed power, and their ruin seemed completed under the Celtic Stuarts.

Our last literary period begins with the year 1600, shortly before the accession of James I. Up to this time, the Pale has been a small fraction of the island, so far as language and letters were concerned. It lay outside the genuine intellectual life of the land, which went on, with great interruptions no doubt, as before. Even in the year 1604, a Contention of the Bards showed their spirit lived, the great Annals were compiled, good works written, and Schools of Ancient Learning were maintained. But in 1627 Conell Ma Geoghegan, wrote that many, whose profession it was to keep the chronicles, could no longer obtain respect and profit by their profession, and set their children to learn English. They neglected their books, and some even sold them as vellum to tailors to be cut in strips—a worse misdeed than the alleged "drowning" of books by Norsemen.

Yet five years later "The Annals of the Four Masters" were begun, and in four years completed, 1636. Thirty years later, Mac Firbis had concluded his well-known "Book of Genealogies," and fortunately came into friendly relations with an erudite Palesman, Sir James Ware. But "the war of chicane followed the war of the sword," as Edmund Burke says, and was more fatal. The enforced flight of the northern earls of Tyrone and Tirconnell, and the plantation of their fertile lands by alien peasants, and plotting owners, careless of culture, paralyzed the intellect for the time and place. There was little light of home during the perfidious reign of Charles I., or the Egyptian rule of Cromwell. If a brief glimmer followed, it closed in the darker night of the penal code of William and Anne, which was an effort made to annihilate the intellect of a nation that had generously fostered the development of all other peoples, and liberally enlightened the world.

Hence it is not surprising there should be a note of deeper sorrow heard. Yet the literature of the period is wonderfully diversified, and it is not the Gael only who mourn. Many bards bear foreign names. Their fathers had crossed with the Normans, or with later settlers, yet they claimed the country's history as their heritage, and they make appeal to all its ancient traditions. So every generation fuses with the great Past, in the adopted land they love. A Norman Nugent feels the pang of exile as keenly as an O'Neill. A singular illustration of this commingling of race is illustrated in connection with the Dirge of Oliver Grace. He was a descendant of Raymond le Gros ; the bard who laments him in Gaelic is of Welsh extraction, yet no dirge is more completely representative of the Irish characteristics and superstitions, as now understood.

The fine poem on " The Desolation," is by Mac Marcuis,

whose name betrays his foreign race, yet his spirit is Irish of the Irish. Clarence Mangan gave a beautiful paraphrase of Mac an Baird's (or Mac Ward's) lament for the northern chieftains, dead at Rome, which begins " O Woman of the piercing Wail." In the elegy for Eogan Rua O'Neill, whose chivalrous and romantic life has been told so well by Mr. J. F. Taylor, Q.C., there are only the simple accents of the untutored heart.

The penal code of William and Anne which forbade education to the Irish people should have suppressed all literary expression. If anything could have made them a nation of illiterate boors, this should. But the soul is stronger than statutes. The penal code seems to have caused the whole island to blossom into music and song. Under it flourished those fine minstrels, O'Connellan and O'Carolan, who gave some of its most delightful airs to the country.

-The eighteenth century abounded in minor bards, some of whose lays are very wells of poetry. Impassioned and refined, with words modulated to music, they offer a great variety of verse forms. They retain the euphonious vowel end-rime, alliteration sometimes, and not infrequently internal rime. Sometimes feats of force are accomplished. The old alphabetical form, where each stanza began with a letter of the alphabet (as in " A solis ortus " of Sedulius), was adopted and excelled. For, at times, the Gaelic bard would make each word in the line —nay, every word in a stanza—begin with the same initial. Another initial had currency in the next verse, and so on. Then, there were interwoven rimes. Again, each word of one line rimed to the word above it, in the preceding line. Such playing with rime, and such mastery over it are only discoverable in mediæval latinity, and the resemblance is so close and exceptional as to prove relationship. The Irish monks of a previous epoch had set the ball rolling—parallels may be found in Irish modern verse (not of course in the same metre) for such riming arrangements as these of Everhardus:

> " Virgo beata salusque parata benigna precanti
> Dona rogata dabis cumulata tibi fabulanti."

Also for these—*adonici alterne relati:*

> " Theca pudoris virgo decoris gemma valoris
> Omnibus horis es decus oris stella nitoris."

For these, where the entire word-series of one line rimes with that of the next:—*Rhythmici retrogradi singulis relati:*

> " Doctorum documen diversorum superasti,
> Multorum nocumen tormentorum tolerasti."

Even for these where all the words rimed together— *Rhythmici retrogradi undique relati:*—a most difficult form:

> "Plura precatura, pura cura valitura,
> Cura mansura, procura jura futura."

The modern Irish bards went still further. In Latin, such efforts fatigue the ear, because there is no variation : the consonants riming as well as the vowels. In Irish, vowel-rime sufficing, there was variety of consonants with increased power of phrasing. Sometimes, then, the poet would run one stanza on two vowel sounds—and then another on two other sounds—still maintaining perfect sense. The Munster poets were especially given to this mellifluous mode, nothing could well be more melodious than their verse, nothing more impossible to render completely into English.

Some of the recent poetry of Mr. Swinburne, with its happy alliteration and melodious flow recalls on a loftier level the musical manner of these later Gael. Tennyson, who effected a revival of interest in ancient British literature, was attracted by that of Ireland. He gave it the homage of an exquisite poem, and set an example which other men of genius, strong enough to enter fresh woods, will surely follow. But long before this poem, his mode of expression was, occasionally, curiously like that of the Gael. Thus, in his early poems, he is fond of compound adjectives: "clear-pointed flame," "low-cowering," "fair-fronted." This was an Irish characteristic. In the Battle of Moyléana, for instance, we find "fierce-fronted, sportive-topped billows." It was a favourite figure with recent Irish bards to describe a maiden as a "blossom of the Apple-tree"—"Bright flower of the fragrant apple." Tennyson, in "The Brook," sings of the "fresh apple-blossom." There is a lyric given in Hardiman's Minstrelsy, where the lover, having waited lonely and long for his beloved, exclaims: "Arise, O bright Sun, give forth the light of day and disperse my clouds, afar." Does not this suggest:

" Shine out, little head, sunning over with curls
To the flowers, and be their sun ? "

At her coming tread, her lover's heart would hear her and
beat, had it lain for a century dead.

So also, the blind bard O'Hearnain, were he laid in
the tomb, would awake, hear and arise, did the Voice of
Freedom sound above his grave.   Then Tennyson's
poem "Crossing the Bar" embodies the central thought
of the King-bishop of Cashel's pilot poem.

There is, I think, conclusive proof that Tennyson read
what had been translated of Irish verse, and derived a
few suggestions from it.   There is a poem in Hardi-
man's work (published in 1831) which contains these lines
of eulogy on John McDonnell the bard.   He was

" A druid, in whose mind her honey-dew
As in a comb did science richly store."

Tennyson wrote in " Edwin Morris " (1856)

"Was he not
A full-celled honey-comb of eloquence
Stored of all flowers ? "

The metaphor is the same : the verb "store" is repeated,
so that this cannot be a chance coincidence.   Strangely
enough the English poet represents the Irish bard's
metaphor more exactly than the translator : for the literal
version is " A sage, and a honeycomb of knowledge." [1]

---

[1] Among the more curious anticipations of the latter-day Gael is
the "Parliament na m-ban," or "Parliament of Women," which
displays in actual work that which is scarcely yet even a dream to
the advanced advocates of Woman's Rights.

XI. The Irish lyrical poetry of the eighteenth century may be conveniently divided into the patriotic or political and that expressive of the more domestic affections.

The former may be fitly introduced by a poem of passionate love : "The Fair Hills of Eiré." It was written in exile, on the dull shores of the Elbe, and never was the devotion of an exile more ardently expressed. Versions of it have been given by Sir Samuel Ferguson and Clarence Mangan, and none would be presented here, were it not that the former had but a fragment of the poem. His noble rendering almost makes it complete. Neither version, however, gives the exact measure and internal rime of the original, which are of literary interest :

> " Behold, in the valley, cress and berries bland,
> Where streams love to dally, in that wondrous land,
> While the great river-voices roll their music grand
> Round the Fair Hills of Eiré, O ! "

Specimens of Jacobite songs follow. In times when great national events strike away the customary or conventional surroundings, man's mind stands naked, unarmed, subject anew to the influences of the invisible. " Her young men shall see visions, and her old men shall dream dreams." Was it because the Irish bards saw visions, and could take refuge in a more ethereal world from hard realities, that the tone of Irish Jacobite poetry is so buoyant ? Spirits came to comfort them, in the days of desolation. Under branches of flowers, in a wood, appeared the Goddess of Song, to her despairing votary :

> "My heart beat with rapture and brightened
>   My soul to that Sprite from above,
> The smile from her blue eyes that lightened
>   Sent my bosom a-thrilling with love.
> O berry-red cheeks !—and, O cluster
>   Of curling gold hair to the knee !
> I could gaze the whole night on your lustre,
>   And the night seem a minute to me."

Or Erinn herself comes radiant upon the waters, but pale with sorrow :

> "Lo, all the splendour of sunshine dancing
>   Through snowy lilies her cheeks upon."

When the bard gave her tidings of future triumph :

> "Her sorrows fleeted—she struck the golden
>   High-ringing harp with her snowy hand,
> And poured in music, the regal, olden,
>   The lofty lays of a free-made Land :
> The birds, the brooks, and the breeze seemed springing
>   From grief to gladness that sunny dawn,
> And all the woods with delight were ringing
>   So sweet her singing for *Buahil Bawn !*"

Or she comes, for her name is banned, in disguise as "Shiela gal ni Connollan," or as "Grannia Wael," as "Kathaleen ni Holohan," or as "Dark Rosaleen." Always the fairest of the fair, the most beautiful being on earth, the most beloved of all the world. This theme was put to almost every tune, so that every air sang her praise. In these poems, the Stuart Prince was a subsidiary personage, the agent of Erinn's deliverance. There are other lays, though few, which show a persona affection, as " Over the Hills and far away," and " Health to the Chief."

In form these are remarkable contrasts to the older poetry, and probably the most noticeable, in that respect is the "Cruiskeen Laun." This is the oldest and only Irish song of the name, which I know. It is political ; the drinking song was written within the English-speaking Pale.

Nothing reveals the feelings of the people so faithfully as its poetry. When their chieftains, nobles, and friends were driven to foreign lands,—there rising by merit to honours—the persecuted remnant of Ireland looked abroad for redemption. At home, strangers ruled in every parish over the confiscated lands, and recreants advanced themselves to wealth and dignities over the wreck of honour. Apart, the remnant of the bards. sang, sorrowed, predicted, and satirized.

It surprises one at first to find they took little or no note of the patriots in the Irish Parliament. These seemed still all strangers, or renegades ; they were not yet fused, though in process of fusion, and now creating a new Irish literature in English.

There are fewer Gaelic ballads in connection with the insurrection of Ninety Eight than one might expect. Some of them are simple peasant verses : others, like " The Slight Red Steed," show mystic faculty. This Republican movement originated in the Anglo-Irish Pale (the Lowlands of Ireland), and was sung in English. It extended to the Gael, and mingled both peoples in

suffering, but the Southerners, from whose kindred chiefly
the Irish Brigade in France was recruited, were royalist
at heart.

XII. In the second section of the poetry of the Penal
Days—the seventeenth and eighteenth centuries—are
grouped a number of songs of the Affections, Elegies,
short epigrammatic verses, etc.   The three Elegies given
are classic in form.   One deplores the death of O'Carolan,
the famous minstrel; and the bard, with the old devotional
boldness, bids the Saints:

> "Give welcome to Toralach's spirit
>   Your ramparts among,—
> And the voice of his harp ye shall hear it,
>   With glorious song."

The second is by a bard, Feilim McCarthy, who, driven
by persecution into the mountain wilderness, discovered,
one fatal morning, that all his four children had been
killed.   I know of nothing which depicts, with such
intense feeling, the anguish of a parent's heart, not
expressed in wailing, but deepened in expression by its
reserve, and its contrast with remembered hopes.   Then
comes that mystic power which grief gives the Gael, break-
ing down the bounds of the invisible.   He sees his lost
children stretching their hands to him in the night-
time:

> "In husht midnight of heavy sleeping,
> When I am watching, sobbing, weeping,
> My children glide before my woe—
> Seeking that I should with them go.

> I see them in the night-time ever,
> From me in no place do they sever ;
> At home, abroad, still near are they,
> Till I go with them to the clay."

Callanan has given an excellent version of this poem ; but it lacks some stanzas, and is not quite close to the metre. The third elegy, by a bard of the Gael on the descendant of a Norseman, shows Conaclon ; here the last words of each stanza begin the succeeding stanza, and the last words of the entire poem are a repetition of its first. Though nearly two centuries later than that on Eoghan Rua, it is more classic in form, because composed by a skilled bard.

Love-songs in Irish literature date from the days of Fand and Deirdré. Here we have some which were composed during the last two centuries. They are chiefly Southern songs, some of which were published many years ago, in a small volume, long out of print. Several are anonymous, and may be found North and South. Munster has produced many others, finely translated by Callanan, Ferguson, Mangan and Walsh—this must be remembered when reading Dr. Douglas Hyde's fascinating book, " The Love Songs of Connaught," itself an " Island of all Delight."

These songs show great diversity in metre, rime, and mood. The pliancy of the language is proved by the ease with which it may be adapted to the most varied airs, and its open vowels and soft sounds make it welcome to vocalists as Italian. The lines may now be long, as in the "Dark Girl of the Glen," or in "A Far Fare-well:"

> " Ah, many a wild and watery way, and many a ridge of foam
> Keep far apart my lonely heart and the maid I love at home,"

and :

> " If you go from me, Vourneen, safe may you depart.
> Within my bosom, I feel it, you've killed my very heart.
> No arm can swim, no boat can row, nor bark can mariner guide
> O'er the waves of that Woeful Ocean that our two lives divide."

They may be but four syllables in length, as in the "Dells of Orrerie," to suit a lighter mood, or varied, long and short, thus:

> " There's a maiden fair to see,
> A fair maid known to me,
>   With tresses bright
>   With looks of light,
> All gladsome grace is she."

In "Doreen Le Poer" the lines are shorter yet, being constructed of five and three syllables.   This is the verse-structure of "Since Celia's my foe," which sings to "The Irish Air" preserved in Queen Elizabeth's Virginal Book. Hence this verse-form must date back to the sixteenth century: perhaps farther.   It would, therefore, be erro-neous to infer that the other verse-forms are recent, merely because they may not be preserved in old and grave manu-scripts.   Here, too, are instances of "re-narration," such as lecturers expounded in their Commentaries on Dallan:

> " 'Tis delight unto the earth, when thy little feet press it,
> 'Tis delight unto the earth when thy sweet singings bless it.

Often several lines of equal length are followed by a shorter line, as in the antique " Envoys : "

> " Her very glance would fill with light
> The darkest dell of the misty South,—
> And sweeter a kiss from her little mouth
> Than all the honey of Erinn."

Or inversely, one long line may follow short lines :

> " Her mind is a dove
> And the wit of my love
> Is more supple and swift than a bird on the wing."

These Irish bards always placed beauty of mind above bodily beauty ; this is shown even in the little simple song, " Birds on a bough." They did not fail, in due times, to extoll the maiden's skill in embroidery, painting, and song—which gives a glimpse into brighter homes, and at more accomplished people than one would think possible, under the Penal *régime*. They were, however, in constant contact with the culture of the Continent, where they had many colleges. They were superior to most of the settlers, but some of these, bearing such names as " Inglis" (or English) and " Conway," became skilful bards.

There are not wanting examples of " vers de société," madrigals, light verses of praise, compliment or raillery, which were popular in that age. Behind these, more simple in structure, are passionate peasant heart-poems by unknown authors. There, for instance, is the weird dramatic ballad of " Mauria ni Millone," with its unexpected and tragic conclusion.

The natural simplicity of the strain allows the heart to speak with undisguised earnestness, as in this verse of a forsaken maid :

> " You promised me purely
> You'd love me while green grasses grew ;
> You promised me surely
> One home between me, Love, and you.
> :   My woe to that even
> When I gave up my heart unto thee.
> O black, O bitter grieving !
> The World 's between you, Love, and me."

The apposition between the home shared between them, and the world interposed between them, makes a marked contrast. In another poem, " Death's Visit," the forlorn maid reminds her lover of his broken promise, sends to him as her envoy the Most High, yet concludes :

> " You've broke death's wall before me,
> The grave's cold breath blows o'er me ;
> Yet, take one kiss, my darling !
> Before you leave me so."

But of all love poems, that of O'Curnain, entitled " Love's Despair," appears to me the most intense and impassioned. It is one of the latest as regards date, being of the nineteenth century : the author is said to have been of low estate, but his desperate emotion gives the poem a rare elevation of thought and dignity of diction. It should be read in its entirety. Nothing but the hand that wounded him can heal the desolation of his life :

> " I know not night from day,
> Nor thrush from cuckoo gray,

Nor cloud from the sun that shines above thee :
    Nor freezing cold from heat,
    Nor friend—if friend I meet—
I but know—heart's love !—I love thee.

    " Love that my life began,
    Love that will close life's span,
Love that grows ever by love-giving :
    Love from the first to last,
    Love, till all life be past,
Love that loves on after living.

    *   *   *   *   *

    " Bear all things evidence
    Thou art my very sense,
My past, my present, and my morrow.
    All else on earth is crost,
    All in the world is lost—
Lost all—but the great love-gift of sorrow."

XIII. The final group comprises lullabies and songs of occupation. These are always of interest, for they open the inner doors, and admit us to the hearth. How old are they? Possibly Spinners' Songs, like these, were sung by the maidens in the youth of the world : in the woman's chamber of Amergin's household, the girl-children may have rimed to the line :

    "Oro, O darling fair, O lamb, and O love ! "

The lullabies are two, differing strangely. One is the crooning song of a happy mother to her babe, whom she would put to sleep :

    "On sunniest day of the pleasant summer,
    Your golden cradle on smooth lawn laying
    'Neath murmuring boughs that the birds are swaying."

The other, the "Fairy Lullaby," is the song of a most unhappy mother, who had been borne away by the invisible creatures to their fortress in the green hill. Her duty is to nurse children in the fairy kingdom, whilst her own child is forsaken. Now, on the eve of the last day when deliverance is yet possible, she chants her message to another woman, whilst anxiously hushing to sleep the fairy babe, that she may reveal the means of deliverance. This is a dramatic conception. Nor must it be taken as a mere poetic fancy: the deep conviction of the reality of such scenes has been fatally illustrated within the past few years.

The collection is concluded by a boat-song, the language of which is older than much of the later verse, but cannot be very ancient, on account of a reference to the Indies. The original imparts a sense of vehemence, buoyancy, and wave-tumult. The author, whoever he was, loved the sea. Is not this a bright picture?

> "With robes from the Indies I dighted my fair,
> How swells her white bosom against the blue air!
> Right buoyant the craft below, shapely the sail,
> O God, but to see her rise out of the gale
> On the high, bright tide! the high, bright tide!
> Queen of my heart, my joy, my pride!
> My beautiful bark on the high, bright tide!"

Accepting a suggestion of Mr. Alfred Perceval Graves, who has done so much for Irish literature, I have added two paraphrases, "The King's Lay," and "The Blessing of Dublin;" the former had the advantage of coming under the notice of Matthew Arnold, and the privilege of his approval.

This concludes a series which cannot be regarded as in any sense complete; but it will add something to what has been already accomplished, and may induce other and better qualified workers to do more.

The subject is one affecting many interests. How can the historian write of a nation if he know nothing of its culture? How can the novelist revive its past, if deaf to its harmonies and blind to its picturesque colouring? How can the statesman comprehend its spirit, the educationist develop its mental forces, the patriot feel and guide its higher instincts, if they be ignorant of its inherited powers and aptitudes?

To the student of European literature it is essential to know the literature of a nation which, when Rome had fallen, held the literary sceptre of Europe for three centuries. That nation imparted its higher culture and methods to the Norse, the Anglo-Saxons, the Germans, the French, and the Spanish, directly or indirectly, in varying degrees. Their earliest essays in verse, for all its crudeness, bear true traces of the ancient master minds, which created, organized, and taught the verse-system of the modern world.

In so far, it may be stated that Ancient Ireland was the Mother of Literatures.

I.—LAYS OF MILESIAN INVADERS.

THE INCANTATION.[1]

AMERGIN.

FAIN we ask Erinn,
Faring o'er ocean's
Motions to mountains,
Fountains and bowers,
Showers, rills rushing,
Gushing waves welling,
Swelling streams calling,
Falling foam-thunder,
Under lakes filling :
Willing—(abiding
Riding rounds, holding
Olden fairs meetly)—
Fleet to lift loyal
Royal king's towers,[2]

[1] When the Milesians, on the second occasion, had approached
the shores of Erinn, they were driven back by a strange magic wind.
Amergin, their poet-druid and judge then made this incantation.
[2] At Tara.

Bowers for crowning ;
Frowning foes over—
Rover Mil's warlike
Starlike sons therein.
Erinn shall longer,
Stronger, show honour,
On our Milesians.—
Wishing, in trouble,
Noble isle's wooing,
Suing, we stay here ;—
Pray here to sail in,
Wailing maids royal !
Loyal chief-leaders,
Pleaders, blend pray'r in.
So we seek Erinn.

FIRST TRIUMPH-SONG.[1]

AMERGIN.

I, THE Wind at Sea,
I, the rolling Billow,
I, the roar of Ocean,
I, the seven Cohorts,
I, the Ox upholding,
I, the rock-borne Osprey,

[1] When Amergin of the Fair Knee first placed his right foot on
the land of Erinn he composed this song in Rosg metre. See
Appendix. This poem gives the first example of blank verse.

I, the flash of Sunlight,
I, the Ray in Mazes,
I, the rushing Wild Boar,
I, the river-Salmon,
I, the Lake o'er plains,
I, the Strength of Song.
I, the Spear for smiting Foemen,
I, the God for forming Fortune!
Whither wend by glen or mountain?
Whither tend beneath the Sunset?
Whither wander seeking safety?
Who can lead to falling waters?
Who can tell the white Moon's ages?
Who can draw the deep sea fishes?
Who can show the fire-top headlands?
I, the poet, prophet, pray'rful,
Weapons wield for warriors' slaying:
Tell of triumph, laud forthcoming
Future fame in soaring story!

THE FIRST ELEGY.

Lugai, Son of Ith.[1]

Sate we sole, in cliff-bower—
　　Chill winds shower—
I tremble yet—shock of dread
　　Sped death's power.
The tale I tell : fate has felled
　　Fáil most fine.
She a man, bare, beheld,
　　In sun shine,
Shock of death, death's dread power,
　　Lowered fell fate,
Bare I came, hence her shame,
　　Stilled she sate.

---

[1] The wife of Lugai, nephew of Milesius, saw her husband naked, whilst bathing, and died of shame, thinking him a stranger. He composed her death-song, which was the first elegy ever composed in Erinn by a Milesian.

The metre and rime-sounds of the original are reproduced in the English version. See Appendix.

II.—THE CUCHULAINN PERIOD.

FAND'S WELCOME TO CUCHULAINN.[1]

STATELY stands the Charioteer,
Beardless, young, who hasteth here;
Splendid o'er the plain he speeds
His careering chariot steeds.

Not to him soft strains are good,
Riding, red with battle blood;
Than loud car that rushing reels
Louder whirr his whirling wheels.

At sight of those steeds, fleeing,
I stand still, silent, seeing:
Never hoofs like these shall ring
Rapid as the winds of Spring.

---

[1] Cuchulainn, allured by fairy power, went to the mystic Isle of Emain; there he assisted Labraid, "quick hand at sword," to overthrow his enemies. Then coming in his chariot, victorious, to the mansion of fair Fand, the princess who loved him, she welcomed his approach in this lay. From "The Sick-bed of Cuchulainn and only jealousy of Emer."—O'CURRY, *Atlantis*, Vols. I., II. See Appendix.

H

Fifty apples of fair gold
Glitter o'er his mantle's fold ;
Never king, on sea or strand,
Won their like, by battle brand.

On his cheeks four dimples be :
One is gray as shallow sea,
One purple pale, one like blood,
Brown is one as forest flood.

In his eyes shine seven rays,
Not forgot in poet's praise ;
Brown his eye-brows' noble track,
Long his lashes, chafer black.

His high head, what head so good?—
Erinn knows it, hill and wood—
Doth three waves of colour hold,
Brown, blood-red, and crowning gold.[1]

Crimsoned is his cleaving blade,
Bright the hilt of silver made ;
Golden bosses gem the shield
White-rimmed, radiant o'er the field.

---

[1] This is taken (in the translation) from the description in the
"Táin Bo," where Cuchulainn is said to have three chevelures :
" Brown at the skin of the head, blood-red in the middle, a diadem
of yellow-gold at the surface."—O'CURRY.

Foremost he in van of war,
Flashing first where dangers are:
There is none who bears a brand
Can with true Cuchulainn stand.

Cuchulainn comes to greet us!
Murtemni's chief to meet us!—
They who bring him from afar
Daughters of Aed Abrat are.

Blood drips from his lofty lance,
In his glance gleams battle fire;
Haughty, high, the victor goes
Woe to those who wake his ire.[1]

LIBAN'S SONG.

WELCOME Cuchulainn,
Dawn of Deliv'rance,
Proud prince of Murtemni's plain,
Mind noble and great,
Chieftain victorious,
Heart of Honour,
Strong Stone of Valour,
In battle-wrath glorious,

[1] The metre of the original is reproduced: it changes in the last
verse. "Liban's Song" is rhythmic blank verse, known as "Rosg."

Guide of courage in Ulad.
　　All beauty arrayed in,
　　Light on the eyes of each maiden
　　　Welcome !
　　Welcome, Cuchulainn !

FAND'S FAREWELL TO CUCHULAINN.[1]

I IT is who shall depart,
Though I leave with heavy heart ;
Though a hero waits me, fain,
Rather would I here remain.

Rather would I linger here,
Happy serving thee, and near ;
Than, though strange to thee it seem,
Rule Aed's court of sunny beam.

Emer, thine be this man still,
Thou shalt garner at thy will ;
What my hand reach not, no less
Am I bound in wish to bless.

[1] Emer, Cuchulainn's mortal spouse, came upon the lovers with fifty maidens armed with knives to slay Fand. Cuchulainn pledged her protection; but on hearing Emer's pathetic plea, he consoled her, declaring she should always be pleasing to him. Fand could not bear a divided love, and asked to be rejected. Emer also asked, but Fand persisted, and, falling into great grief, departed when she had spoken this lay. See Appendix.

Many men for me have sued,
Sought in court, in secret woo'd,
Never one have I come nigh
For my path lay pure and high.

Woe to one whose love has gone,
And finds naught to rest upon ;
Better who rejected roves
Than be loved not as one loves.

CUCHULAINN'S APPEAL TO FERDIAD.[1]

COME not here, nor helmet don,
O Ferdiad, Daman's son ;
Worst for thee will be the blow,
Though it bring a world of woe.

Come not here, with wrongful strife,
My hands hold thy last of life ;
Why hast not bethought thee well
How my mighty foemen fell ?

[1] From the "Táin Bo Cuailgné." Cuchulainn was defending the frontier of Ulster against the aggression of Queen Mave of Connacht and her allies. He had defeated her foremost champions. At last, by threat of satire, taunt, and praise, she induced his fellow pupil, fellow champion, and plighted friend, Ferdiad, to undertake her cause and attack Cuchulainn, guaranteeing great rewards, including arms, armour, large estates, and her beautiful daughter, Findabar. When Ferdiad appeared Cuchulainn appealed to him, as Damon might have appealed to Pythias had he come as a foe.

Art not bought with weapons bright,
Purple belt, and armour light?[1]
She for whom thy weapons shine
Shall not, Daman's son, be thine.

Mave's fair daughter, Findabar,
Brilliant though her beauties are,
Though her form has ev'ry grace,
Her thou never shalt embrace.

King's daughter is Findabar,
Pledged to thee for price of war;
Pledged to other chiefs was she,
Whom she led to death, like thee.

Break our vow of peace not here,
Break not friendship, long and dear;
Break not thou thy plighted word,
Come not hither, with the sword.

They have pledged the peerless maid
Fifty times for battle aid;
Fifty times fit meed I gave
Ev'ry champion found a grave.

[1] A curious anticipation of Browning's reproach to Words-
worth :

" 'Twas just for a handful of silver he left us,
Just for a ribbon to stick in his coat."

Who than Ferbeth was more proud?
Heroes used his court to crowd;
His high rage was soon brought low,
Him I slew with but a blow.

Daré, too, how rude his fate!
Loved by maids of high estate;
Fame afar his name had told,
His robe glowed with threaded gold.

Should she be mine, on whom smiles
All the isle's most valiant youth,—
I would crimson not *thy* breast
East or West, or North or South!

CUCHULAINN LAMENTS FERDIAD.[1]

PLAY was each, pleasure each,
Till Ferdiad faced the beach;
One had been our student life,

---

[1] From the "Táin Bo Cuailgné." In the Fight at the Ford, after
mighty deeds, Ferdiad at last is slain. Cuchulainn, grievously
wounded, bewails his friend. His charioteer at last beseeches him
to leave; he consents, declaring that each contest and each combat
which he had waged before was play and pleasure compared to this
battle with Ferdiad. Then he speaks this lay. The original metre is
reproduced. It will be observed that iterated or burthen lines
appear in this poem, which was probably composed before the sixth
century.

One in strife of school our place,
One our gentle teacher's grace
    Loved o'er all and each.

Play was each, pleasure each,
Till Ferdiad faced the beach ;
One had been our wonted ways,
One the praise for feat of fields,
Scatach gave two victor shields
    Equal prize to each.

Play was each, pleasure each,
Till Ferdiad faced the beach ;
Dear that pillar of pure gold
Who fell cold beside the ford.
Hosts of heroes felt his sword
    First in battle's breach.

Play was each, pleasure each,
Till Ferdiad faced the beach ;
Lion fiery, fierce, and bright,
Wave whose might no thing withstands,
Sweeping, with the shrinking sands,
    Horror o'er the beach.

Play was each, pleasure each,
Till Ferdiad faced the beach ;
Loved Ferdiad, dear to me :

I shall dree his death for aye
Yesterday a Mountain he,—
But a Shade to-day.

QUEEN MAVE'S ENVOYS.[1]

QUEEN.

"COME ye home with honour,
Envoys to King Conor ;
How fared ye afar ?
Doth Emania stay him ?
Do its feasts delay him ?
Fears he that we slay him ?
Comes he wild for war ?

ENVOYS.

" Ulster is not sitting,
Feasting were not fitting,
Foes they face at Brea :
They will never sunder
Till they take their plunder,
Till they reach like thunder
Cairbré and the sea."

[1] From " The Battle of Ros-na-ree," translated by Rev. Professor Hogan, S. J. Todd, Lecture Series, 1895. The saga seems redacted after the Norse invasion, but the poem may be much more ancient, and date from pre-Christian times. The metre and rime are reproduced, and show a curious similarity to Moore's " Go where glory waits thee," as first noticed by Mr. T. O'N. Russell.

QUEEN.

"They shall flee and fear us,
If they venture near us,
    How their heads shall fall!
If that man [1] advances,
Strong are Leinster's lances,
I disdain his glances,
    Stir I not at all."

ENVOYS.

" Great our champions' story
If they share the glory,
Weapons shall be gory
    Red on Ros-na-ree."

QUEEN.

" Here, if come King Conor,
Back shall turn his banner,
Low shall lie his honour,
    Vanquished shall he be."

[1] Her divorced husband, Concobar.

DEIRDRÉ'S FAREWELL TO ALBA.[1]

" And Deirdré looked back at the shores of Alba, and she said :
' My love to thee, O land in the east, and 'tis ill for me to leave
thee, for delightful are thy coves and havens, thy kind soft flowery
fields, thy pleasant green-sided hills, and little was our need for
departing,' and she said this lay : "

LOVELY Land, yon eastern Land !
Alba of the wondrous strand !
I had not come from her, now,
Came I not in Naisi's prow.

Dear is Dunfi, Dunfinn dear,
Dear the high Dun [2] rising near :
Dear is Draina, in the sea,
Suivni's Dun is dear to me.

Cuan Wood !
Where, alas ! oft Ainli stood.
Short to me appeared the time
With Naisi, in Alba's clime.

Glen Lay !
Where I used sleep happily.
Prime of badger, fish, and deer,
Were my cheer still in Glen Lay.

---

[1] From "The Fate of the Children of Usnach," one of " The
Three Sorrows of Story."   See Appendix. Alba is the Gaelic
name of Scotland.

[2] Dun (pronounced Dun or Doon), an ancient fort.

Glen Massin !
Fair the ferns, green the grass in !
We slept with moving pillows
On billows in Glen Massin.

Glen Urcheen !
Straight vale of ridge serene,
No man than Naisi brighter
In the light air of Urcheen.

Glen Itty !
There my first house, my pity !
Lovely woods, at morn, unrolled.
The Sun's Fold [1] was Glen Itty.

Glen Da Roe !
Love to all who thither go,
Cuckoos call from bending bough
O'er the brow of Glen Da Roe.

Dear is Draigan o'er the strand,
Dear its waters on pure sand ;
I would ne'er from Alba rove
Came I not thence with my Love.

---

[1] This is a literal translation of the poetic Irish words, "buaile greine"; as the herdsman inclosed his herd in a fold, so the sun inclosed his rays in Glen Itty. "Buaile," anglicized "Boolie," came to mean the mountain places to which (as still in Norway and Switzerland) cattle were driven in summer for pasture. Glen Itty was the sun's "boolie."

THE CLOUD OVER EMAIN.[1]

Foreboding treachery, Deirdré sought to dissuade the Sons of
Usnach from accepting King Concobar's invitation, in vain.   As
they drew near his court at Emain, she sang her last lay of warning:

Lo, Naisi, the cloud on high
Which I see in yonder sky :
I see, o'er Emain's tower,
A crimson blood-cloud lower.

Chilled with sudden fear am I,
Seeing that cloud in the sky ;
Like gout of gore it showeth,
The thin cloud dreadful groweth.

I would give you counsel here,
Sons of Usnach, fair and dear :
Wend not Emain-ward this night
Under omen of affright.

To Dundelgan [2] be our way,
With Cuchulainn let us stay ;
Then, upon the morrow, forth
Hie with him unto the north."

Naisi, in a wrath, replied
To fair Deirdré, prophet-eyed :

[1] In his song, beginning " Avenging and bright," Moore refers to
this omen in the line, " By the red cloud that hung over Conor's
dark dwelling."   [2] Now, Dundalk.

" Fear frights not us, unshaken,
Thy course shall not be taken."

Seldom was it known of old,
Royal sons of Rury bold,
That discord did us sever—
I and thou, Naisi—never !

When Manannan gave the draught,
We and true Cuchulainn quafft,
Thou hadst not, for might of men,
Been against me, Naisi, then.

That day we fled together,
O'er Esroe's stormy weather,
Thou hadst not, I say again,
Been against me, Naisi, then.

LAMENT FOR THE SONS OF USNACH.

After the death of the Sons of Usnach, King Concobar Mac Nessa
sought to win the favour of Deirdré by honours, feasts, and music :
she rejected all, remembering their faithful fellowship, and her love.
In the Court of Emain she sang the defiant dirge of its betrayed guests.

DEIDRÉ.

WAIL the Warriors, and your shame,
Killed at Emain, when they came :
Nobly came they here at once,
Usnach's high heroic sons.

Naisi gallant, gentle, good,—
Mourn with me his murdered blood !
Ardan, victor of the boar,—
Weep too Ainli, strong no more !

Sweet to you the mellow mead
That Mac Nessa loves to speed ;
Ever sweeter seems the fare
I with Usnach's Sons used share.

When that Naisi urged the chase
Through the wood and wilderness,
All was more than honey sweet,
When they fetched the forest meat.

Ye think the wailing mellow
Of pipe and trumpet yellow ;
I have heard,—tell Concobar !
Music more melodious far.

Sweet to Concobar, the King,
When the pipes and trumpets sing ;
Sweeter song made me rejoice—
Usnach's Sons' delightful voice.

Naisi—strong sound of ocean !
Sweet list'ning to its motion !
Great as Ardan's call to roam,
Ainli's cheer was, hying home.

Naisi's grave is made this night,—
Sorrow comes of it and blight!—
He filled foemen, ring on ring,
With red waves of slaughtering.

Lovely was their childhood's flow'r,
Mighty grew their manhood's pow'r :
Sorrow comes of it and scathe—
Usnach's Sons are done to death.

Dear their converse bright !
Dear their strong young lofty might !
When they came from Erinn's war
Dear their welcome forms afar.

Dear their blue eyes, woman-loved,
Praise went round them when they roved ;
When they came from forest chase
'Twas delight their track to trace.

I sleep no more ;
Once of yore my cheek was red ;
Me strains of welcome cheer not,
Now I hear not Naisi's tread.

I sleep never,
Sorrows sever now for naught :
What to me feast or playing,
Whose mind 's straying, all distraught.

Not for me be banquet spread,
Nor mead red, nor welcoming ;
Soft nor sweet, nor song nor sport,
Palace proud, nor court of King.

III.—THE FIONN PERIOD.

DAWN OF SUMMER.[1]

FIRST LAY OF FIONN MAC CUMAL.

SOFT Summer's first day !
How radiant the sky !
Merles lilt their full lay,—
Would Laiga were nigh !
Clear call the cuckoos,
Glad welcomes still greet
Sweet summer's bright hues !
By branchy wood's brim
Swift steeds seek the stream,
Its gleam swallows skim ;
Floweth fine heather's hair,
Bloweth frail bog-down fair,
Flee-eth frown of evil sign,
Planets beam bright benign,
Soft sigh the sleepy seas
Flowers flourish o'er the leas.

The original, with translation by Dr. O'Donovan, appeared in
" The Boyish Exploits of Find Mac Cumall," published in the " Pro-
ceedings of the Ossianic Society," Vol. IV. Find = Finn and Fionn.

WINTER'S APPROACH.[1]

FIONN MAC CUMAL.

LIST my lay : oxen roar,
Winter chides, Summer's o'er,
Sinks the sun, cold winds rise,
Moans assail, ocean cries.

Ferns flush red, change hides all,
Clanging now, gray geese call,
Wild wings cringe, cold with rime,
Drear, most drear, ice-frost time.

A WARRIOR'S DUTIES.

FIONN MAC CUMAL.[2]

THOU, Mac Lugach, shalt discern
What the warrior-order learn :
Keep in hall a courteous mood
Though in brunt of battle rude.

---

[1] The original is quoted in tract on the Amra of Columbcille, edited by Professor O'Beirne Crowe, 1871.

[2] "Silva Gadelica." Mac Lugach was Finn's grandson. When born he was laid in Finn's bosom, then Finn laid the babe in his wife's bosom, who nurtured him 'till his twelfth year had closed, and the age of arms had come. She equipped him, and sent him to Finn, who gave him a very gentle .welcome. The lad plighted service and

Blame thy spouse not, without thought,
Never beat thy hound for naught;
Never strive with senseless loon—
Wouldst thou war with a buffoon?

Gird at none of goodly fame,
Share not in the brawler's shame;
Keep apart thy path, again,
From or mad or evil men.

Two thirds of thy softness show
Women, babes that creep below,
Bards that varied verse evoke—
Nor be fierce with common folk.

Be not first to seek thy sleep
Where awake thy fellows keep;
Rules respect, false friendship shun,
Nor revered be ev'ry one.

Speak not thou mere words of might
Say not thou'lt not yield what's right—
For a shame is mighty speech
When the deed is out of reach.

fealty, striking his hand in Finn's. He was with the Fianna for a
year, but he was so indolent that but nine of his pupils had been
taught to kill deer or boar, and, worse still, he beat his hounds and
his servitors. Then the Fianna, at Ross in Killarney, made their
complaint to Finn, and bade him choose between Mac Lugach and
them. Finn admonished his grandson in this poem, and by its
counsels Mac Lugach guided his life thereafter.

Never thou thy chief forsake
Till red earth thy life shall take;
Nor for gem nor gold reward
Fail in warrant to thy ward.

Never to the chieftain's ear
Blame his household too severe,
It suits no true man's estate
Faulting low folk to the great.

Thou'lt bear no glozing story,
Not thine the carper's glory,
Thine, conduct clear and knightly
Hence men shall serve thee brightly.

Never long the ale horn hold,
Never once deride the old;
What is worthy that maintain,
Make not of misfortune pain.

Food to foodless ne'er refuse,
Nor for friend a niggard choose;
Never on the great intrude,
Nor give cause for censure rude.

Guard thy garments, guard thine arms
Through the heat of battle harms;
Ne'er to frowning fortune bow
Steadfast, stern, and soft be thou.

THINGS DELIGHTFUL.

OISIN.[1]

SWEET is a voice in the land of gold,
Sweet is the calling of wild birds bold,
Sweet is the shriek of the heron hoar,
Sweet fall the billows of Bundatrore.

Sweet is the sound of the blowing breeze,
Sweet is the blackbird's song in the trees,
Lovely the sheen of the shining sun,
Sweet is the thrush over Casacon.

Sweet shouts the eagle of Assaroe,
Where the gray seas of Mac Morna flow,
Sweet calls the cuckoo the valleys o'er,
Sweet, through the silence, the corrie's roar.

Fionn, my father, is chieftain old
Of seven battalions of Fianna bold;
When he sets free all the deerhounds fleet
To rise and to follow with him is sweet.

---

[1] The original appeared in the Dean of Lismore's Book.

THE COLD NIGHT OF INNISFAIL.[1]

COLD, cold,
Chill, this night, is Lurc's wide wold;
Foodless now the gaunt deer goes,
High o'er hills the snows are rolled.

Cold to death
Sweeps the broad'ning tempest's breath;
Round the fords the whirlpools roar,
Rills through ridges pour in wrath.

Each loch now a sea doth make,
And a great lake is each pond;
No steed wins the ford of Ross,
No foot dares to cross beyond.

Fishes Innisfail must flee,
Since there's neither sea nor strand;

[1] Whilst Diarmid and Gráinné were hiding from Finn in the cave of Howth, this lay was composed to induce them to remain there, by their servant. Whilst they were deliberating whether or not to fly from their cave of refuge (which Professor Kuno Meyer thinks to be that on the north side of the Hill of Howth), she went to watch and report. She met Finn; he professed to admire her, and then she betrayed the lovers. She dipped her cloak in the sea, and, on her return, spread it across the door, chanting this lay of a terrible tempest. But Gráinné touched the cloak with her tongue, found it salt, and discovered the treachery in time. The rime and measure are given. This ancient poem was published in the "Revue Celtique," Vol. XI., by Professor Kuno Meyer, with translation.

Bells are dumb, no herons call
Land is none in all the Land.

In their Cuan cove no hound
Yet has found repose or rest ;
Nor may wren of Leiter Lone
Shelter in its own round nest.[1]

On the small bird-comrades beat
Icy darts and sleety winds ;
Not one nook in Cuan's grove,
As 'twould love, the blackbird finds.

Cheerful is our cauldron here,
Cold and drear is Leiter Lone ;
Staff in hand, what toil to go,
Climbing snow where tempests moan.

Even the ancient eagle chief
Shakes in grief 'neath Rigi's [2] peak ;
Pierced with pain, the bitter breeze
Soon may freeze with ice her beak.

From soft down for snows to part,
Hearken heart !—'twere madly bold ;
Ice-heaps cumber every ford,
Hence each word I cry is cold.

[1] The wren builds the warmest nest.
[2] Glen Rigi is the Vale of Newry.

THE FAIR FORT OF CRÉDÉ.

CAEL, SON OF CRIMTANN.

PLEASANT is her fortress fair,
Men and maids and boys are there,
Druids and the Sons of Song,
Cupmen, doormen, skilled and strong.

Men for steed, and men for stall,
Men to rule the roast in hall ;
Supreme o'er all sits Crédé
Bright, beauteous, gold-haired lady.

Dear to me that pleasant dun,
With soft down to sit upon ;
Were the will in Crédé's breast,
Happy here would be my quest.

Full fair the porch, where splendid
Blue wings and yellow blended :
Round the fountain is a wall
Of crystal and carmogal.

Bowl of juice of berry glints,
Whence her eyebrows black she tints ;
Clear vats of ale are flowing,
Rich cups and goblets glowing.

Lime-white is her fortress wall,
Rugs and rushes deck her hall,
Silks are seen and mantles blue,
Gold and horns of glossy hue.

Her bow'r by lakelet beameth,
There gold with silver gleameth,
Wings, brown and crimson, cover
Blent bright, its roof all over.

Pillars twain of green stand there,
By the portal, passing fair ;
Spoil of silver, famed of yore,
Forms the beam above the door.

On thy left is Crédé's chair,
Ever fairer and more fair;
By dainty bed 'tis shining,
Alpine gold round it twining.

O'er this chair, like a bower,
Crédé's couch seems to tower ;
Orient-built by Tuil's device
With pure gold and gems of price.

Yet a bed beams on thy right
Built of gold and silver white ;
From rods of light bronze, looping,
Fall fox-glove curtains drooping.

In that home, the household bright
Seem all destined to delight;
Never mantle dim or bare
'Neath the clusters of their hair.

Wounded men sink to slumbers,
Whilst blood their bodies cumbers,
When they hear birds of Faery
Sing o'er her bower airy.

If she grant me grace at all—
She, for whom the cuckoos call,[1]
Then I, for thanks, will give her
More lays to live for ever.

THE DIRGE OF CAEL.[2]

By Crédé, His Spouse.

Moans the bay—
Billows gray round Ventry roar,
Drowned is Cael Mac Crimtann brave,
'Tis for him sob wave and shore.

---

[1] This is a subtle compliment. The cuckoos call for the approach of summer, hence Crédé's presence is like the coming of young summer.

[2] The rimes and metre of the original are given. For its curious history, see Appendix.

Heron hoar
'Mid the moor of Dromatren,
Found the fox her young attack,
Bleeding, drove him back again.

Sore the sigh
Sobs the stag from Drumlis nigh ;
Dead the hind of high Drumsailin,
Hence the sad stag's wailing cry.

Wild the wail
From the thrush of Drumkeen's dale ;
Not less sad the blackbird's song,
Mourning long in Leitir's vale.

Woe is me !
Dead my Cael is fair and free :
Oft my arms would ward his sleep,
Now it is the deep, dark sea.

Woe, the roar
Rolling round from sea and shore ;
Since he fought the foreign foe,
Mine the woe for Cael no more.

Sad the sound,
From the beach and billows round ;
I have seen my time this day :
Change in form and face is found.

Ever raining
Fall the plaining waves above ;
I have hope of joy no more,
Since 'tis o'er our bond of love.

Dead, the swan
Mourns his mate on waters wan,
Great the grief that makes me know
Share of woe with dying swan.

Drowned was Cael Mac Crimtann brave,
Now I've naught of life mine own :
Heroes fell before his glaive,
His high shield has ceased to moan.

WHERE IS THE SWEETEST MUSIC? [1]

NOBLE news of Song and Valour
　　Bear I Balor's fort within,
Little heed I who may hearken,
　　If my song be heard of Finn.

Men were gay in golden Allin [2]
　　Hill and hall in, far and wide ;
Feast was spread and music flowing
　　And we saw our Finn preside.

[1] Dean of Lismore's Book.
[2] The Fortress of Finn, Commander of the Fianna.

Ossian staunch, and Diarmid stately
  Sate by Luay, greatly strong,
And their friends, at feast and foray :
  Ancient Conan, Oscar young.

"Speak, ye champion chiefs, rejoicing,"
  Rang the voice of Finn around,
"Tell me each, in answer meetest,
  Where is sweetest music found?"

"There's one music fit for faming ;
  Give me gaming," Conan cried,—
Strong his hand for crash of combat,
  But his head was sense denied.

"Song of Swords for war, unsheathing,"—
  With quick breathing came the word,
"Throng of blows when falling fleetest,"—
  Seemed the sweetest Oscar heard.

"There is music more endearing,"
  Dark-eyed Diarmid did declare ;
"Naught comes nigh the voice's cadence—
  When the maiden's soft and fair."

"Sweeter song at dawning dewy—"
  Said Mac Luay, sharp of spear,
"When the bounding dogs are crying,
  And we race the flying deer."

"This is Song, and this is Music—"
  Spoke our lofty Leader old,
" Blowing breeze 'mid moving banners
  And an Army 'neath their gold."

"Then I fear no bardic passion,
  Ossian !" said our Captain strong,
" With my faithful Fianna round me—
  This to me is Harp and Song."

IV.—OSSIANIC: AGE OF LAMENTATIONS.

AFTER THE FIANNA.[1]

OISIN.

LONG, this night, the clouds delay,
And long to me was yesternight,
Long was the dreary day, this day,
Long, yesterday, the light.

Each day that comes to me is long—
Not thus our wont to be of old,
With never music, harp, nor song,
Nor clang of battles bold.

No wooing soft, nor feats of might,
Nor cheer of chase, nor ancient lore,
Nor banquet gay, nor gallant fight—
All things beloved of yore.

No marching now with martial fire—
Alas, the tears that make me blind—
Far other was my heart's desire
A-hunting stag and hind.

[1] Dean of Lismore's Book.

K

Long this night the clouds delay—
No striving now as champions strove,
No run of hounds with mellow bay,
Nor leap in lakes we love.

No hero now where heroes hurled—
Long this night the clouds delay—
No man like me in all the world,
Alone with grief, and gray.

Long this night the clouds delay—
I raise their grave-carn, stone on stone,
For Fionn and Fianna passed away—
I, Ossian, left alone.

THE BLACKBIRD OF DARICARN.[1]

SWEET thy song, in Dari grove,
No sweeter song from east to west,
No music like thy voice of love—
And thou beneath thy nest !

A strain the softest ever heard,
No more shall come its like to men.
O Patrick ! list the wondrous bird—
Thou'lt chant thy hymn again.

[1] " Transactions of Gaelic Society."

If thou, as I, but knew the tale
It sings to all the ancient isle,
Thy tears would rise, and thou wouldst fail
To mind thy God awhile.

In Norroway beyond the wave,
Its forest glades and streams among,
That bird was found by Fionn the brave,
And still we hear its song.

'Tis Daricarn yon western wood—
The Fianna huntsmen loved it best,
And there, on stately oak and good,
Lost Fionn placed its nest.

The tuneful tumult of that bird,
The belling deer on ferny steep—
This welcome in the dawn he heard,
These soothed at eve his sleep.

Dear to him the wind-loved heath,
The whirr of wings, the rustling brake,
Dear the murmuring glens beneath,
And sob of Droma's lake.

The cry of hounds at early morn,
The pattering o'er the pebbly creek
The cuckoo's call, the sounding horn,
The swooping eagle's shriek.

The mountain, not the cell, they sought,
Great Fionn and the Fianna fleet ;—
Than tinkle of the bells, they thought
The blackbird's song more sweet!

THE HOUSEHOLD OF FINN.

OISIN.[1]

I'VE seen the House of Finn,
No housefolk they of humble fame,
Last night—a Vision thin—
The Hero's household came.

I've seen the House of Art
Where towered apart his brown, bright son,
Not one like worth could win—
I've seen the House of Finn.

None sees what I have seen,
Finn wield the wondrous sword of Luin,
What woe, that sight—unseen !
I've seen the House of Finn.

The tale could never cease
Of woes that rend my heart within,
Then let me Thou have peace—
I've seen the House of Finn !

[1] Dean of Lismore's Book.

PLEASANT ARANN.[1]

CAILTÉ.

ARANN !—in deer delighting !
Ocean smiles o'er her shoulders ;
Men have feasts there, and fighting,
Blue darts redden 'mid boulders.

Hinds make merry her mountains,
O'er moss-berries they've morriced ;
Rills flow cool from her fountains,
Nuts fill her brown oak forest.

Hounds are there of high powers,
Fruits are bending the bramble ;
Homes are bough-woven bowers,
Deer in the deep wood ramble.

Red her rock-crop for reaping,
Faultless grass grow her valleys ;
Over smooth wood-lawns leaping,
Fawns dance, dappled, in alleys.

[1] From "Silva Gadelica," edited with translations by Standish
Hayes O'Grady.   London : Williams and Norgate.

Sleek her swine in the musters,
Truly nothing comes nigh her ;
Fair, through the hazel clusters,
Sailing of long ships by her.

Pleasant, when winter 's dying—
With trout 'neath banks not barren,
Fleet gulls, answering, flying—
Pleasant all times is Arann !

SOLACE IN WINTER.[1]

CAILTÉ.

CHILL the winter, cold the wind,
Up the stag springs, stark of mind :
Fierce and bare the mountain fells—
But the brave stag boldly bells.

He will set not side to rest
On Sliav Carna's snowy breast ;
Echta's stag, also rousing,
Hears wail of wolves carousing.

Cailté I, and Diarmid Donn,
Oft, with Oscar apt to run,
When piercing night was paling
Heard rousing wolves a-wailing.

[1] " Silva Gadelica." Colloquy with the Ancients.

Sound may sleep the russet stag,
With his hide hid in the crag;
Him, hidden, nothing aileth
When piercing night prevaileth.

I am aged now and gray,
Few of men I meet this day;
But I hurled the javelin bold
Of a morning, icy cold.

Thanks unto the King of Heaven,
And the Virgin's son be given:
Many men have I made still,
Who this night are very chill.

V.—THE CHRISTIAN DAWN.

THE GUARDSMAN'S CRY.[1]

By St. Patrick.

I BIND me to-day on the Triune a call
With faith on the Trinity—Unity—God over all.
I bind me the might of Christ's birth and baptizing,
His death on the Cross, His grave, His uprising,
His homeward ascent, the power supernal
Of His coming for judgment eternal.
I bind me the might of the Seraphim's love,
The angels' obedience, the hope of arising
    To guerdon above :
The prayers of the Fathers, prophetical teachings,
The virtue of virgins, apostolical preachings
    The acts of the True ;
    I bind to me, too,

---

[1] This is the ancient Irish name given to St. Patrick's hymn,
The original is a " Rosg," a poem of short sentences with irregular
rhythm and rime, imitated in the translation. It is, I think, the
original of the irregular ode.

Heaven's dower, sun's brightness,
Fire's power, snow's whiteness,
Wind's rushing, lightning's motion,
Earth's stability, rock's solidity,
 Depths of Ocean.

I bind me to-day
 God's might to direct me,
 God's power to protect me,
 God's wisdom for learning,
 God's eye for discerning,
 God's ear for my hearing,
 God's word for my clearing,
 God's hand for my cover
 God's path to pass over,
 God's buckler to guard me,
 God's army to ward me
  Against snares of the devils,
  Against vice's temptations,
  Against wrong inclinations,
  Against men who plot evils
   To hurt me anew,
 Anear or afar, with many or few.

I have set all these powers around me,
 Against danger and dole
Of all the foe-powers that would wound me
 In body and soul;

  Against each incantation
   By false prophets breathen,
  Against black legislation—
   The laws of the heathen,
Against idolatry's wares, and heretical snares,
Against spells of the women, smiths, druids, the whole
  Of that knowledge which blindeth the soul.
   Christ keep me to-day
  Against poison and burn,
  Against drowning and wounding,
  Until I may earn
  The guerdon abounding.
   Christ near,
   Christ here,
  Christ be with me
  Christ beneath me,
  Christ within me,
  Christ behind me,
  Christ be o'er me,
  Christ before me,
Christ on the left and the right,
  Christ hither and thither,
  Christ in the sight
Of each eye that shall seek me,
Christ in each ear that shall hear,
Christ in each mouth that shall speak me,
  Christ not the less,
  In each heart I address.
I bind me to-day on the Triune the call

With faith, on the Trinity—Unity—God over all.

    Christi est salus

    Christi est salus

Salus tua, Domine, sit semper nobiscum!

THE CHILDREN OF LIR.[1]

King Lir's wife, Queen Aifa, becoming jealous of her step-children, bade them bathe in Loch Derryvara; then, striking them with a Druid wand, they were changed into four beautiful pure white swans. She doomed them to pass a term of many years on the lake, another term on the current of Cantire, and a third term on the Sea of Erris.

AIFA.

"HENCE, king's offspring, and away,
    Doomed for aye, a blighted race:
Friends your woeful tale shall weep,
    You shall keep with birds your place."

FIONNUALA.

"Witch! thy true name now we know,
    Foul the blow, no boat is nigh;
Doomed to swim from wave to wave,
    Oft from cape to cape we'll fly.

"We shall yet see, manifest,
    Grace and rest of joyous worth:
Though our bound's the gray lake marge,
    Our minds shall, at large, go forth."

[1] This is the name of the second of the "Three Sorrows of Story," O'Curry, "Atlantis," Vol. IV., 1863, text and translation. The original metres are reproduced.

ON THE WATERS OF MOYLE.

Time passed pleasantly with the Swan-Children, on the lake : in the day they conversed with their kindred and friends who had encamped around ; at night they sang "slow, sweet, fairy music," that made sorrow sleep.   This term closed : they bade farewell to all, and went forth to the Waters of Moyle, where they suffered from icy storms.   Fionnuala, covering her young brothers with her wings, sang :

"LIFE is weary here,
Great the snowing here,
Night is dreary here,
Bleak the blowing here."

On a day, they saw a Fairy Cavalcade at the river Banna, and were told that Lir and their friends were celebrating the Feast of Age, happy but for their absence.   Fionnuala made this lay : [1]

Gay this night Lir's royal house,
Chiefs carouse, mead flows amain ;
Cold this night his children roam,
Their chill home the icy main.

For our mantles fair are found
Feathers curving round our breasts,—
Often silken robes we had,
Purple-clad, we sat at feasts.

[1] This theme suggested Moore's "Silent, O Moyle," and the "Song of Fionnuala" of Katherine Tynan (now Mrs. Tynan-Hinkson).

For our viands here and wine—
Bitter brine and pallid sands:
Oft the hazel mead they served
In carved vessels to our hands.

Now our beds are the bare rock
Smit with shock of heavy seas;
Often soft breast-down was spread
For the bed of grateful ease.

Though 'tis now, in frost, our toil
To swim Moyle, with drooping wings;
Oft we rode as Royal Wards
And our guards were sons of Kings.

THE RETURN OF THE CHILDREN OF LIR.

In the extremity of their suffering, frozen in Erris sea, the brothers
were inconsolable. Fionnuala asked them to believe in the true
God, and they were relieved, and suffered no more. At the end of
their final term, they arose and went very lightly and airily towards
the city of their father. "And thus they found the place: void,
desolate, with naught but the bare green paths and forests of nettles,
without house, without fire, without tribes. Then the Four drew
close together, and thrice they raised on high the cry of wailing,
then Fionnuala spoke this lay ":

STRANGE is all this place to me,
No house, no home, no gladness;
As 'tis thus, this place to see—
Alas, my heart, what sadness !

No hound, no sound, no ember,
No group where princes gather;
Not thus do we remember
Its old days with our father.

No horn, no goblet glancing,
No halls of light, each morrow:
No youth, no proud steed prancing—
All signs portend us sorrow.

All the void that here I see—
Alas, my pain grows stronger!
Makes it, this night, clear to me
Its loved lord lives no longer.

City, where of old we knew
All arts of joy exerted,
What a fate of woe and rue—
Thou art, this night, deserted!

Dark our doom and tragical—
Condemned the waves to wander,
Ne'er such ill fate magical
Did mortal yet fall under.

Now, the City populous
Gives weeds and woods its favour:
No man lives who'd welcome us
To this, our homestead, ever.

THE ISLE OF DELIGHT.[1]

SIXTH CENTURY.

THERE's an island far away,
Round it swift sea-horses play;
Four pillars bear it gracious,
O'er surge of ocean spacious.

Joy of eyes, that plain where are
Hosts at gay games near and far;
Barks there with chariots vying
Race oft, for triumph trying.

Whitest bronze, the pillars fair
Gleam through happy ages there,
Lovely land o'er whose bosom
Soft falls the sweetest blossom.

Tall stands the Tree of Flowers
Where birds call in its bowers;
Call to Hours the leaves among
At due times, with choral song.

---

[1] "Voyage of Bran" (Nutt). On a day, Bran heard entrancing music; when he awoke, he saw a woman with a flowering apple-branch of silver and crystal, who sang this lay. It gives a picture of the Ancient Paradise of the Gael—their "limbus patrum." The bard endeavours to harmonize it with the new doctrine of Christianity.

O'er the plains, sweet-voiced, tender,
Beam many hues in splendour,
Joys, with music, gently crowd
The south plain of Silver Cloud.

There deceit nor wailing is
In that fruitful land of bliss,
Naught rude or rugged showeth
But soft, sweet music floweth.

Grief or darkness none, nor death,
Ill, nor any harm it hath.[1]
This tells of Emain's[2] glory;
Where else such wondrous story?

'Tis the beauty of things bright,
Loveliness is in its sight,

---

[1] These and other verses are evidently the originals of passages in " The Pricke of Conscience " and in the " Land of Cokaigne," *e.g.* :

> " Under heaven n'is land I wiss
> Of so mochil joy and bliss.
> There is many swete sight :
> All is day, n'is there no night ;
> There is baret, nother strife,
> N'is there no death, ac ever life.
> There n'is lack of meat, no cloth,
> There n'is man no woman wroth.
>
>   *   *   *   *   *   *
>
> Ok all is game, joy, and glee,
> Well is him that there may be."

[2] Emain is here the name of the Irish (pagan) paradise.

Cheer it gives hearts all cheerless,
Its halo-haze is peerless.

In the Valley Bountiful
Rubies show'r, and gems we cull;
Billows beat the shore, and rain
Crystal hairs from ocean's mane.[1]

Wealth, health, and varied treasures
Dower this mild Land of Pleasures,
Mellow tunes ever flowing,
Lucent wines always glowing.

In Moy Réin, gold chariots ride,
Rising sunward with the tide;
Moy Mon's cars are silver white,
And bronze chariots beaming bright.

Gold-hued steeds fly o'er the strand,
Crimson steeds along the land;
Fleecy steeds are bounding too,
Azure as the heavens blue.

There shall come, with dawn's whiteness,
One fair man, shedding brightness;
He will ride the wave-beat flood,
Stirring ocean till 'tis blood.

---

[1] From such metaphors often enigmatical, the Norse Skalds got models for the synonyms so common in their Court verses.

There shall come a host with oars,
Rowing to these happy shores,
To the Splendid Rock [1] they'll row
Whence a hundred sweet strains flow.

To the hosts 'twill ever sing,
Making all the ages ring:
Rising with a myriad choirs,—
Death shall never dim their fires!

Happiness shall hereafter
Hither come, girt with laughter,
Health will come, ne'er to sever,
Joy comes that lasts for ever.

What a day of sunlit hours,
Silver o'er the land it showers!
That Rock stands the shore upon,
Taking radiance from the Sun. [2]

In Moy Mon, the hosts that came
Urge the great and noble game;
O'er its varied beauty they
Meet nor death nor slow decay.

They hear music in the night,
Through this Isle of all Delight—

[1] Possibly the Church is thus symbolized.
[2] *I.e.* God, the Sun of Heaven.

Flash of beauty's diadem—
With the white cloud over them.

*   *   *   *   *

There shall be a wondrous birth
In no lofty place of earth,
Hence a Virgin's Son shall take
Rule o'er myriads for their sake.

Rule that ends not, nor began ;
He has made the world and man,
His the earth and the great sea ;
Woe, who His unfriend shall be.

He made heaven high and bright,
(Happy he whose heart is white !)
He will cleanse with waters clean,
And make whole who sick hath been.

BRAN'S VOYAGE TO THE ISLE OF DELIGHT.[1]

SIXTH CENTURY.

"BRAN beholds a shining sea,
From his curach, fair and free,—

[1] Bran sailed forth to seek the Island of Delight—the very Gentle
Land.   When he had been at sea two days, he saw one in a chariot
driving over the waters who was Manannan, the son of Lir, the
Ocean-God, who sang this lay.

"Voyage of Bran, son of Febal to the Land of the Living," by
Kuno Meyer, and Alfred Nutt, London : Nutt, 1895.

I, in chariot driving there
See a flow'ring meadow fair.

"The sea is clear,
So thinks Bran when sailing here,—
I, in car, with purer pow'rs
Know the happy Plain of Flow'rs,

"Bran beholds
Flowing billows, fold on folds,—
O'er the plain I have in sight
Waving blossoms red and bright.

"Summer sea-steeds [1] leapt and ran
Far as reach the eyes of Bran,—
Rivers, run with honey clear
In the fair land of Mac Lir.

"He, the ocean's gleaming glint
Sees, and billows' pallid tint—
I, the bounteous land behold
Decked with azure and with gold,

"Speckled salmon leap for him
From the water's bitter brim,—
I can see, o'er lovely lawns,
Lambkins play and frolic fawns,

---

[1] *I.e.* waves.

"Thine eyes mark one charioteer
O'er Moy Mell in light appear—
Many chariots race, I ween
O'er the plain, by thee, unseen.

"Wide the plain, the hosts are great,
Bright their colours, high their state,
Streams of silver, gleams of gold
Welcome and abundance hold.

"Beauteous their delightful game,
Flows the wine like ruddy flame,
Noble men and gentle maids
Stainless in the sinless shades.

"O'er the finest forest trees
Swam thy curach, cleaving seas,
Bright fruit on boughs are glancing
Now, 'neath thy prow advancing.

"Branches rich with fruit and bloom
Breathing forth the vine's perfume ;
Woods moulder not, tho' olden,
Faultless, with foliage golden.

"We are here since Time had birth,
Aging not, nor called to earth ;
Nor fear we aught should wither
Since the Sin came not hither.

For the snake went,—ill the hour !
To the Father's [1] fortress bow'r ;—
An ill change on earth was wrought
Gray decay, unknown, it brought.

He has slain us, in disgrace,
Greed has wrecked his noble race,
Thence, with'ring Body wasteth,
Hence oft to torment hasteth.

Law of worldlings is Pride's nod,
Minding creatures and not God :
Hence decay, disease, defeat,
Age, and soul-death through deceit.

Yet, our Maker-king shall send
Great deliverance ere the end,
There shall come White Law [2] o'er sea,
And He God and Man shall be.

---

[1] *I.e.* Adam's.
[2] The Norse apparently got the term White Christ from the Irish.

VI.-VII.—EARLY CHRISTIAN.

JESUKIN.[1]

St. Ita (b. 480—d. 570).

Jesukin
Lives my little cell within ;
What were wealth of cleric high—
All is lie but Jesukin.

Nursling nurtured, as 'tis right—
Harbours here no servile spright—
Jesu of the skies, who art
Next my heart thro' every night !

Jesukin, my good for aye,
Calling and will not have nay,
King of all things, ever true,
He shall rue who will away.

Jesu, more than angels aid,
Fosterling not formed to fade,

---

[1] Whitley Stokes, LL.D. "On the Calendar of Œngus," "Royal Irish Academy's Transactions," 1880. Note, p. xxxv.

Isucan : loving diminutive of Isa—in modern Irish, Iosa—applied to the Child Jesus.

Nursed by me in desert wild,
Jesu, child of Judah's Maid.

Sons of Kings and kingly kin,
To my land may enter in ;
Guest of none I hope to be,
Save of Thee, my Jesukin !

Unto heaven's High King confest
Sing a chorus, maidens blest !
He is o'er us, though within
Jesukin is on my breast !

KING CELLACH REGRETS HIS STUDENT-LIFE.[1]

CIRCA 540.

WOE to him who leaveth lore
For the red World's arts or ore ;
Who the True God's love would leave
With the false World's kings to cleave.

---

[1] "Silva Gadelica.—A Collection of Irish Tales." Edited and translated by Standish Hayes O'Grady. London: Williams and Norgate. King Eogan of Connaght, being wounded to death, advised that his chieftains should beseech his elder son Cellach to leave his Student-life at Clonmicnóis, and assume arms and kingship, for the safety of the State. Reluctantly he consented. Then arose a rival (Guairé) who, at a tryst, treacherously fell upon Cellach's company. Cellach (pronounced Kellach) and a small band escaped to the woods as outlaws : there he composed this poem.

Woe, who taketh arms in life
And repenteth not of strife,
Better far books of whiteness
Where psalms are seen in brightness.

Though great the war-man's glory
Much the toil and short his story :
Swift and sharp his life hath past
In exchange for hell at last.

Still stealth of trades is meanest,
Murky, lorn, lankest, leanest ;
Whosoe'er hath good at first
Soon he seemeth wicked-worst.

Such the stains that fell upon
Hapless Cellach, Eogan's son :
Roaming now from place to place
With a band of outlaws base.

Woe, who leave high heav'n of saints
For dark hell and horrid plaints.
Christ, our Light o'er combats dim,
Who forsakes Thee, woe to him.

ST. CELLACH'S DEATH SONG.[1]

A.D. 540.

'TIS my Love, the Morning fair,
Floating, flame-like, through the air :
'Tis my Love who sends her, too,
Victor Morning, ever new !

O Morning, fair and tender !
O Sister of Sun's splendour !
Welcome thou, O Morning fair !
Beaming on my booklet there.

At ev'ry house-guest glancing—
All tribes of earth entrancing—
Welcome here, O White-neck rare !
Winsome, wondrous, golden-fair !

Soon my small fleckt book shall tell
That not well my life went past ;
Now Maelcrón, set on murther,
Fares to further death at last.

---

[1] " Silva Gadelica." Cellach, persecuted by King Guairé, fled ;
the king bribed the Saint's pupils to betray him. They seized and
wounded him, but spared his life for one night in a wood. On open-
ing his prison door, he saw the fatal dawn, and closed it again ; but,
through faith and in resignation he re-opened it, and welcomed the
morning in this lay. Here he foretells his fate. The rime, measure,
and rapid transitions are reproduced.

Grim fellow,
Gray, grip-beak, gleam-eye yellow,—
Thou, Scall-crow! watchful sitter
Tak'st bitter care of Cellach.

O constant-croaking Raven!
Is thy hunger-craving fresh?
Rise not from this rath-topt hill,
Thou shalt have thy fill of flesh.

The keen Kite of far Cluanó
Swiftly for the spoil shall go;
Thence, with strong claws full, will start—
Nor from me will meekly part.

Fox in forest, lurking low,
He shall hear and hail the blow;
He will bear my flesh and blood
Through the wild, dark, dreary wood.

The red Wolf will leave his lair
In the rath of Drumicdair,
And rush here, quick and quiet,
Chief o'er the robbers' riot. .

I saw in sleep a Vision!—
In a recent night of dread:
Four wild dogs rent me, racking,
East and West, through bracken red.

I saw in sleep a Vision !—
On a mission came four men ;
Me to one gray glen they bore,
Nevermore to come again.

I saw in sleep a Vision !—
In derision I was brought,
With my Wards to feast, methought,
Each to each, we quaffed of naught.

Little Wren of feeble flight,
Sad thy promise sung a-right ;
Methinks to those would slay me
Thou'dst betray me in the night.

O, Maelcrón !—
What a deed of ill thou'st done !
Eogan's son would plot thy fall
Not for all of wealth unwon.

O, Maelcrón !—
Wealth to own my life thou'dst sell—
For the world thou hast done well,
Thou hast bargained high for Hell.

I'd give of gold a river,
Sleek steeds and jewels greater,
Thee, Maelcrón, to deliver
That *thou* shouldst be no traitor.

Lo, Mary's Son of glory
Hath said me this sooth story:
"Thou'lt have earth,—thou shalt have heav'n,
I to thee have welcome giv'n!"

REMEMBERING ERINN.

St. Columba [1] (A.D. 563).

'Twere delightful, O Son of God,
    Forward faring,
Sail to hoist o'er swelling surges,
    Home to Erinn!
O'er Moyn-Olarg, past Benevna,
    Foyle-ward winging,
Where we'd hear the pleasant music
    Swans are singing.
Hosts of sea-gulls would give welcome,
    With white pinions,
Did "Red Dewy" [2] reach, rejoiceful,
    Their dominions.
Much I have here—but not Erinn—
    Were that gladness!

[1] St. Columba was born in the year 521. He went into exile to Iona in 563. Having submitted the question of his responsibility for the battle of Cuil-dreimne to St. Molaisi, he was ordered to leave Erinn, and to see it no more. He returned once, it is said, blind-folded, to save the bards from expulsion. He died in 597.

[2] "Derg Dructach"—"Red Dewy"—St. Columba's sea-ship.

On this unsung shore of exile,—
        Shrouded sadness !
Woeful was mine ordered voyage,
        King of Heaven !
Cuil's red combat leaves me lonely
        Here, bereaven.
Dima's son is happy yonder,
        Down in Durrow ;
All his mind desires he heareth,
        Night and morrow :
'Mid the elms the swooning breezes
        Ever playing,
Joyous note of blackbird's voice, its
        Wings displaying,
Lowing of Ros-grena's kine, at
        Dewy dawning,
Cuckoo's call at Summer's brink, from
        Forest awning.
Of this peopled world I've left three
        Dear things only :
Durrow, Derry's grove of Angels,
        Lewy, lonely ;
I've loved Erinn's cascade-land, not
        Rule unrightful,—
Days with Congall, feast with Caindech
        Were delightful.

THE FALL OF THE BOOK-SATCHELS.

St. Columba.

"Now when Longarad was dead, men of lore say this, that the book-satchels of Erinn fell down on that night. Or it is the satchels wherein were books of every science in the cell where Columbcille was that fell then, and everyone in that house marvelled at the noisy shaking of the books. So then said Columbcille, 'Longarad in Ossory,' quoth he, 'a sage of every science has now died' . . . . *et dixit :*"[1]

DEAD is Lón
Of Kilgarad ; make ye moan.
Now must Erinn's tribes deplore
Loss of Lore and Schools o'erthrown.

Died hath Lón
Of Kilgarad ; make ye moan.
Loss of Lore and Schools o'erthrown
Leave all Erinn's borders lone.[2]

---

[1] Whitley Stokes, LL.D., "On the Calendar of Œngus," Dublin ; "Royal Irish Academy's Transactions," 1880; Note from Lebor breac. Œngus speaks of the "Hosts of the Books of Erinn." The manuscript books were preserved in leather satchels, often ornamented.

[2] The varied repetition of the first line, and of the last two in each stanza entitle St. Columba to be regarded, I believe, as the inventor of the Rondeau.

M

DELIGHTS IN ERINN.

St. Columba (A.D. 563).

Lovely Edar's Hill[1] to me,
Ere we sail the pale, pale sea :
Billows breaking at its base,
Bare and lone its lofty face.

Lovely Edar's Hill to me,
After the bright-bosomed sea :
There to row our boatlet o'er
White waves racing round the shore.

Fleet my Curach's flying track,
When on Derry turns its back ;
I lament the happy havens,
Seeking Alba of the ravens.

My foot 's in my tuneful Curach,
My heart bleeds in constant sorrow ;
Men must lead, or feebly follow,
Ignorance is blind and hollow.

[1] Benn Edair, *i.e.*, the Bluff of Edar, that Dublin hill which the
Norsemen called Hoved, the Head, whence its present name of
Howth.

There's an eye of gray
Looks back to Erinn far away :
While life lasts, 'twill see no more
Man or maid on Erinn's shore !

I gaze o'er the bitter brine,
From these oaken planks of mine,
Big tears wet that eye of gray—
Seeking Erinn, far away.

Still on Erinn rests my mind—
Lene and Linné left behind,
On Ultonian mountains wild,
Meath and Muman smooth and mild.

Many heroes eastward are,
Many an ail, ill and scar,
Many scant of garb and art,
Many a hard, jealous heart.

Many, west, sweet apples shine,
Many kings and princes fine,
Many snowy-blossomed sloes,
Many oak trees, few the woes.

Sweet her birds, her clerics sage,
Soft her youth are, wise is age—
Noble men who glad the sight,
Noble maids for nuptial rite.

Westward is sweet Brendan now,
Colam, son of Crimtan's vow.
(Westward shall fair Baithin be,
And Adamnan after me.) [1]

Bear my greetings, noble youth !
O'er to Congall's soul of truth,
Bear my greetings home again,
To Emania's king of men.

Blessings bear, benedictions,
From this heart of afflictions,
Half for Erinn—seven times !
Half for Alba's eastern climes.

Bear my blessing with thy sail
To the Nobles of the Gael ;
Let them never more give ear
When Molaisi's words they hear.

Were it not Molaisi's speech,
I should stand on Imlais' beach,
Keeping constant watch, to ward
Ail and ill from Erinn's sward.

Bear my blessing to the West,
Broke my heart is in my breast ;

[1] This is an interpolation by a later bard.

Should a quick death be my bale,
'Tis for great love of the Gael.

Gael, O Gael! O name most dear!
Wish I've none but that to hear;
Dear fair Cumin o'er the brine,
Caindech dear, and Comgall mine.

Came all Alba's cess to me,
From its centre to its sea,
I would choose a better part—
One house set in Derry's heart!

Dear for these things Derry fair:
Purity and peace are there,
Hosts are there of angels white,
Moving through it, noon and night.

Derry mine! my small oak-grove!
Little cell, my home, my love!
O thou Lord of lasting life,
Woe to him who brings it strife!

Dear is Durrow, Derry dear,
Dear Raphœ is, calm and clear,
Dear Drumholme, where sweet fruit swells,
Dear to me are Swords and Kells.

Dear too, westward, evermore,
Drumcliffe on Culkinny's shore—
O to see fair Foyle in might,
'Mid its woodlands were delight!

Delight is there.—There's delight
Where flash ocean's sea-gulls white—
Far I bear from Derry's grove,
Quiet peace and lasting love.

CONALL DEAD.

By His Spouse (A.D. 634).[1]

OCHAGON![2]—here is the head
Of Conall of the keen blue blade:
The head of understanding clear,
The noble, dear, devoted head.

Ochagón! here are the eyes
Of Conall's wise and generous head;
From these the lashes used to rise
And flashes mild and manly sped.

---

[1] Dean of Lismore's Book.   Congall Claen, son of Scanlan, Prince of Ulster, was killed at the battle of Moira (Magh Rath), A.D. 634.   Conall is the phonetic form, in the Dean's Book.

[2] Ochagón is an exclamation of grief like Ullagone.   It is written Ochagan.

Ochagón ! here is the mouth
That north and south the poets praise,
Of slender grace and apple-red,
Like honey shed was Conall's mouth.

Ochagón ! here is the hand
Bore Conall son of Scanlan's brand,
The hand that strong in conflict strove,
The hand of Conall—my first love !

Ochagón ! here is the side
Where oftentimes ours nobly lay ;
From Moyle's gray tide there came a hound
With wile to wound that stainless side.

Ochagón ! here are the feet
That ne'er gave way where warriors meet :
Feet still first in fiery fray,
The battle-bravest Conall's feet !

Och ! and here his Fort for aye,
The strong cold Clay for all the years,
Conall's Fort—where I deplore
Whose tale is o'er—the House of Tears !

THE MOTHERS OF BETHLEHEM.[1]

FIRST WOMAN.

WHY tear my love's son from me,
Me, who reared him?
My breast fed him,
My womb bore him,
My veins did suckle him,
My heart he filled,
My life was he.
My death his taking,
My strength is gone;
My voice is choked,
My eyes are blind.

SECOND WOMAN.

My son ye snatch,
I'm guiltless of ill,
But kill even me,
Kill not my son;
My breasts are milkless,
My eyes are flowing,
My hands are trembling,

[1] Professor Kuno Meyer, "Gaelic Journal," Dublin, May, 1891.
Text and Translation.   It is in "rosg," Irish blank verse.

My body stumbles;
My husband's sonless,
Myself am strengthless,
My life—a death.
O God, my one son!
My fost'ring worthless,
My sickness sterile
Till Doomsday lost;
My bosom silenced,
My heart crushed.

THIRD WOMAN.

One ye seek slaying,
Numbers ye slaughter,
Nurslings smiting,
Fathers gashing—
Mothers murd'ring.
Hell ye were filling,
Heaven's gate closing,
Wantonly shedding
The blood of the righteous.

FOURTH WOMAN.

Come to me, O Christ,
Take swiftly my soul,
Alike with my son.
Ah, Mary of night,
Mother of God's son,

See, sonless am I,
For *thy* son are slaughtered
My mind and my sense,
I'm made a mad woman
For want of my son ;
My heart is a death-froth,
Because of sad slaughter,
From now till the judgment.

THE SONG OF SATAN.[1]

AUTHOR UNKNOWN.

GOLD is he—a sun-lit sky,
Silvern cup where wine is high,
Wisdom, which the angels praise—
Who obeys the Godhead nigh.

---

[1] St. Moling was at prayer, when a dignified youth in purple approached and said, "That is well, O Cleric." "Amen," said Moling. "Why dost thou not bless me?" says the youth. "Who art thou?" quoth Moling. "I am Christ, Son of God," says he. "That cannot be," says Moling, "when Christ used to come to converse with the servants of God, not in purple, nor royally did he come, but in the shape of the wretched, to wit, of the sick and of the lepers." "Is it unbelief thou hast in me?" asked the youth, "who is it seems to thee to be here?" "Meseems," says Moling, "that it is the Devil for my hurt." "Ill for thee is the unbelief," says the youth. "Well," says Moling, "[if thou art Christ] here is thy successor," raising the Gospel. "Raise it not, O Cleric, likelier 'tis I whom thou

Bird that's brought within the snare,
Leaking bark that dangers dare,
Broken branch that withered sways ·
He who God's will disobeys.

Fragrant bough, and full of bloom,
Honey cup of sweet perfume,
Precious stone of shining rays,
Who obeys the King of Doom.

Nut of dust, decayed and sour,
Bitter crab-branch, void of flow'r,
Leafless tree that hurts the gaze,
Who the King's will disobeys.

Whoso hears the Lord divine,
Summer-girt, a Sun shall shine,
God's true image here is seen—
Vessel clean of crystal fine.

thinkest I am, the Man of Tribulation." He had sought to obtain the
saint's blessing because its fragrance would be around him, as if one
rose from a bath of honey. Failing, he asked a curse, because its
venom would return on Moling. Then he asked how be might earn
the blessing. "By service unto God," quoth Moling. "Woe is me,"
he said, "I have not chosen it." "Even a little reading," says
Moling. "My reading saveth me not and helpeth me not."
"Fasting then," says Moling. "Fasting I am since the world's
beginning, not the better am I." "To make genuflections," says
Moling. "I cannot bend forward, for backward are my knees."
"Go forth," says Moling, "I cannot teach thee or save thee."
Then the Devil said this lay.—Stokes, "Felire of Œngus." "Notes
from Irish, cv."

He's a swift steed o'er the plain
Who seeks God's gate to attain,
He's a chariot 'neath a king
Which shall bring gold gifts amain.

Sun to warm the heaven of bliss,
Man for whom God thankful is !—
Temple, light-lit ev'ry line,
Shrine that sacred lips shall kiss.

Altar he where wine is shed,
Round it choral song is said ;—
Cleanséd chalice he, behold !
Chased and carved of purest gold.

TRIUMPH OF FAITH,

By ŒNGUS THE CELE DE,[1] 8TH CENTURY

Low is Tara's tower[2]
Closed its sovran story—
Crowds with wisdom dower
Ardmagh's growing glory.

Lofty Laeré's splendour
Has, alas, gone under,—
Patrick's name, more tender,
Glows, a great world-wonder.

[1] Stokes, "The Calendar of Œngus." In reference to a passage relating to Œngus, Matthew Arnold writes: "A Greek epitaph could not show a finer perception of what constitutes propriety and felicity of style in compositions of this nature:

> Œngus out of the assembly of heaven,
> Here are his tomb and his bed ;
> It is hence he went to death,
> On the Friday, to holy heaven.
> It is in Cluain Eidnech he was reared,
> It is in Cluain Eidnech he was buried ;
> In Cluain Eidnech of many crosses
> He first read his psalms."

[2] Tara was the abode of the Over-King of Erinn ; Rath-Cruachain, the fortress of the Kings of Connacht ; Emania was the northern royal city in the days of King Concobar, and Aillin the stronghold of Leinster.

Faith has flow'red and flourished,
This shall fail us never,
Raths which Gentiles nourished
Now are empty ever.

Gone Rath Cruachain from us
Aillil's fame—a pity!
See in sov'reign promise
Cluain's excelling city.

Hark the chantings choral
Rise round Ciaran glorious,
Clonmicnóis its carol
Rolls in rime victorious.[1]

Never shall it perish—
God's love, night or morrow,
This cheer if you cherish
Shamed shall be all sorrow.

Aillin high and hoary
With its hosts is shrouded—,
Great is Brigit's glory,
Fair her city crowded.

---

[1] Œngus, who says he milked into his Calendar "the vast tome of Ambrose, Hilary's pious 'Sensus,' Jerome's 'Antigraph,' Eusebius's 'Martyrology,'" also adds "the hosts of the books of Erinn." Foreign literature was cultivated, whilst native letters were fostered in Erinn—a thousand years ago.

Ruins strew the region
Once Emania's palace,—
Rome revives its legion
In Glenlocha's valleys.

Like a lamp of light is
Ferna great and glowing,
Lost in clouded night is
All the host of Eoghan.

Haughty heathen cities,
Built for everlasting,
Fall, and no one pities,
Like to Lugai's wasting.

Pagan power is over,
False its fair devotion ;
God rules, Lord and Lover,
Earth and sky and ocean !

Doncad, dread in danger,
Bran, in battle bravest,
Seek their graves, O stranger !
Vainly help thou cravest.

Maelruain, nothing warlike,
Served with faith and feeling,—
At his tomb, the Star-like
Every heart has healing.

Just the Judge is, truly,
When his rule's regarded :
Foes are punished duly,
Friends, at last, rewarded.

Gone the despots; gory
Kings have downward drifted,
Ciarans rise to glory—
Cronans are uplifted.

Sunk the summits olden,
Hewn by swords asunder :
Raised the glens, as golden
Peaks above the thunder !

VIII.—GAEL AND NORSE.

From the Ninth to the Thirteenth Century.

THE BLACKBIRD'S SONG.[1]

A.D. 850.

GREAT woods gird me now around,
With sweet sound merle sings to me :
My much-lined pages over
Sings its lover minstrelsie.

[1] " Reliquie Celtiche. Il manoscritto irlandese di S. Gallo."
Firenze, Torino, Roma, 1872. Cavaliere Nigra found the original Irish
verses on the margin of an ancient manuscript of St. Gall's. The
monk had been copying, when the merle (or blackbird) sang, and he
paused to write this little lay. See Introduction. Love of animals
was a characteristic of the ancient Irish saints. Various charming
anecdotes show this. St. Ciaran of Saighir (the first resident native
saint) is related to have formed his first community of animals : a
furious wild boar came to assist him, then a fox, a wolf, a badger,
and a fawn. Thus he made a little monastery in the forest, amongst
pagans. When the fox gave way to appetite, and carried off the
saint's shoes to gnaw, the badger brought him back. "O brother,"
said Ciaran gently, "why hast thou done this theft, so unbecoming
to a monk, for there are wholesome water and food for the com-
munity, and if thy nature made thee prefer meat, God would have
made it thee of the tree-bark around." Here is another example
from the Lebor Breac (Stokes, "Calendar of Œngus," Note xl.).
"Maelanfaid saw, on a day, a little bird a wailing and lamenting.
'Ah, my God,' quoth he, 'what has happened here? I vow,'
quoth he, 'I will not eat food till it is revealed to me." So while

N

Soft it sings its measured song,
Hid among the tree-tops green :
May God on high thus love me,
Thus approve me, all unseen.

THE HEAVENLY PILOT.[1]

CORMAC, KING-BISHOP OF CASHEL (837—903).

WILT thou steer my frail black bark
O'er the dark broad ocean's foam?
Wilt thou come, Lord, to my boat,
Where afloat, my will would roam?
Thine the mighty: Thine the small:
Thine to mark men fall, like rain ;
God ! wilt Thou grant aid to me
Who come o'er th' upheaving main?

he was there he beheld an angel (coming) to him.   'That is well,
O cleric,' saith the angel, 'let this not give thee grief any more.
Molua Mac Ocha is dead, and therefore it is that the living crea-
tures bewail him, for he never killed a living creature, whether
small or great.   So that not more of the people bewail him than the
other living creatures, and the little bird which thou seest.'"

[1] "Book of Leinster." In O'Curry's "Manners and Customs,"
Vol. III., p. 388. This Irish poem, composed in the ninth century,
anticipates the central thought of Tennyson's exquisite verses,
"Crossing the Bar." O'Curry says that Cormac, who wrote the
"Psalter of Cashel" has always been considered "one of the most
distinguished scholars of Europe of his time. Besides the know-
ledge he is recorded to have acquired of the Hebrew, Greek, and
Latin, the British, Saxon, and Danish" (*rectè* Norse) "and other
northern languages, he is regarded as having been one of the
greatest Gaedhelic scholars that ever lived."

NIALL'S DIRGE.[1]

BY QUEEN GORMLAI, HIS SPOUSE, A.D. 919.

Move, O monk, thy foot away,
Lift it now from Niall's side,
Over-much thou'st cast the clay
Where I would, with him, abide.

Over-long thy task, this day,
Strewing clay o'er Niall slain ;
Tread no further, friend, delay,—
Raise it not to meet the plain.

Ah, close not for aye the grave,
Cleric sad, with solemn lay ;
From o'er Niall bright and brave
Move, O monk, thy foot away.

Golden King, not thus wert bound
Had I power thy strength to stay,
Leave his pillar, leave his mound,
Move thy foot, O monk, away.

I am Gormlai, who, in gloom,
Sing for him the sorrowing lay ;
Stand not there upon his tomb,
Move, O monk, thy foot away.

---

[1] The Dean of Lismore's Book. Edited by the Rev. Thomas McLauchlan. Edinburgh : Edmonston and Douglas. Niall was slain in battle by the Norsemen, A.D. 919. See account of the tragic fate of the "most unhappy Lady Gormlai," in Appendix.

THE RUINED NEST.[1]

AUTHOR UNKNOWN.

SAD is yonder blackbird's song,
Well I know what wrought it wrong;
Whosoe'er the deed has done,
Now its nestlings all are gone.

Such a sorrow I, too, know
For such loss, not long ago;
Well, O bird! I read thy state
For a home laid desolate.

How thy heart has burned, nigh broke,
At the rude and reckless stroke!
To lay waste thy little nest
Seems to cowboys but a jest.

Thy clear note called together
Flutt'ring young in new feather;
From thy nest comes now not one—
O'er its mouth the nettle's gone.

[1] The original of this touching poem is found in "the famous
fourteenth century manuscript, known as the Lebor Breac," writes
Prof. Kuno Meyer, who first edited and translated it for the "Gaelic
Journal," 1890. It was composed long before the fourteenth century.

Sudden came the callous boys,
Their deed all thy young destroys :
Thou and I one fate deplore—
For my children are no more.

By thy side there used to be
Thy sweet mate from o'er the sea ;
The herd's net ensnared her head—
She is gone from thee, and dead.

O, Ruler of high heaven !
Thou'st laid our loads uneven :
For our friends on ev'ry side
'Mid their mates and children bide.

Hither came hosts of Faery
To waste our home unwary ;
Though they left no wound to tell
Brunt of battle were less fell.

Woe for wife ; for children, woe !
I, in sorrow's shadow, go ;
Not a trace of them I had
Hence my heavy heart is sad.

THE SEA-MAIDEN'S VENGEANCE.[1]

AUTHOR UNKNOWN.

A GREAT gallant king of yore
Ruled shore and sea of Erinn ;
Noble then all sections shone
'Neath Rigdon's son of daring.

O'er the mane of slow gray seas,
With the breeze, lay his hoar way ;
To behold his foreign friend
He would wend north to Norway.

Sped his splendid vessels three,
When the sea calmed its motion ;
Till they, sailing, sudden stop
On the ridgy top of ocean.

They refused to wend away—
Fixed they lay, no where faring !

---

[1] "Book of Ballymote." In "Atlantis," Vol. IV. O'Curry :
note, pp. 235-240. This singular lay, if presented in German,
might pass for a Teutonic poem. It cannot be doubted that it was
owing to Irish teaching that a pupil of St. Gall's introduced rime
into German. How far its literature has been otherwise affected is
insufficiently known. It would be very curious if the germ of the
legend of the Lorelei had been carried and naturalized on the Rhine
by St. Goar (Guaire), or some other of its many Irish pilgrims.

Then into the dark dread deeps
Ruad leaps, greatly daring.

When he dived for their release,
Through the sea's surging waters ;
There he found the forms divine
Of its nine beauteous daughters.

These with clear soft accents said,
It was they stay'd his sailing :
That to leave nine maidens sweet
Were a feat few prevail in.

He with these nine nymphs remained,
Where there reigned shade nor sadness ;
'Neath the waters, where no wave
Ever gave gloom to gladness.

One of these his bride became,
Still his fame forced him forward ;
But he vow'd to greet her lips
When his ships came from norward.

Once on board, he bade them sail
Past the pale billows breaking ;
And, with one bound, make their course
To the Norse of quick speaking.

O'er the salt sea then they rode,
And abode, sweet the story,

Till the seventh glad year ends
With their friends, great in glory.

Ruad then ran out, once more,
On the hoar salt sea faring;
Speeding forth his ships to reach
The bright far beach of Erinn.

Warped and wrong the royal will,—
Solemn still is promise spoken:
He should have gone to the maid
As he said, nor pledge have broken.

When the prince of Tuired's name
Unto Muired's[1] borders came,
Around the shore—foul his fame!
A sound arose of sad acclaim.

'Twas the sweet-voiced women's song
Borne along in music's motion,
Following Ruad's fleeing sail
O'er wail of wave-worn ocean.

Sailing, in bronze boat, they came—
No plank-frame, made by mortal—
Those nine maidens, fair and fierce,
Till they pierce Ollbin's[2] portal.

[1] The region between Howth and the Boyne.
[2] Mouth of the River Ollbin, now Dilvin.

Dire and dread the deed then done
There by one, 'mid the water,
Ruad's son—her own—she slew,
Vengeance knew, sweet in slaughter !

Then, upraising high her hand,
Forth she cast him on the strand,—
Shrank the shore and shudd'ring foam
From King Ruad's welcome home !

LAY OF NORSE-IRISH SEA-KINGS.[1]

ARTUR MAC GURCAICH, THE BLIND.

FAIR our fleet at Castle Sweyn—
Glad good news for Innisfail !—
Never rode on bounding brine
Barks so fine with soaring sail.

Tall men urge the ships and steer
Our light, leaping, valiant van ;
Each hand holds a champion's spear—
Gay of cheer is ev'ry man.

---

[1] Dean of Lismore's book, pp. 117-151. Sweyn has been Gaelicized Suivne and Sweeney—but this is a confusion of the Norse with a somewhat similar Gaelic name.

Coats of black the warriors wear
On the barks with tree-mast tall;
Broad the brown belts that they bear,
Norse and Nobles are they all.

Sword-hilts gold and iv'ry gleam
On our barks with banners high;
Hung on hooks the bucklers beam,
Sheaves of spears are standing nigh.

Purple wings our ships expand
O'er the fleckt and flowing wave;
'Mid the masts the champions stand
Fit for foray, mild and brave.

Blue is the sea surrounding
Prows o'er the billows bounding;
Swords in their sheaths are glowing,
The lances thrill for throwing.

Fair are the forms reclining
On the cushioned couches high,
Wives in their beauty shining
'Neath the chequered canopy.

Silks in varied fold on fold,
Clothe our king-ship sailing fast;
Silks of purple splendour hold
Wells of wind at every mast.

There is seen no hardened hand—
Waist of worker belted tight;
High-voiced heroes hold command,
Fond of music, play, and fight.

Ne'er did Finn or Fianna know
Gallant chiefs of deeds more grand,
Nor could Erinn braver show
Than this fair-haired battle band.

Swifter ship of ships there's none—
None shall go, and none has gone;
Here comes nor sigh nor sorrow
Night or noon, day or morrow.

Fleeter bark of barks ne'er fared—
Full of princely folk she goes;
Gold with bards they've, gen'rous, shared
While the foam-topt ocean flows.

Who took this fleet together
Close to the high hill heather?
Dauntless he; he braves the blast—
Claims his right with upraised mast.

Sail the ship, Ion, son of Sweyn!
O'er the hard-backed brilliant brine;
Raise aloft its conq'ring crown
O'er the billows' fret and frown.

Many welcomes, many smiles,
Greet our ship, 'mid Alba's isles;
Bards, the narrow seas among,
Welcome us with harp and song.

Then we came to Castle Sweyn,
Like a bright hawk o'er the brine;
By that rock we raised the fight,
Facing foes with fierce delight.

There we pierced the foreign foes
As the stinging serpent goes;
Sore we smote them, men and lords,
With our thin, sharp, shearing swords,

Chanting Sweyn-son's battle-song,
All the surging seas along;
Till the shore-rock tall and black,
Over ocean sends it back.

Vain their spears and swords and darts,—
Our brown bucklers hold our hearts;
Rocky Rathlin,[1] rousing, hears
Singing of our swords and spears.

That thin sword is Europe's best,
That swift spear serves each behest;
Where were shield safe in the world
When the victor weapon 's hurled?

---

[1] An isle off the north coast of Ireland.

Son of Sweyn, whose ways are wide,
These keen arms keeps at his side ;
Be it now the blind bard's care
Him to sing, strong, sage, and fair.

"TAKE THESE HEADS."

Having achieved their feats, the Children of Tuirenn sailed homeward, wounded to death, Brian alone upstanding. At last he spoke : "I see Benn Edair, and Dun Tuirenn, and Tara of the Kings." "We should be full of health could we see that," said another ; "for thine honour's love, O brother," said they, "take these heads on thy breast that we may see Erinn afar, and we care not be it death or life thereafter." And one spoke this lay : [1]

TAKE these heads upon thy breast,—
Son of Tuirenn brave and best,
Torch of Valour, void of guile !—
That we may see Erinn's isle.

Raise upon thy shoulder, too,
These our heads, thou champion true !
That from o'er the waters, we
Usna, Taltin, Tara, see.

Boyne's Bru [2] and Dublin darkling,
Freman and Tlacta sparkling,

[1] The Fate of the Children of Tuireann, " Atlantis," Vol. IV. See Appendix.
[2] Brugh : a fort.

Liffey's plain, and Bregia's air,
And the hills round Taltin's Fair.

If I saw Benn Edair forth,
And Dun Tuirenn in the north,—
Welcome then were death to me,
Were it death with agony.

THE FAIRY FOREWARNING AT CLONTARF.[1]

Dublaing [2] O'Hartagan wished to assist his friend Prince Murcad, at Clontarf, though he had been banished by King Brian. Dublaing's spirit-bride, *leanàn sighe*, covered him with the cloak of invisibility, and he made havoc of the Norse-Irish round Murcad. "Methinks I hear the battle-blows of Dublaing, but I see him not," said Murcad. "'Tis fitting I should put off what prevents thee seeing me," said Dublaing, and he did. Then they retired to consult with Aeibel, his spirit-bride, who warned Prince Murcad that he, his son, his father the King, and many chiefs would die that day. Thus they spake:

SPIRIT-BRIDE.

"THOUGH thy heart be high, O Love,
When the hosts move forth to fight,
Though thy face be flushed, its glow
Change shall know, ere come the night."

[1] "Proceedings of the Ossianic Society," Vol. II., p. 99. Dublin, 1855. The poem was of course composed some time after the battle (1014), but the presence of Spirits is mentioned in the prose account, "The Wars of the Gael and Gall." The Orkney Norse also saw phantom omens.

[2] Dublaing, pronounced Dulaing.

PRINCE MURCAD.

" I could tell, ere that befall,
Story small, indeed, but true :
Fear for fate of life in war
Ne'er shall mar my face's hue.

If we die, so die the Gall—
Gael shall all their strongholds share ;
None may count the crowded dead
Hewn beneath my red sword there."

SPIRIT-BRIDE.

" Thou, O Dublaing ! keep from fight
Till the light of morning's ray:
Thou shalt live an hundred years,—
Shun the spears for but one day."

DUBLAING.

" I would not quit Murcad bold,
Not for silver,—not for gold ;
Nor would bear dishonour's breath
For inevitable death.

All the steeds in Lurc that live
He would for my body give :
I that body's bulwark bring
For the Heir of Erinn's king."

SPIRIT-BRIDE.

" Fall shall Murcad—Brian shall fall—
Fall, in one career, shall all,—

Gory the field of sorrow
With haughty blood to-morrow."[1]

HOLY SPIRIT.

MAEL-ISU.[2]

HOLY Spirit of Love
In us, round us, above ;
Holy Spirit, we pray
Send, sweet Jesus ! this day.

[1] The remarkable resemblance between this dramatic poem and
"Lochiel's Warning" is obvious.   In Campbell's poem a Wizard
foretells the doom ; these lines might be a free paraphrase of the
last Irish stanza :

> " For a field of the dead rushes red on my sight,
> And the clans of Culloden are scattered in fight."

Lochiel's answer gives the very spirit of Murcad's refusal.   His
clan come like reapers : woe to his enemy.   Though their ranks
perish,

> "Lochiel, untainted by flight or by chains,
> While the kindling of life in his bosom remains,
> Shall victor exult or in death be laid low."

Again, Lochiel offers a mantle to the Wizard.   "Draw," he says :

> " This mantle, to cover the phantoms of fright."

The coincidences are such that I am induced to think Campbell,
who showed his sympathy with Ireland in some fine poems, may
have heard this Irish legend, and taken its suggestive spirit.

[2] Maelisu, grandson of Brolcan, of Derry, died in the year 1038.
"Mael-Isu " means " Client of Jesus " (literally, the " Tonsured of
Jesus ").

Holy Spirit, to win
Body and soul within,
To guard us that we be
From ills and illness free,

From sin and demons' snare,
From Hell and evils there,
O Holy Spirit, come !
Hallow our heart, thy home.

DEUS MEUS.

MAELISU.

Deus meus adiuva me,[1]
Give me thy love, O Christ, I pray,
Give me thy love, O Christ, I pray,
'Deus meus adiuva me.

In meum cor ut sanum sit,[2]
Pour, loving King, Thy love in it,
Pour, loving King, Thy love in it,
In meum cor ut sanum sit.

Domine, da ut peto a te,[3]
O, pure bright sun, give, give to-day,
O, pure bright sun, give, give to-day,
Domine, da, ut peto a te.

[1] My God, assist thou me.
[2] Into my heart that it sound may be.
[3] Lord, grant thou what I ask of thee.

O

Hanc spero rem et quæro quam [1]
Thy love to have where'er I am,
Thy love to have where'er I am,
Hanc spero rem et quæro quam.

Tuum amorem sicut uis, [2]
Give to me swiftly, strongly, this,
Give to me swiftly, strongly, this,
Tuum amorem sicut uis.

Quæro, postulo, peto a te [3]
That I in heaven, dear Christ, may stay,
That I in heaven, dear Christ, may stay,
Quæro, postulo, peto a te.

Domine, Domine, exaudi me, [4]
Fill my soul, Lord, with Thy love's ray,
Fill my soul, Lord, with Thy love's ray,
Domine, Domine, exaudi me.
        Deus meus adiuva me,
        Deus meus adiuva me. [5]

---

[1] This thing I hope and seek of thee.
[2] Thy love as Thou mayst will.
[3] I seek, I claim, and I ask of Thee.
[4] Lord, Lord, hearken to me.
[5] This poem, written on the margin of " Lebor Breac." p. 101,
is quoted by Dr. Whitley Stokes, " Calendar of Œngus," clxxxv.
Alliteration is observed in the Latin lines.   In the first verse it
seems obtained by the reading " ad-iuva," and in the fifth "amorem"
alliterates with " uis " [vis].

ALEXANDER THE GREAT.[1]

AUTHOR UNKNOWN.

FOUR men stood beside a grave,
Alexander's, great and brave;
There the song of truth they said
O'er the mighty monarch dead.

" Yesterday," the first man spoke,
" All the world lay 'neath his yoke,
Myriad hosts were then his own,
To-day, he lieth all alone."

The second : " Yesterday he hurl'd
Royal edicts o'er the world,
Rode the earth from rim to rim,
To-day, earth rideth over him."

" Yesterday," so spake the third,
" All things hung upon his word,
Naught save his of earth was found,
To-day, scarce seven feet of ground."

" Alexander, brave and bold,
Alexander treasured gold "—

---

[1] The Dean of Lismore's Book, edited by the Rev. T.
McLauchlan. Edinburgh : Edmonston and Douglas.

Thus the fourth man said his say—
" The gold, it treasures him to-day."

Like the Palm o'er all the trees,
Like Leviathan in seas,
Like the Moon above the stars,
Shone the Conqueror of wars.

Like as Sion to all hills,
Like the Ocean to the rills,
Like the Eagle's victor head,
Like the Lion on his dead :

Greatest he of all things great,
Loftiest on earth his state,
Mightiest Man that ever trod,
None above him,—only God !

Truth they told beside the grave,
Of the High King bold and brave,
Not as foolish dames deplore,
Sang the wisdom of the Four.

THE VISION OF VIANDS.

ANIAR MAC CONGLINNE [1] (TWELFTH CENTURY).

IN a slumber visional,
Wonders apparitional
 Sudden shone on me :
Was it not a miracle?
Built of lard, a coracle
 Swam a sweet milk sea.

With high hearts heroical,
We stepped in it, stoical,
 Braving billow-bounds ;
Then we rode so dashingly,
Smote the sea so splashingly,
That the surge sent, washingly,
 Honey up for grounds.

---

[1] "The Vision of Mac Conglinne," edited by Professor Kuno Meyer, and David Nutt. London : Nutt, 1894. See Appendix. The Irish metre is reproduced. This curious poem evidently suggested passages in "The Land of Cokaigne." Compare the first two stanzas with these verses :

> "Up a river of sweet milk
> Where is plenty great of silk,
> When the summer's day is hot,
> The young nunnes taketh a boat

Ramparts rose of custard all
Where a castle muster'd all
    Forces o'er the lake ;
Butter was the bridge of it,
Wheaten meal the ridge of it,
    Bacon every stake.

Strong it stood, and pleasantly
There I entered presently
    Hying to the hosts ;

And doth ham forth in that rivere,
Both with oares and with steere."

Again, compare with the third, fourth, and fifth stanzas these verses :

" There is a well fair Abbey
Of white monks and of grey :
There beth bowrs and halls,
All of pasties beth the walls,
Of flesh, of fish, and a rich meat
The likefullest that man may eat,
Flouren cakes beth the shingles all
Of church, cloister, bowrs and hall,
The pinnes beth fat puddings
Rich meat to princes and kings."

The Irish original was at least partly rimed into Lowland
Scotch, judging by an old verse I heard in Ulster, concerning a
house :

" Weel I mind the biggin' o't,
Bread and cheese were the door cheek
And pancakes the riggin' o't."

This forms part of the Jacobite song : " This is no my ain house,"
but may come from an older song.

Dry beef was the door of it,
Bare bread was the floor of it,
  Whey-curds were the posts.

Old cheese-columns happily,
Pork that pillared sappily,
  Raised their heads aloof;
While curd-rafters mellowly
Crossing cream-beams yellowly,
  Held aloft the roof.

Wine in well rose sparklingly,
Beer was rolling darklingly,
  Bragget brimmed the pond.
Lard was oozing heavily,
Merry malt moved wavily,
  Through the floor beyond.

Lake of broth lay spicily,
Fat froze o'er it icily,
  'Tween the wall and shore;
Butter rose in hedges high,
Cloaking all its edges high
  White lard blossomed o'er.

Apple alleys bowering,
Pink-topped orchards flowering,
  Fenced off hill and wind;

Leek tree forests loftily,
Carrots branching tuftily,
  Guarded it behind.

Ruddy warders rosily
Welcomed us right cosily
  To the fire and rest;
Seven coils of sausages,
Twined in twisted passages,
  Round each brawny breast.

Their chief I discover him,
Suet mantle over him,
  By his lady bland;
Where the cauldron boiled away,
The Dispenser toiled away,
  With his fork in hand.

Good King Cathal, royally,
Surely will enjoy a lay,
  Fair and fine as silk;
From his heart his woe I call,
When I sing, heroical,
How we rode, so stoical,
  O'er the Sea of Milk.

IX.—GAEL AND NORMAN, ETC.

FROM THE THIRTEENTH TO THE SEVENTEENTH CENTURIES.

IN THE HEART OF JESUS.

MUIREADACH (ALBANACH) O'DALY.[1]

CIRCA 1215.

THAT in Jesus' heart should be
One like me is marvellous ;
Sin has made my life a loss
But his Cross shall speak for us.

---

[1] The bard had a romantic history. In 1213 O'Donnell's steward entered Connacht to collect tribute. He acted so offensively to the bard at Lissadill, that the latter smote him, and he fell. The poet fled for refuge to the De Burghos, thence to the O'Briens, thence (O'Donnell pursuing) to Dublin, whence he was conveyed to Scotland, where he resided until he succeeded in making his peace. These poems were preserved in Scotland in the Dean of Lismore's Book, and the editor, the Rev. Mr. McLauchlan says Muireadach Albanach (*i.e.*, the Albanian) was the ancestor of the Mac Vurrichs, bards to the Mac Donalds of Clanranald. He was cotemporary with Cahal Mor of the Red Hand (O'Connor of Connacht) who addressed a poem to him, which has been translated by Professor Blackie.

As of old, O Jesus sweet !
Bless my feet and hands thine own ;
Of thy bounty, bless to good
These my blood, and flesh, and bone.

Never now I keep from ill
Since my body will take part ;
Make it hallowed by thy love
From above, in head and heart.

Sweet and great one ! grant relief,
All my grief take quite away ;
So that ere my life be spent
Thou'lt have sent and cleared my way.

TEACH, O TRINITY !

By Muireadach (Albanach) O'Daly.

Teach thou me, O Trinity !
O Lord, whose speech is sweet,
Teach my tongue, O Trinity !
Bless it with blessing meet.

Holy o'er the heavens free
Make strong my arms and sure,
In my heart abide with me,
Thou Prince of all things pure.

Take my heart and teach my hand,
So may'st Thou, king of truth !
Eye and ear and voice command,—
Bless Thou my lips with ruth.

These my lips which wrought thee wrong
Nor warring words reproved
This my tongue which lapsed too long—
Bless these, my soul's Beloved !

Thee, O Trinity, from thee
Ah, Lord, grant healing balm,
Like a fair and fine oak tree
With cankered core I am.

Yet of blood I bear no stain,
No stain of spoil I bear ;
Then, for Mary's love, O deign
Give answer to my prayer.

Thou, who gavest prayer its birth,
Is 't wrong to pray thee now ?
Not the kings or lords of earth
Can comfort give, but Thou.

None such knowledge sweet hath given
But thou, O Lord ! alone—
Thine is truth, O King of heaven !
No wisdom like thine own.

If I on the right way bide
No less my vow commands,
If I stray, be Thou my guide,
Who am within thy hands.

Clay nor rock can refuge yield
From fire of doom above,
Thou, thyself, shalt be my shield
And guard me, with thy love.

THE HARP THAT RANSOMED.

By Gillabride Mac Conmide,[1] a.d. 1230.

Bring my King's harp here to me,
That my grief, forgot, may flee;
Full soon shall pass man's sadness
When wakes that voice of gladness.

[1] Pronounced (and now written) Mac Conmee. This bard was a
native of Ulster, but was known as Albanach, the Albanian (or
Scottish) because of his oft sojourning in Alba. Commissioned by
Prince Doncad O'Brian to win back, for a price, the harp which had
been sent as ransom for the return of the poet O'Daly, he failed in
his object. The "jewel of the O'Briens," a small or hand-harp,
would not be surrendered for flocks of sheep. At last, the bard
called for it and touched its chords whilst he sang to it this farewell
song. O'Curry thought it may have been taken to Westminster by
Edward I., and suggested the insertion of the harp on the Irish
escutcheon, under Henry VIII. He argued that this may possibly
be the instrument now erroneously called " Brian Borumha's Harp."

Noble he, and skilled in all,
Who owned this tree[1] musical;
Many lofty songs he sang
While its soft sweet numbers rang.

Many jewels he bestowed,
Seated, where this fair gem glowed;
Oft he guerdoned the beholder,
Its curved neck on his shoulder.

Dear the hand that smote the chords
Of the slight, smooth, polished boards;
Bright and brave, the tall youth played,
True his hand, for music made.

When his hand o'er this would roam—
Music's meet and perfect home—
Then its great soft tender sigh
Bore away man's misery.

When the curled Dalcassians came,
Guests, within his hall of fame,
Then its deep voice, woke again,
Welcomed Cashel's comely men.

All men admired the Maiden,
Banba[2] with praise was laden:

---

[1] Tree, *i.e.*, harp, because of its wood, a bold synonym.
[2] Ireland.

" Doncad's harp," they all exclaim,
" The fair, fragrant tree of fame ! "

" O'Brian's harp ! clear its call
O'er the feast in Gabran's hall ;
How the heir of Gabran's Kings
Shook deep music from its strings ! "

Son of Gael, of weapon sharp,
Wins not now O'Brian's harp :
Son of stranger shall not gain
From this gem its Spirit's strain.

What woe to come a pleader
For harp of Lim'rick's Leader !
What woe to come a-dreaming
That flocks were thy redeeming !

Sweet thy full melodious voice,
Maid, who wast a Monarch's choice :
Thy blithe voice would woe beguile,
Maiden of my Erinn's isle !

Could I live the yew tree's time
In this deer-loved eastern clime,
I would serve her gladly still,—
The Chief's harp of Brendon Hill.

Dear to me—of right it should—
Alba's ever-winsome wood,
Yet, though strange, more dear I love
This one tree of Erinn's grove !

THE EXILED HEAD.

GILLABRIDE MAC CONMIDE,[1] A.D. 1260.

DEATH of my heart !—Brian's head
Far in foreign land is laid :
High head of dauntless daring
An Orphan Isle is Erinn.

To their king of Saxon they
Bore our Gael king's head away ;
What could enemy wish more—
Thou, O Head ! art triumphed o'er.

This peers all that foes have wrought—
Brian's head to London brought !
Now hath Fate fulfilled all woes,—
Brian's head lies 'mid his foes !

---

[1] Pronounced Mac Conmee (sometimes made Mac Namee). He
was Chief Bard of Ulster, and friend of King Brian O'Neill, whose
claim to the Over-Kingship was contested by an O'Brien. Brian
was killed at the battle of Down, in 1260, by the Norman Lord
Justice Stephen de Longe Espée. These are the first verses of a
lengthy poem, in "Miscellany of the Celtic Society," Dublin, 1849.

WOMANKIND.[1]

GERALD THE BARD, FOURTH EARL OF DESMOND.

SHAME, who overleaps his steed,
Rightly rede and understand ;
Love with land goes swift behind,
Weigh the worth of Womankind.

Them may malisons enfold,
Though of old we used to mix,
Youth, their tricks are as the wind—
Ware the wiles of Womankind.

He who early looks abroad
Shall a load of ills discern,
Wouldst thou learn the worst to find,
Watch the heart of Womankind.

Married man with witless wife,
Fails in strife with foreign foe ;
Bad for hart is belling hind,
Worse the tongue of Womankind.

Dame who hears but does not heed—
Walled indeed her ears with wax,

---

[1] The Dean of Lismore's Book.   See Appendix.

See her tax her spouse too blind,
Wont to rouse is Womankind.

Show a stranger,—off she trips,
Wreathes her lips with smiles resigned,
Him beguiles with martyred air—
False as fair is Womankind.

Wedded wife from altar rail,
Pious-pale before the priest,
After feast shows bitter rind—
Best beware of Womankind.

Best beware of Womankind,
Meetly mind, this truth proclaim :
He who fails full soon shall find
Bondage blind and bitter shame.

THE FAILING ART.[1]

Doncad Mor of Lennox.

14th—15th Century.

Grieve for him whose voice is o'er
When called once more to meet with men ;

[1] The Dean of Lismore's Book.—In this pathetic poem
Doncad Mor anticipates, by four centuries, the plot of Balzac's
novel, " Le Chef d'Œuvre," which Mr. Kipling recalls in " The

Him whose words come slow as sighs,
Who ever tries, and fails again.

Never now he swells the air,
Nor rolls the fair and faultless lay,—
Harp he cannot set aside,
Nor wake, when tried, its minstrelsy.

Yet his tinkling will not cease,
Nor bide in peace ; he still would sing—
When no man can tell his words
Nor hear the frail chords, faltering.

Grieve for him who fails in fame,
Nor keeps his name where none impeach ;
Him who strives, and still in vain,
That fruit to gain he cannot reach.

Did I yearn such fruit to gain,
I should not strain without reprieve ;
I would tear the tree from clay
Let whoso pray, or rage, or grieve.

Light that Failed." In all three cases, the interest centres on the
failure of an artist's powers. Balzac and Kipling depict a painter
with decaying faculties : but the painter is not aware of the ruin of
his work. Doncad's minstrel must be supposed conscious of his
wrecked powers, and his despairing efforts against inevitable fate
make this a greater tragedy. It is one Balzac should have dealt
with.

LOVE UNTOLD.

ISABEL STUART, FIRST COUNTESS OF ARGYLL, A.D. 1459.

WOE to one whose wound is love,
Be the reason what may be ;
Who can heart from heart remove ?
Sad the fate that follows me.

Love I gave my Love unknown,
Never tongue the tale may speak ;
Soon, unhealed, it shall be shown
In fading face and thinning cheek.

He, to whom I gave my love
(Ear shall hear not, none shall know),
He has bonds eternal wove
For me,—an hundred fold of woe.

[1] Dean of Lismore's Book. Isabel, second daughter of
Stuart, Lord of Lorn, married Archibald, first Earl of Argyll (title
granted A.D. 1457). The verses indicate a hidden romance.

A KING'S LESSON.[1]

TADG O'BRUADIN, A.D. 1580.

GREAT the teaching of a King,
He prosperity may bring,
May the land with order grace,
Raise his country or abase.

*   *   *   *   *

Know whose pow'r is o'er thy head,
Follow Him, with faithful tread;
In thy heart still let Him be
From whom *thou* hast royalty.

Mind thou this, o'er everything:
Love and honour the High King;
Faithful fear of God gave force
To all wisdom, and its source.

---

[1] This is part of a poem addressed by the bard to Doncad O'Brien (fourth Earl of Thomond) when the latter was elected Chieftain of his clan. The bold freedom of the bardic lesson contrasts with the adulation of the contemporary court-poets of England, as with the doctrine of James I. The modernity of the Irish bard's teaching is due to its antiquity; mankind has moved round on its tracks. The syllabic measure of the original is given, but not certain peculiarities which would make a faithful translation impossible. It is related that the bard was ultimately murdered by a Cromwellian soldier, who coveted his inheritance.

Run not on a wanton will,
Chief of Thomond, heedful still :
Be the people's cause thy care—
Not an idler's task is there !

Let no banquet, drink, nor game,
Maids, nor music thee inflame ;
Make the ill-deed manifest
Spite of potent chief's protest.

Not for love, nor fear, nor hate,
Give thou, Judge deliberate,
Wrongful sentence ; calmly cold,
Silver sways it not, nor gold.

Then crowds shall come to sue thee,
Bring all their quarrels to thee ;
Nor from thee fear any wrong,
Full of wisdom, skilled and strong.

Let thy fort be full of men,
Few should of thy secrets ken ;
Many courtiers gleam and flit
Who for secrets are unfit.

Let thy rule not swerve away
From one noble 'neath thy sway :
This is Erinn's right and root,
This her first law absolute.

Should thy friends impose, be thou,
Till they're humble, stern of brow :
Should for peace thy foemen sue
Feuds forget in friendship true.

Fierce shall be thy countenance
When thy hosts to war advance ;
Bright at banquet, when thou'lt share
To each guest due honour there.

Haughty be with men of blood,
Mild with learning's lettered brood ;
Be thy young face grave, thy speech
Kind and courteous still to each.

High in deed, be low in pride,
Staunch in rush of terror's tide ;
Manful keep thy soul, my son,
Till the battle 's lost or won.

Claim thy homage, none omit,
Place in power no man unfit ;
When loose men in office stand,
King, contempt will stir the land.

Never threaten, in thy wrath,
War if no true cause it hath :
Nor abandon right for peace,
Or thou'lt dwindle and decrease.

Curb thy will, nor come perforce ;
Bear at times to thwart its course :
That the land draw to thy will
Patience show in anger still.

Surest word the word that's slow.—
Lower the lofty, lift the low,
Quell the mob, make peace to sing—
Such the true signs of a king.

Son, for thee no song I raise,
Though thou be designed for praise ;
I for thee stand silent still
Till our teaching thou fulfil.

* * * * *

Then the sun of day, the sky,
Earth and water, birds on high,
Every element shall sing
To the praises of the king.

On the boughs shall swarm the bees,
Salmon leap from shining seas,
All the fair tribes of the flood
Praise with me the chieftain good.

Then the warriors, and the bard,
Then the king shall praise award,
They shall laud thy high estate,
Nor deem any king so great.

FAREWELL TO INNISFAIL.

GERALD NUGENT.[1]

WOE, to part from Innisfail,
Woe from Erinn's side to sail ;
Land of the bee-glad mountains !
Isle of the steeds and fountains !

Now I cleave the foreign foam
Facing east from Fintan's home :
My heart leaves me, faring o'er,
Dear no shore but Erinn's shore.

Shore of fine fruit-bended trees,
Shore of green grass-covered leas ;
Old plain of Ir, soft, show'ry,
Wheatful, fruitful, fair, flow'ry !

Home of priest, and gallant knight,
Isle of gold-haired maidens bright,
Banba of the clear blue wave,
Of bold hearts and heroes brave.

---

[1] A bard of a noble Anglo-Norman family (de Nogent) who became
Irish, and victims to later invaders. It is noticeable how appeal
is made to old Gaelic heroes, whose feelings they assumed as part of
their heritage. The Irish Nugents became illustrious leaders on the
continent. Field-Marshal Nugent, of the Austrian service, defeated
Murat. The poet's praise of the valour of Irishmen was supported
by his contemporary, Edmund Spenser, who said " no man cometh

If God bless my flag, unfurled,
I'll yet reach my native world;
But I come not from abroad
'Neath the shunnéd Saxons' rod.

Not deeps I dread, upheaving,
But leaving Laeré's mountains
'Tis quitting Delvin, grieving,
That fills all sorrow's fountains.

Fare ye well, who watch my sail
Youths of honoured Innisfail!
Farewell Meath, the nest of song,
Noble, knightly, steadfast, strong!

on more bravely at a charge." The Irish cavalier, finely apparelled, resembled Sir Topas "in his robe of sheklaton, which is that kind of guilded leather with which they used to embroyder their Irish jackets. And there, likewise, by that description, you may see the very fashion and manner of the Irish horseman most truly set forth in his long hose, his ryding showes of costly cordwaine, his hocqueton, and his haberion, and all the rest." . . . Sir Topas, in Chaucer, wore fine "cloth of lake," "sherte," and " breche " next his white skin :

" And next his sherte an haketon
And over them an habergeon,
    For piercing of his herte.

" And over them a fin hauberk
Was all ywrought of Jewes werk,
    Ful strong it was of plate ;
And over that his cote armoure,
As white as is the lily floure,
    In which he would debate."

X.—SEVENTEENTH CENTURY.

DIRGE OF OLIVER GRACE.

Sean Mac Walter Walsh (1604).[1]

Dark the cloud our mountains o'er,
A cloud that never came before;
Stern the noon-hush, broken lowly
By the voice of sorrow solely.

Floats the death knell on the wind,
Grief, alas! comes close behind;
Harshly hoarse the raven's croaking,
Warning that man's life is broken.

For thee, O noble youth! for thee
Wails the banshee mournfullie;
In the midnight, still and lone,
Sadly swells her Caeiné's moan.

---

[1] This very Gaelic dirge was composed by the descendant of a Welshman for the descendant of an Anglo-Norman (of Raymond Le Gros, or Le Gras, whence Grace), and is rendered into English by the descendant of a Norseman. Here is evidence of how complex may be the Irish nature and the "Celtic note" at times.

The Rock's Son [1] answers to her wail,
Grieving from gray rock and vale ;
The cock no longer hails the pearly
Morn, nor cheers us late or early.

Ah, my Oliver óg, mo chree ! [2]
'Tis thy death wakes the weird banshee ;
'Tis it that brings—both night and morrow—
'Tis it that brings the bitter sorrow !

What fills thy place to us, our chief?
Naught but Tears and sobbing Grief !
There 's naught for us since he is taken
But weeping tears and sore heart-breaking.

Death ! thou'st smote for ever, now,
Fairest flower from highest bough ;
Mo nuar ! could nothing stay thy doom,
And save our dear one from the tomb ?

Sword of brightness, strong and sure,
Shield of justice and the poor,
'Neath thy noble father's banner
High thou'st won, in Ormond, honour.

Ne'er till came this darkest day
Thy home in sorrow hopeless lay ;

[1] Echo.
[2] Young Oliver, my heart.

Good thou wast, O heir ! and noble,—
Thee they mourn in bitter trouble.

Rightful heir, in truth, still bearing
High their name and love for Erinn,
An oak-tree, thou wast fair to see,
And like to spread thy branches free.

Such was not thy fate's designing,
Low in earth thou'rt now reclining,
Ruin of joy, each day for all—
For thy love a black heart-pall !

She, a mother, ever weepeth
For the long, lone sleep he sleepeth,—
Her children's sire, her first love, dearest,
Ah, 'tis she has anguish drearest.

Never again the chase he'll follow,
O'er misty mount or dewy hollow ;
Never be heard his clear horn ringing,
Never his dog's cry, gaily springing.

Never he'll urge his swift young steed
Over the mount and over the mead ;
Change is o'er his beauty bowed,
O'er his glory falls a cloud.

O gen'rous hand, thou'rt weak for aye !
Magnanimous heart, thou art but clay !
Seed of knighthood, friend of the bard,
    O'er thee the Spirit of Song keeps ward.

Bright beam of song ! not quencht thy fame,
My lay shall live with thy radiant name,
And win a tear, in the after morrows,
For thee, perchance, and thy bard of sorrows.

THE FLIGHT OF THE EARLS.[1]

ANDREAS MAC MARCUIS, A.D. 1607.

Lo, our Land this night is lone !
Hear ye not sad Erinn's moan ?
Maidens weep and true men sorrow,
Lone the Brave Race night and morrow.

---

[1] O'Neill and O'Donnell, Earls of Tyrone and Tyrconnell. The great plunder obtained, by the confiscation of the Earl of Desmond's estates in South Munster, in Elizabeth's reign, sharpened the appetite for more spoils. Hence in the reign of James I., a conspiracy was formed and a sham plot was alleged against the Earls of Tyrone and Tyrconnell : they fled, and the lands they had ruled were shared among the spoilers. In the next reign an attempt was made to annul the titles of the old Anglo-Norman nobility of Connaught, for the new-comers spared no race.

Lone this night is Fola's plain,—
Though the foemen swarm amain—
Far from Erinn, generous-hearted,
Far her Flower of Sons is parted.

They have crossed the Spanish foam,
To their great Forefather's home;
Though from populous Erinn gone,
They have left behind not one.

Great the hardship! great the grief!
Ulster wails Tirconaill's Chief,
From Emain west to Assarue
Wails gallant, gentle, generous Hugh.

Children's joy no more rejoices,—
Fetters silence Song's sweet voices—
Change upon our chiefs, alas!
Bare the altar, banned the Mass.

Homes are hearthless, harps in fetters,
Guerdons none for men of letters,
Banquets none, nor merry meetings,
Hills ring not the chase's greetings.

Songs of war make no heart stronger,
Song of peace inspire no longer,—
In great halls, at close of days,
Sound no more our Fathers' lays.

Bregia's plain now hears no more
Great Milesian deeds of yore;
Unsung the rout, o'er hill and hollow
When Denmark flees and gay Gael follow.

Thus is Erinn's sad estate,
This henceforth must be her fate;
Long the ban will lie upon her,—
Helpless long in hard dishonour.

Now come,—it must, alas! be said—
Egyptian rule upon her head;
The faithless host round Troja's walls,
The fate of Babylonian halls.

Foemen camp in Neimid's plains;
Who shall break our heavy chains?
What Naisi, son of Conn, shall prove
A Moses to the land we love.

She has none who now can aid her,
All have gone before the invader;
Banba's bonds and cruel cross
Steal the very soul from us!

TWO CHAMPIONS OF CHRISTENDOM.[1]

DONNCAD O'FUTAIL, A.D. 1619.

O'ER the fair sea they set sail,
Two tried chiefs from Innis Gael,[2]
Free of will they left the shore—
We shall see them never more.

Why did our comrades leave us,
That wistful woe should grieve us?
Each went, with hero's ardour,
To serve as Europe's warder!

Forth they fared across the foam
For the fame of Christendom;
They in high emprise succeed
By true worth and dauntless deed.

---

[1] Extract from a long poem in "Miscellany of the Celtic Society."
Concobar was the son and heir of Sir Fingein O h-Edirsceóil,—
which name was altered to Florence O'Driscoll. This chief had
done homage to the Lord Deputy, but the son took service and rose
to distinction abroad, like so many other Irishmen. His son's first
name seems to have been curiously latinized Cornelius, hence Corneil.
The two champions of Christendom against the Turks were father
and son : the latter, O'Donovan says, was killed at the mouth of the
Mediterranean, in June, 1619, in a battle between the Turkish and
Spanish Fleets.
[2] Isle of the Gael.

Their names shine clear in story,
Shore and sea speak their glory:
Nothing dimmed their valour's glow
Till an ill fate laid them low.

Conall Cearnach,[1] no, nor Cu[2]
Greater courage never knew;
Nor fair Oscar, first in war,
Braver was than Concobar.

Oliver[3] hath noble name,
Fortibras is fair of fame;
Yet, 'mid surge and spray of spears,
These our princes were their peers.

Conall Gulban,[4] great of yore,
Waged the war from shore to shore—
Though he urged the forays far,
Farther still came Concobar.

Nor doth very Hector, he—
Nor Achilles, in degree,
Though aloft each shone a star,
Beat the blade from Concobar.

[1] Greatest of the Red Branch Knights, in the first century.
[2] *I.e.*, Cuchulainn.
[3] One of Charlemagne's paladins, and frequently mentioned in Irish romance.
[4] Famous son of King Niall of the Nine Hostages.

They have sent, hand over hand,
The renown through ev'ry land
Of their high heroic deeds,
Faring far where honour leads.

Well the Saxes know the name—
Well the Franks the flying fame
Of the bare-armed heroes' might,[1]
Of their far-resounding fight.

Nobles speak their praise in Spain,
And the Emp'ror in Almaine,
Fair the feats on.honour's roll
Of the Heir of Edirskeól.

The champion chiefs of Flanders
Lament the dead Commanders,
Alba, Erinn, both deplore
The brave men who come no more.

But th' exulting Turks take breath,
They have rest with Corneil's death;
They fear not now his warning,—
He sleepeth sound till Morning.

*　　*　　*　　*　　*

[1] They bared the arm for battle, disdaining the encumbrance of armour.

How dark the clouds of heaven,
By flash of red fires riven,
No boughs bend [1] above the dell
Since the two famed heroes fell.

The shores and seas are wailing,
The moon and stars are paling,
And loud the cascade's calling,—
Because the knights have fallen.

The earth and air, all over,
The angel birds [2] that hover,
Each mournful night and morrow
Lament with lovers' sorrow.

There's no country, clan, nor home,
There's no heart in Christendom,
But shall feel as fell two stars
In the fate-killed Concobars.

[1] *I.e.* with fruit.　　　　　[2] Literal.

LAMENT FOR EOGHAN RUA O'NEILL.[1]

A.D. 1649.

How great the loss is thy loss to me !
A loss to all who had speech with thee :—
On earth can so hard a heart there be
As not to weep for the death of Eoghan ?
    Och, ochón ! 'tis I am stricken,
    Unto death the isle may sicken,
    Thine the Soul which all did quicken ;
    —And Thou 'neath the sod !

I stood at Cavan o'er thy tomb,
Thou spok'st no word through all my gloom;
O want ! O ruin ! O bitter doom!
O great, lost Heir of the House of Niall!
    I care not now whom Death may borrow,
    Despair sits by me, night and morrow,
    My life henceforth is one long sorrow ;
    —And Thou 'neath the sod !

---

[1] There are at least three dirges for Eoghan Rua : one, of recent
date, by Thomas Davis ; a Gaelic lament, translated by Mangan,
somewhat formal in tone ; and this, which evidently expresses the
sincere feelings of a personal friend, whose name is lost to us.

O child of heroes, heroic child!
Thou'dst smite our foe in battle wild,
Thou'dst right all wrong, O just and mild!
And who lives now—since dead is Eoghan?
 In place of feasts, alas! there's crying,
 In place of song, sad woe and sighing,
 Alas, I live with my heart a-dying,
 —And Thou 'neath the sod!

My woe, was ever so cruel woe?
My heart is torn with rending throe!
I grieve that I am not lying low
In silent death by thy side, Eoghan!
 Thou wast skilled all straits to ravel,
 And thousands broughtst from death and cavil,
 They journey safe who with thee travel,
 —And Thou with thy God!

My days shall count but a short, sad space,
Till I, 'mid saints, shall behold thy face;
Nor meet to mourn in that holy place,
In joy before the self-chosen Lamb.
 O then I ne'er shall fear to sever,
 O from thy side I'll wander never,
 Singing the glory and peace for ever;
 —And we, with our God!

SHAUN O'DWYER OF THE GLEN.

Air: "*Sean O'Duibir an Gleanna.*"[1]

A.D. 1651.

OFT, at pleasant morning,
Sunshine all adorning,
I've heard the horn give warning
   With bird's mellow call—
Badgers flee before us,
Woodcocks startle o'er us,
Guns make ringing chorus,
   'Mid the echoes all ;
The fox run high and higher,
Horsemen shouting nigher,
The maiden mourning by her
   Fowl he left in gore.
Now, they fell the wild-wood :
Farewell, home of childhood,
Ah, Shaun O'Dwyer a' Glanna,—
   Thy day is o'er !

---

[1] Pronounce: Shaun O Dyer a glanna. Colonel John O'Dwyer
was a distinguished officer, who, in 1651, commanded in Tipperary
and Waterford, and subsequently left Waterford for Spain with 500
followers.

It is my sorrow sorest,
Woe,—the falling forest !
The north wind gives me no rest,
   And death's in the sky :
My faithful hound's tied tightly,
Never sporting brightly,
Who'd make a child laugh lightly,
   With tears in his eye.
The antlered, noble-hearted
Stags are never started,
Never chased nor parted
   From the furzy hills.
If peace came, but a small way,
I'd journey down on Galway,
And leave, tho' not for alway,
   My Erinn of Ills.

The land of streamy valleys
Hath no head nor rallies—
In city, camp, or palace,
   They never toast her name.
Alas, no warrior column,—
From Cloyne to peaks of Colum,
O'er wasted fields and solemn,
   The shy hares grow tame :
O ! when shall come the routing,
The flight of churls and flouting ?
We hear no joyous shouting
   From the blackbird brave ;

More warlike is the omen,
Justice comes to no men,
Priests must flee the foemen
    To the mountain cave.

It is my woe and ruin
That sinless death's undoing
Came not, ere the strewing
    Of all my bright hopes.
How oft, at sunny morning,
I've watched the Spring returning,
The Autumn apples burning,
    And dew on woodland slopes !
Now my lands are plunder,
Far my friends asunder,
I must hide me under
    Branch and bramble screen—
If soon I cannot save me
By flight from foes who crave me,
O Death, at last I'll brave thee
    My bitter foes between !

THE MUNSTER KNIGHT.[1]

Richard O'Broin.

" Hail, O fair maiden, this morning fair,
Calm are thy slumbers,—and I in despair ;
Rise and make ready, and turning our steeds
We'll travel together to Munster's meads."

" Tell first thy Christian and clan-name too,
Lest what said about Munstermen might come true :
They'd take me in joy and they'd leave me in rue
To bear my kin's scorn my whole life through."

" I'll tell first my Christian and clan-name true :—
Ristard O'Broin from o'er Munster's dew,
I'm heir to an Earl and to tall towers white,
And for me dies the child of the Greenwood-Knight."

" If thou'rt heir to an Earl and to tall towers white,
Thou'lt have choice of rich damsels to be thy delight,
Who've peers as their fathers and hold the high cheer,
Thou need'st my humble self not, Cavalier ! '

---

[1] This poem may date from Elizabethan days.

"Come with me and thou, too, shalt sit with peers,
Come with me and thou, too, shalt hold high cheers;
Thou'lt have halls where are dances and music old,
Thou'lt have couches the third of each red with gold!"

"I'm not used at my father's to sit with hosts,
I'm not used at the board to have wines and toasts,
I'm not used to the dance-halls, with music old,
Nor to couches the third of each red with gold."

"O would we were speeding in chariot fine,
A glitter of gold in the gay sunshine,
More welcome than sunlight thy gold tresses are,
And long I have pined for my Morning Star."

THE FLOWER OF MAIDENS BROWN.

To the county of Leitrim—if you would come over!
    O Flower of Maidens Brown!
I'd bring you sweet meud [1] and honey of the clover,
    O Flower of Maidens Brown!
Beneath the green boughs, along the sunny shore,
You'd see the ships sail and watch the dipping oar,
And sadness or grief you never should know more,
    O Flower of Maidens Brown!

[1] Metheglin.

"I will not flee with you, in vain your imploring,"
   Saith Flower of Maidens Brown!
"A banquet of praises would leave me deploring,"
   Saith Flower of Maidens Brown!
"A thousand times better live without a love,
Than walking the dew, in valley or in grove,
The pulse of my heart for you did never move,"
   Saith Flower of Maidens Brown!

I saw her—she came across the mountain heather,
   As a star through mist shines down,
I told her my love, and we roved on together,
   Till the green milking field we found;
Then, seated awhile, where blossomed boughs grew,
I plighted my pledge that she should never rue,
All dangers I'd bear and ever would prove true
   To Flower of Maidens Brown!

'Tis my grief, 'tis my ruin—she will not come hither,
   The Flower of Maidens Brown!
The spouse of my heart to be, for aye together
   With Flower of Maidens Brown!
From mankind afar, in a glen out of sight,
All happy, all joyful, by day and by night,—
O God! what a fate if I win not my delight,
   The Flower of Maidens Brown!

EIVLIN A RUIN.

AUTHOR UNKNOWN.

Air: "Eiblin a Ruin." [1]

I AM dazzled with love for thee,
            Eivlin a ruin!
To praise you is joy to me,
            Eivlin a ruin!
My Glory of Light art thou!
My Solace most bright art thou!
My Mirth and my Might art thou!
            Eivlin a ruin!

O, Fosterer sure art thou!
O, Wood-dove all pure art thou!
My heart's only Cure art thou!
            Eivlin a ruin!

With frankness and spotless youth,
            Eivlin a ruin!
Could you deceive my truth?
            Eivlin a ruin!
More beauteous than Venus far,
More fair than the Morning Star,

---

[1] "Eiblin a ruin."   Pronounced Eivleen or Eileen a rooin—*i.e.*,
Eivleen, O, secret treasure.

My Helen, unstained, you are
      Eivlin a ruin !

My red Rose, my Lily white,
My treasure for ever bright,
Darling ! my soul's delight !
      Eivlin a ruin !

I'd cross the salt sea with you,
      Eivlin a ruin !
And ne'er—ne'er I'd flee from you,
      Eivlin a ruin !
What soft tales I'd tell to you,
I'd taste your lips' sweetness, too,
I'd sing 'mid the falling dew,
      " Eivlin a ruin ! "

I'd bring you where rivers glide,
Where green boughs o'ershade the tide,
'Neath music of birds to bide,
      Eivlin a ruin !

O ! joy beyond life would bless,—
      Eivlin a ruin !
Should I wed your loveliness,
      Eivlin a ruin !
My fond arm would circle you,
My heart be your guardian true,
Ne'er maiden were loved like you,
      Eivlin a ruin !

My beauteous Star, mild and clear,
Sooner than cause a tear,
O Death,—it were welcome here !
Eivlin a ruin !

THE FAIRY LAND OF PROMISE.

ART MAC CUMAIGH.[1]

ON the clay of Creggan churchyard, I slept all the night
in woe,
With the rise of morn, a Maiden came and kissed me,
bending low :
Her cheek had the blush of beauty, her tresses the
golden sheen,
'Twas the world's delight to gaze on the face of that fair
young Queen !

"O true heart," she said, "and constant ! Consume not
in grief for aye,
But arise and make ready swiftly, and come to the West
away :

[1] This pathetic ballad was composed by an Ulster bard, after the
last struggles of the independent Irish. All night he had lain
amongst the graves of his chieftains, and is comforted by an ethereal
Spirit which allures from hopeless grief to an Ideal World. The
Spirit of Poetry has thus often comforted the Gael. Another version
is given in Mr. McCall's "Noinins" (Dublin : Seely, Bryers and
Walker) with some true Irish songs.

In that fair Land of Promise, strangers bear sway o'er no
    sea nor shore,
But the sweetness of airy music shall entrance thee for
    evermore."

"Not for all of the gold that monarchs could heap on the
    round of earth
Would I stay when you seek me, Princess!—but this lone
    land of my birth
Keeps yet on its hills some kindred my heart would be
    loath to leave,
And the bride that in youth I wedded, were I gone,
    would, it may be, grieve."

"Methinks that, of all thy kindred, no friend hast thou
    living now,—
None speaks but to deride thee, none grieves for thy
    stricken brow;
No hand goes to clasp a comrade's, no eyes to look into
    thine—
Why tarry in snows of sorrow, when I call to a life
    divine?"

"Ah, my anguish, my wound! we've lost them the Gael
    of our true Tyrone,
And the Heir of the Fews, unhonoured, sleeps under the
    cold gray stone;

Brave branches of Niall Frasach, whose delight were the
    lays of old,
Whose hearts gave the minstrels welcome, whose hands
    gave the poets gold!"

"Since at Aughrim all were vanquished, and the Boyne—
    alas, my woe!
And fallen the great Milesians, and every chieftain low,—
Were't not better to fairy fortress to flee, in our love,
    away,
Than to suffer Clan William's [1] arrows in thy torn heart
    ev'ry day."

"One pledge I shall ask you only, one promise, O Queen
    divine!
And then I will follow faithful,—still follow each step of
    thine,—
Should I die, in some far-off country, in our wanderings
    east and west,
In the fragrant clay of Creggan, let my weary heart have
    rest."

[1] The partisans of William III.

MABEL NI KELLY.[1]

Toralach O'Carolan (1670-1738).

Whomever Fate may favour
To have his right hand 'neath thy head,
For all his life, he never
Will think of death or danger dread.
O head of the beauteous curling hair!
O breast like the swimming swan so fair!
Love and hope of Lover,
All the island over,
Fairest maid is Mabel, here and everywhere!

No song the sweetest,
No music meetest,
But she sings its melody, full, soft, and true;
Her cheek the rose a-blowing,
With comrade lily glowing,

[1] The genius of O'Carolan infused fresh and vigorous life into Irish Song. Three versions of this lyric have been published, but none in the metre of the original. Hardiman, who considered it one of the Bard's finest pieces, supplies the reason: "The difficulty of adapting English verse, in any variation of metre, to the complicated modulations of several of his surviving melodies is generally acknowledged. . . . His lively style, so different from the slow plaintive strains of our ancient music, the rapidity of his turns, his abrupt changes and terminations, so unexpected yet so pleasing could be followed only in the language in which he thought, composed, and sung."

In this version, the original metre of O'Carolan's irregular lyric is reproduced, in English, with its complicated modulations.

Her glancing eyes, like opening blossoms blue.
   And a bard has sung how herons keen
On hearing her victor-voice slumber serene.
      Her eyes of splendour
      Are wells of candour.—
Here's thy health, go leór, a stór, our beauty bright
   queen !

   Since they have passed death's portals
   Those heroines of world-wide name,
      Methinks, their place 'mid mortals
   Is Mabel's now by right and fame.
Lively and lovely all hearts she has won,
Fortune of song and its sweet paragon,
      Curling Cooleen fairest,
      Down-white shoulder rarest,
Chord of music ringing, after she has gone !

      None can espy her,
      Such charm is nigh her,
But will startle, and will flutter, like wings in the air—
      And the lamp will lose its light
      Before the maiden bright,
Of all the Gaelic nation most winsome and most fair :
For foot or hand or eye or mouth, nothing can compare !
Her tresses, like a sunbeam, to the grasses fall,
      Then let the palm be mine
      ·Of minstrelsy divine,—
Because I sing the Sovereign of all !

XI.—EIGHTEENTH CENTURY: PATRIOTIC.

THE FAIR HILLS OF EIRÉ.

By Doncad Mac Conmara.   Circa 1736.[1]

Air : " Uileacan Dub O."

TAKE my heart's blessing over to dear Eiré's strand—
    Fair Hills of Eiré O !
To the Remnant that love her—our Forefathers' Land !
    Fair Hills of Eiré O !
How sweet sing the birds, o'er mount there and vale,
Like soft sounding chords, that lament for the Gael,—
And I, o'er the surge, far, far away must wail
    The Fair Hills of Eiré O !

[1] Composed whilst the poet was in exile, on the Continent (at Hamburg), during the Penal Régime. The name Eiré (Ireland) is dissyllabic, and may be pronounced as "eyrie." The bard was born at Cratloe, Clare County, about 1710, and outlived the century. In spite of the penal laws against education, he succeeded in acquiring, at home and on the Continent, a mastery of classic and foreign languages. Besides short poems, he wrote a mock-heroic Æneid, detailing his adventures. In his old age he became blind, and the Irish teachers and pupils in Waterford, with old-time liberality and appreciativeness, laid a tribute on themselves for his maintenance.

How fair are the flow'rs on the dear daring peaks,
  Fair Hills of Eiré O !
Far o'er foreign bowers I love her barest reeks,
  Fair Hills of Eiré O !
Triumphant her trees, that rise on ev'ry height,
Bloom-kissed, the breeze comes odorous and bright,
The love of my heart !—O my very soul's delight !
  The Fair Hills of Eiré O !

Still numerous and noble her sons who survive,
  Fair Hills of Eiré O !
The true hearts in trouble,—the strong hands to strive—
  Fair Hills of Eiré O !
Ah, 'tis this makes my grief, my wounding and my woe
To think that each chief is now a vassal low,
And my Country divided amongst the Foreign Foe—
  The Fair Hills of Eiré O !

In purple they gleam, like our High Kings of yore,
  The Fair Hills of Eiré O !
With honey and cream are her plains flowing o'er,
  Fair Hills of Eiré O !
Once more I will come, or very life shall fail,
To the heart-haunted home of the ever-faithful Gael,
Than king's boon more welcome the swift swelling sail—
  For the Fair Hills of Eiré O !

The dew-drops sparkle, like diamonds on the corn,
  Fair Hills of Eiré O !

Where green boughs darkle the bright apples burn
    Fair Hills of Eiré O !
Behold, in the valley, cress and berries bland,
Where streams love to dally, in that Wondrous Land,
While the great River-voices roll their music grand
    Round the Fair Hills of Eiré O !

O, 'tis welcoming, wide-hearted, that dear land of love !
    Fair Hills of Eiré O !
New life unto the martyred is the pure breeze above
    The Fair Hills of Eiré O !
More sweet than tune flowing o'er the chords of gold
Comes the kine's soft lowing, from the mountain fold,—
O, the Splendour of the Sunshine on them all,—Young
    and Old,
        'Mid the Fair Hills of Eiré O !

THE BRIGHTNESS OF BRIGHTNESS.

Egan O'Reilly.[1]

Brightness of Brightness came, in loneliness, advancing,
Crystal of Crystal her clear gray eyes were glancing,
Sweetness of Sweetness her soft words flowed, entrancing,
Redness and Whiteness her cheek's fair form enhancing.

---

[1] John Mor O'Reilly, the son of a gentleman farmer, was sent
from Crosserlough, Cavan, at the beginning of the eighteenth

Cluster of Clusters, her hair descended flowing,
Swept o'er the flowers in showers of golden glowing;
Round her a raiment more pure than purest snowing,
Lofty her radiant race far beyond our knowing.

Lore of all Lores, she there swift to me imparted,
Lore of his sailing, from whom we long were parted;
Lore of their wailing, who to wreak his ruin started,
Lore not for song, but a trust for the true-hearted !

Thrills after thrills came as I drew nigh this Wonder,
Captor she captured, and bound my senses under;
When for His aid I cried, who ruleth thought and
        thunder,
Flashing she fled to the Peaks of Luachra, yonder.

Throbbing I follow, o'er hollow, height, and river,
Through many unknown ways, where lone waters shiver,
Oped the Druid Fort, a passage free to give her,
Where, in its core of cores, me she did deliver.

Laughter, thereafter, broke forth in harsh derision,
Wizardry, Witchery, kept watch in sour suspicion,

century, to learn classics in Kerry, where the Penal Code did not
operate efficiently, and communication with the continent was fre-
quent.   Having, in self-defence, slain one of several men who way-
laid him, he was tried and acquitted at law; but, by the Church
canons, he was forbidden admission to its ministry.   He settled in
Kerry, married a Miss Egan : their son Egan O'Reilly (often made
O'Rahilly in Munster) was the bard.

Chaining they chained me, then showed her sad position,
Bound to a Clown,—the Maid of Maids elysian !

Forth rushed my words of wrath and indignation :
" Thine not to brook such base humiliation,
When the noblest knight of all the Scotic nation
Thrice sought to raise Thee to right royal station."

Hearing my voice she wept, noble sorrow showing,
Tears fell in silence, like bitter torrents flowing ;
Guerdon she gave, as my guide through gloom, bestowing
Brightness of Brightness I'd seen, in loneliness, when
      going.[1]

THE DAWN OF DAY.

Egan O'Reilly.[2]

The Fair Maid Morning moved o'er the ocean,
   The flow'rs grew fragrant on ev'ry bough ;
Sweet rose the voices of birds in motion,
   And joy in all breathed around me now :—

---

[1] The argument, of course, is that the bard, in solitude, met the
Spirit of Song, which led him over all obstacles to his Queenly
Erinn, fettered and degraded : then Erinn, in guerdon for his loyalty,
bestowed on him the Spirit of Poetry, whose light and sweetness
gave him purer vision and consolation.

[2] O'Kearney MSS., Royal Irish Academy. O'Kearney states
that, every seventh year, the fishermen off the Black Rocks, near

Slow sound of waves, where the swans were gliding,
  Soft call of cuckoos in greenwood gay,
Smooth shimm'ring gleams from the billows sliding,
  And the heavens smiling the Dawn of Day!

The bees o'er meadows went seeking sweetness,
  The splendid fish gleamed o'er ocean's brow,
The white lambs played in a happy fleetness,
  And ripples ran from the rushing prow;
When, lo! there shone, on the surface sunny,
  Our Hero-champions in war's array,
The dew that fell was of newest honey—
  How gay and gladsome the Dawn of Day!

Floating Sea-nymphs were round them glancing,
  The blowing breeze bade their banners hail—
Hosts on hosts of our friends advancing,
  In gleaming arms, came to free the Gael.
Loud rang the trumps o'er ranks victorious
  Of noble knights for the noble fray,
Our brave defence in the battle glorious—
  Great God! how radiant the Dawn of Day!

Dundalk, may see the splendid vision of an ancient city, with a fair
space of fruitful lands around it. It is noteworthy that the dawning
(not the midnight) hour, was the propitious time for fairy appear-
ances. Tradition seems, in this and other visions, to have preserved
the memory of the pagan paradise visited of old by Cuchulainn, and
later by Bran and others. Clarence Mangan gave a free paraphrase
of the original Irish in "The Dawning of Day," in a quite different
metre, but full of melody.

Through wondrous forests the hosts came marching,
   Through glades that glowed with all berries sweet,
The very brambles that rose, o'er-arching,
   Rained scented blossoms before their feet.
'Twas Paradise, methought, in glory,
   With gate thrown wide to the Gael for aye!
I looked again—ah, the cruel story!
   There was naught, my grief! but the Dawn of Day!

OVER THE HILLS AND FAR AWAY.

Sean Clarach Mac Donnell.[1]

Once I was a maiden fair,
Now a widow's weeds I wear,
My true Love cleaves the billows' spray,
Over the hills and far away!

Chorus.

This were the choice of the world for me,
To sail with him the shining sea,
With him to be, at the dawn of day,
Over the hills and far away.

---

[1] Born in Cork County, 1691, the poet died in 1751. The historian O'Halloran writes: "Mr. Mac Donnell, a man of great erudition, a profound antiquarian and poet, whose death I sensibly

O, to hear my true Love come,
With pealing of bell and roll of drum,
While trumpets sound the gathering gay
Over the hills and far away !
    Chorus.

O, to see my true Love bold,
And on his brow the crown of gold !
His country's joy, his foes' dismay,
Over the hills and far away !
    Chorus.

Love of my heart, my prince, my king !
Sweeter than song the wild birds sing,
Brighter to me than star of day,
Over the hills and far away !
    Chorus.

I'll stand yon mountain peak above,
And sing the praise of my own true Love,
Till heaven itself shall help the fray,
For the sake of him who is far away.

feel, and from whom, when a boy, I learned the rudiments of our
language, continually kept up this custom "—of holding Sessions
of Bards.   He was well versed in Greek and Latin, and proposed to
translate Homer into Irish.   Yet, it was the penal time, and " on
more occasions than one, he saved his life by hasty retreats from his
enemies, the bard-hunters."—HARDIMAN.

CHORUS.

This were the choice of the world for me,
To sail with him the shining sea,
With him to be, at the dawn of day,
Over the hills and far away !

THE SPIRIT OF SONG.

PATRICK MAC GEAROIT (FITZGERALD), A.D. 1764.

A DARK mist druidic closed o'er me
  As, wearied of woods and astray,
I saw the weird lake gleam before me
  Of Blarney, and fain I would stay :
The branches of blossoms drooped over
  When, sudden, She came to my side,
In beauty far fairer than lover
  Had ever, since Eden, espied !

My heart beat with rapture, and brightened
  My soul to that Sprite from above ;
The smile from her blue eyes that lightened
  Sent my bosom a-thrilling with love.
O berry-red cheeks ! and O cluster
  Of curling gold hair to the knee !
I could gaze the whole night on your lustre
  And the night seem a minute to me !

" The Brink of White Rocks[1] has it been a
  Retreat for thy beauty?" I said,
" Art thou Ainé, or Miorras, or Cliona,
  O gentle and snowy-palmed maid?
Art thou Deirdré, whose wonderful fairness
  Lured a Crimson Branch Knight o'er the sea?
Hast thou tidings of rue or of rareness
  From wand'rings to whisper to me?"

" For the clans of high Miled I'm grieving,
  Of that flower of the brave is my race,
And long I have mourned in Bán-eeving[2]
  To hear their gay cheer in the chase.
But hark! of the Viscount of Blarney
  Soon the voice in yon turrets shall ring,
And our Exile be victor in war, nay!
  Three islands shall crown him their king.

" These tidings thy kinsmen to charm or
  To frighten their foes bear away,
Our warriors in Spain don their armour,
  And swift sailing barks fill the bay:

---

[1] Aeivil was the Fairy Queen of the North, Mab (Madb) was
the Fairy Queen of Connaught, and Cliona (pronounced Cleena) of
the South. The Wave of Cliona is off Cape Clear, but her chief
residence, the headquarters of all the Munster fairies, was in
a wild mountain region, near Mallow and the Cross of Donoch-
more.

[2] " Bán aeibinn "—the pleasant " bawn " or mead of Blarney,
which belonged to McCarthy Mór.

They'll wing to green Erinn, their way, tide
    And tempest shall scatter the foe,
And Freedom shall gladden ere May-tide
    The true-hearted Lordly and Low.

" O Bard, skilled in musical cadence,
    Come flee with me down to Tyrone,
Where an hundred of silken-bright maidens,
    In druid enchantment are thrown.
We'll have festivals, dancing, and gladness,
    The harps shall their melodies pour,
The fairest shall love thee to madness,
    And youth shall rejoice thee once more."

"O Bridi,[1] of Fairies the fairest!
    An thou give but a month and a day,
To prepare for the life thou preparest,
    I'll haste to thy side and away.
The beloved of my youth I must give her
    Farewell, and my blessing for aye ;
Then from thee, Spirit sweet, if I sever,
    May I swiftly go down to the clay ! "

---

[1] The Gaelic goddess of poetry.

THE DEAR WHITE YOUTH.

SEAN O'COILEANN.[1]

Air: "*An Cáilin donn.*"

THE golden gleaming of dawn shone streaming
  O'er leafy oaks by the lonely shore,
Where to me came, in my visioned dreaming,
  A Maid celestial the south sea o'er.
Her brow was brighter than stars that light our
  Dim dewy earth ere the summer dawn;
But she sighed, deploring, "My heart of sorrow!
  Ne'er brings a morrow, *Mo Buachaill Bán.*[2]

Her teeth were pearlets, her curling tresses
  All golden flowed to the shining sea,
Soft hands and spray white, such brows as traces
  The artist's pen with most grace, had she.
Lo, all the splendour of sunshine dancing
  Thro' snowy lilies her cheeks upon!
But the royal light of her clear eyes' glancing
  With tears was darkened for *Buachaill Bán!*

---

[1] Sometimes written O'Cullane, and (wrongly) Collins. The bard, one of the O'Coileanns, chiefs of Castlelyons, was born about the year 1754, in Cork County, and died in 1816. He composed several fine poems, *e.g.*, a "Lament for Timoleague Abbey," translated by Sir Samuel Ferguson.

[2] Buachaill Bán (pronounced Bohill Bawn) means fair or white Youth.

I lowly bowed to this Maid of glory,
   The bright, the beauteous, the faultless flow'r !—
And sought the lay of her sorrow's story,
   The race that owned such a peerless dow'r.
" Art child of gods of the olden sky? is 't
   An earthly King who thy love has won ?
O name this Highest, whose fate thou sighest,
   For whom thou diest, thy *Buachaill Bán.*

" Art thou that Star of all maids for beauty,
   Though clouded now in a night of grief,
Since false King Connor broke faith and duty
   And Naisi slew—thy heroic chief?
Or wailing Spirit who, on Moyle's water,
   Lir's lovely daughter, wert once a swan,—
A Red Branch Knight who lies low in slaughter,
   Was he thy darling, thy *Buachaill Bán ?* "

" O none of these," said the wondrous Maiden,
   " I am Fola, Queen of the Gael !
With foreign fetters my clans are laden,
   My chiefs are bondsmen in Innisfail !
In wasting woe I've been long a griever
   For one—true heir to victorious Conn,
The exiled offspring of royal Eiver,
   My love for ever, my *Buachaill Bán.*"

" O, noble Lady ! weep now no longer,
   Take comfort, heart, all so worn with grief !

S

He comes, thy champion, from exile stronger
  With arms and armies to thy relief;
Their hosts are nearing the shores of Erinn,
  In tall barks steering the seas upon,
Soon thou shalt crown with thy hand victorious
  Thy lover glorious, thy *Buachaill Bán!*"

Her sorrow fleeted, she struck the golden
  High ringing harp with her snowy hand,
And poured in music the regal, olden,
  The lofty lays of a free-made land,
The birds, the brooks, and the breeze seemed springing
  From grief to gladness that sunny dawn,
And all the woods with delight were ringing—
  So sweet her singing for *Buachaill Bán!*

THE CRUISKEEN LAUN.

AUTHOR UNKNOWN.

O sons of noble Erinn,
I've tidings of high daring
    To brighten now your faces pale and wan:
Then hearken, gather nearer,
In Gaelic ringing clearer,
    We'll pledge them in a cruiskeen lán, lán, lán,[1]
    We'll pledge them in a cruiskeen lán!

[1] Crusga is a jar (compare the German *krug*, and French *cruche*),
and cruisgin, its diminutive, is a little jar : lán (pronounced laun)
means full, and slán (pronounced slaun) safe.

Olfameed an cruiskeen,
Sláinté gal mo vuirneen ! [1]
In motion, over ocean, slán, slán, slán !

In exile dark and dreary,
Wandering far and weary,
    With friends that never failed, I have gone,
The trusted and true-hearted,—
Would God, we'd never parted
    Our brothers, boys, a cruiskeen lán, lán, lán !
    Our heroes in a cruiskeen lán.

Heav'n speed them over ocean,
With breeze of rapid motion,
    The ships that King Charles sails upon ;
With troops the frank and fearless,
To win our Freedom peerless,
    Our Freedom, boys, a cruiskeen lán, lán, lán !
    Our Freedom, in a cruiskeen lán !

Young men who now are sharing
The toast we raise to Erinn,
    With hope that the King is coming on,
Grasp your guns and lances
For swift his host advances,
    We'll toast them in a cruiskeen lán, lán, lán !
    We'll toast them in a cruiskeen lán !

[1] " Let us drink the cruiskeen—the bright health of my darling."
This is the earliest Irish song which I have seen of this name : it
must have suggested the popular song in English.

The tribe who would destroy all
Our rightful princes royal
    Shall hence end their rule and begone ;
The Gael shall live in gladness,
And banished be all sadness.
To that time, then, a cruiskeen lán, lán, lán !
    That time, boys, a cruiskeen lán !
    Olfameed an cruiskeen,
    Sláinté gal mo vuirneen,
In motion, over ocean, slán, slán, slán !

SHIELA GAL NI CONNOLAN.[1]

WILLIAM O'LEANAIN,[2] 1750.

Air : " Móirin ni Chuillionain."

ALONE, at dim dawn early,
    I stood within the islet bowers,
Where Lawin's stream flows pearly
    'Mid wavy grass and fragrant flowers ;
Green earth gave fruits unchary,
    And rosy wines, they over-ran
For me, from nymphs of faery
    Like Shiela gal ni Connolan !

---

[1] Bright Shiela ni Connolan.
[2] This name is now sometimes written Lenane, Lennon, and (wrongly) Leonard.

Fair flocks of birds sang sweetly
  'Mid floods of flowers, their pleasant home,
And in the stream-isle meetly
  I broke the golden honey-comb :
When lo ! on brink tree-shady,
  A Child of Glory on me shone,
With features like our Lady—
  Our Shiela gal ni Connolan !

In beauty white, this daughter
  Of graceful majesty was drest,
Like swans above the water
  The snowy radiance of her breast.
On her cheek the crimson berry
  Lay in the lily's bosom wan,
And forth my love did hurry
  To Shiela gal ni Connolan !

Her teeth were small and pearl-like,
  And white as brightness of the blooms ;
Her lustrous palms were fair like
  Downy silk from finest looms ;
No gems or 'broidered glove or
  Red gold her fingers glittered on,—
O, in meanest garb I'd love her
  Fair Shiela gal ni Connolan !

Her rose-red lips beguiling
  Spake words more than honey sweet,

And o'er her glad eyes smiling
  Were pencilled eyebrows arching meet,—
As if some artist loreful
  Twin bows with compass fine had drawn.
I'd not leave for empires oreful
  Sweet Shiela gal ni Connolan !

In truth, I'll lose all gladness
  With wasting love for her, the Sprite
Who clings with yearning sadness
  To Eiré's woods and valleys bright.
My arrowy piercing sorrow
  Would vanish swiftly, blue-eyed one !
If far and free to-morrow
  With Shiela gal ni Connolan !

Her clustering, loosened tresses
  Flowed glossily, enwreathed with pearls,
To veil her breast with kisses
  And sunny rays of golden curls !
But grief has pierced my bosom—
  My weary days lag 'neath a ban—
Thro' thy beauty, O white Blossom !
  O Shiela gal ni Connolan.

When birds, 'mid branches twining,
  Beheld her eyes, they thought them, sure,
Two rays of sun, or shining
  Beams from the crystal pure ;

When rose her sweet voice ringing,
   They strove to peer its mellow tone,
But were vanquished by the singing
   Of Shiela gal ni Connolan !

While o'er the smooth stream glancing,
   A moment ere her form I spied,
I saw her shadows dancing
   Deep in the glassy limpid tide—
I thought some fairy rarest,
   Had playful 'mid the waters gone,
Till I saw thee near, my Fairest
   Bright Shiela gal ni Connolan !

As sunbeam through the blue air,
   Or light above the ocean's tide,
Her flashing glances flew there,
   And thrilled my very heart inside.
O theirs was all the brightness
   That shines from heaven's starry van.
Their light has darked my lightness—
   Dear Shiela gal ni Connolan !

I thought to win her graces
   And love-smile on that rosy morn,
In those green islet-places
   Beneath the shady forest-thorn.
But she vowed, with fiery fervour,
   To never grant her love to man,

Till came her Strong to serve her
   True Shiela gal ni Connolan !

"No foreign tyrant lover
   Nor slave who bends to him the knee,
Till judgment day be over,
   Need hope to win a smile from me ;
I'll brook not lord in age or
   In youth, of whatsoever clan,
Till come the Gael to wage war
   For Shiela gal ni Connolan.

Then bards and books shall flourish,
   And gladness light the looks of all,
Then gen'rous knights shall nourish
   Our olden fame of open hall.
Brave men and chiefs to lead them
   Shall flash their spears in valour's van,
And glorious days of freedom
   Crown Shiela gal ni Connolan !"

THE JOYFUL RETURNING.

TADG O'NEACHTAIN.[1]

HEALTH to the Chief ! the Chief ! the Chief !
Health to the Chief returning—

---

[1] This name is sometimes written Naughton, and (wrongly) Norton.
The bard was probably akin to Sean O'Neachtain, who was born in

Over the wave,
Back to the Brave,
Home to the House of Mourning !

Cormac and Conn, and Diarmad Donn,
Up and away with sleeping !
Night has ended,
Dawn descended,
Up, to your lances leaping !

This is the time for testing men,—
This is the time for trial—
Silken store,
Gold *go leór*,
Beer, too, and banquets royal—

Horns of the wine, and cups that shine,
Brim for the men who need 'em,
Money and mirth,—
For Joy of Earth !
Hither again comes Freedom !

Bells a-tolling, drums a-rolling,
Trumpets tell the story !
Damsels dancing,
Bonfires glancing,—
Bright is the path of glory !

Meath at the beginning of the eighteenth century, and who was (says
Hardiman) a distinguished and learned author.

Health to the Exile, banished long—
Health to our Chief returning
With weal for woe !
Friend for foe !
And joyful Hope for Mourning !

THE SONG OF ECHO.[1]

BRIAN MAC GIOLLA MEIDRE.[2]

DAWN came softly, as a dove,
O'er the cove of slumb'ring ocean ;
Bending boughs were thrilled, above,
With cooing love and sweet commotion.
All around, from blossomed bowers,
Fragrant flow'rs sent odours airy ;
Lo, there shone a radiant light—
A brilliant, bright, and noble Fairy !

Ah, she wept in weary woe,
Her accents low, her full tears flowing,

---

[1] Echo, in Irish, is "Mac Alla :" "Son of the Rock."
[2] This name may be pronounced Mac Gillamery, but is usually (and wrongly) made "Merryman." The bard, who died in 1808, was a native of Clare. He is chiefly known by a long poem, composed in classic metre, the "Midnight Court," in which are told the proceeding of a "Cour d'Amour," which sate to solve problems pertaining to love and marriage. The conception of Echo sorrowing with her Country is surely that of a true poet.

Her sobbing sighs came sad and slow,
  Her tresses go on breezes blowing,
Bowed the head that once was high,
  Dim her eye, with woe and worry,
It rent the heart to hear her sigh—
  So sad, and sick, and sore, and sorry.

"Now," she said, "I'm lorn and lone,
  As, 'neath stone, a corpse of coldness;
Darts go through me, friends I've none,
  Gone is Thomond's ancient boldness.
Faint my spirit now and sore,
  Strength is o'er, my heart is breaking;
Down the breeze a venom blows—
  Cause of woes—a Shrew is shrieking!

" Long I've lain 'neath Druid sway,
  Whose cry was gay, from hill to hollow;
All I've answered, night or day,
  Faithful still their fate I follow.
No horn of Chieftain on the height,—
  No murmur slight of billow dying,
But found responses, loud or light—
  Thou, aright, heard my replying.

" Once my accents bore command
  O'er the land, like mellow thunder:
Conn I sang, and Eoghan's fight,
  Mac Morna's might, and Finn, our Wonder!

From wood and scar, I sped afar
   Of noble war the rolling clangour,
My bosom's sword !—now, no such lord
   Starts from the sward in awful anger.

" Last I told our grief of griefs,
   The Flight of Chiefs o'er foreign water ;
The Fall of Erinn's fairest flow'r,
   William's power, and Aughrim's slaughter :
The bullet flies,—my wild notes rise
   With battle's cries, and cannon's roaring ;
They kill, they kill ;—my wail is shrill
   A wounded Nation still deploring.

" Vaunt not yet, though faint I seem,
   Ye shall not deem me lost for ever ;
Though ruin roll in sullen stream,
   And Morning's beam appeareth never.
I a thousand fights have seen,—
   And I have been, by fetters, bounded,—
And I have served and sung My Queen
   When foe on foe went under, wounded ! "

THE FOREST FAIR.

Sean O'Coileain.

Once beside the corrie,
Musing sad and sorry,

I saw within the forest
    The fairest maiden dear.
The song of sweet bird follows,
    Fawn and doe draw near,
And from the river hollows
    The fish leap up to hear.

How curling, gleaming, glowing,
Softly, smoothly, blowing,
Her tresses full and flowing—
    A shining Golden Fleece!
More fair her teeth and shoulder
    Than glint of snowy geese,
'Twas star-like to behold her
    With small rose-lips of peace.

She sang her race and story,—
Not hers the Gentiles gory—
Her heart glowed with the glory
    Of Heber high and free:
Though long her Royal lover
    Did ban of exile dree,
Now Conqu'ror he comes over,
    And Crowned across the sea!

IN PRAISE OF THE GAELIC.

Our Gaelic speech has high repute,
It speaks as soft as breathes the flute,
It sings like love-notes of the lute,
   And shines in letters golden.
No tongue on earth could e'er compare
In tuneful tone and cadence rare,
And, O to hear its accents, where
     In song and tale
     Through Innisfail,
Of mighty kings and chiefs it sings
   For Erinn's nation olden !

And Erinn yet shall have her own
Right royal princes on the throne,
To whom the Gaelic speech is known,
   And welcome in our sireland.
The gentle harp shall sound once more,
And prosp'rous be the sons of lore,
And, proud, the gallant deeds of yore
     Before the king
     The bards will sing
And there recall the stories all
   That give renown to Ireland !

GRÁINNÉ MAEL.[1]

SEAN CLARACH MAC DONNEL.

ABOVE the bay, at dawn of day, I dreamt there came
The beautiful—the wonderful—the dear, bright dame !
Her clustered hair, with lustre fair, lit all the vale—
She came a Star, with fame afar, Our Gráinné Mael !

"I pray thee hear, O Lady dear, O faultless Fair !
Rejoice our souls, with voice that rolls, like music rare ;
We're sorrowful,—we're weariful—our Hope grows pale,
For the coming of her promised Love to Gráinné Mael."

"O faithfullest and gratefullest of friends, I vow
The Night is past, the Light at last will beam forth now,
Our warriors, long tarriers, will set swift sail
In motion true, o'er ocean blue, to Gráinné Mael !

"The thrushes seen, in bushes green, are singing loud—
'Bid sadness go, and gladness glow,—give welcome proud !
The Rover comes, the Lover, whom you long bewail,
O'er sunny seas, with honey breeze, to Gráinné Mael !'"

[1] Pronounced Graunia Wael, the m being modified.   This is one
of the endearing names given to Ireland, in the Penal times.

THE SKY-MAIDEN.

David O'Herlihy.[1]

THE Flesg's fairy numbers
Had sung me to slumbers,
'Neath the wide leafy boughs of the wood;
Till I heard sweeter singing
Than bird-song or harp-ringing,
And beside me a Sky-maiden stood.
Young Love tarried nigh her,
On man making war
With his arrows of fire,
Till my heart did unbar—
Till he left me a capture
To wild-throbbing rapture,
In the ray of that bright beaming Star!

The lily of whiteness,
The berry of brightness,
In combat her fair cheek contest;
Her teeth were the fairest,
Her small rose-lips rarest,
Her blue eyes made beauty their guest;

[1] Of Glenflesk, in western Cork. The bard was hereditary
Warden of St. Gobnet's church. The Vision is that of Erinn.

Her bosom, soft, beaming,
   Was snowy and free ;
Her neck was, in seeming,
   The swan on the sea ;
From brow, bright and pearly,
Her gold curls flowed fairly
To her small twinkling feet on the lea.

My heart had been teeming
   With grief, for in dreaming,
I had dreamed of the World and its guile ;
   But my waking was splendid,
   My Love-Star had descended,
'Mid the green leafy grove of the isle !
   The sun-sheen poured light on
      Each bough of each tree,
   The sun-sheen fell bright on
      Each grass-tip in glee,—
And my Pearl's sheen was streaming
With such brilliance of beaming
That good Fortune gave pledges to me !

Where the river is ringing,
   That Sky-maid is singing,
And the birds' mellow music flows clear ;
   The branches are bowers
   Of sweet-scented flowers,
There is honey in mossy banks near.
   And hither hares peeping,

T

'Mid wood-creatures stare,
The foxes come creeping
From out of their lair—
All come full of gladness,
For Her voice would chase sadness,
'Twould give joy to the Clansmen of Care!

FLORA McDONALD.[1]

HAD you seen Flora at dew-dawn alone,
Her tresses of gold by the sea-breezes blown,
No jewel she wore, but lamenting did go
And smiting her fair hands in sorrow and woe.

The briars of the mountains had wounded her sore,
Her eyes were like fountains with tears flowing o'er,
Her troubled heart forced her a watcher to be
In hope of beholding some ship on the sea.

I hearkened, with grieving, the plaint that she made,
And fain would have freed her from sorrow's cold shade.
She spoke, and her sigh would have rended a stone,
" O dark darling Charles, 'tis for thee I make moan.

[1] It is interesting to discover, in Irish, this tribute of song to the brave and loyal Scottish heroine, and to find that it was popular over all Ulster. O'Kearney, Irish MSS. Royal Irish Academy.

"They'll follow thee over the heather and scar,
A-thirsting for blood like the wolves that they are ;
Nor e'en let thee lie on the rock cold and bare,
To the cave by the billows, they'd follow thee there !

"Why fear they a fugitive, lorn, in defeat—
No sentry, save hunger, to guard thy retreat?
Yet 'tis oft in thy perils, by forest and field,
The hosts of high Heaven were thy shelter and shield !

" But with Might over Right now oppressors prevail,—
Stay, stay !—on the ocean there flashes a sail !—
'Tis the foam ! "—and in tears died the smile bright and
    gay,
And I turned from her sorrow in silence away.

A HEALTH TO KING PHILIP.[1]

Now, friends, grasp glasses and fill up,
    Let your bumpers brimful be ;
We'll drink to the health of King Philip
    And the Child who strays o'er-sea.

[1] Only portion of this Jacobite song is given ; it is a type of several ballads, varying in metre rather than in ideas. The air to which it is sung supplies an element of interest. O'Daly (" Munster Poets," Second Series) says it is contained in O'Farrell's " Collection of Irish Airs," p. 150—a scarce book. Dr. W. K. Sullivan, when

Too long, he wanders in sorrow,
　　Forgetting our land and lance ;
To raise grief from us, to-morrow,
　　I travel to Spain and France.

I pray the bright King of Heaven
　　To cause the oppressors to quail,
Exiled from the Woman Bereaven—
　　Our Lady,—our Innis Fail !

Let Stuart sail the seas over,
　　Bring homeward the gallant Lord Clare,—
Then joyful she'll greet her True Lover,
　　And foreigners forth shall fare !

THE ROVER.

Peasant Ballad, 1797.[1]

No more—no more in Cashel town
　　I'll barter health a-raking,

treating of Irish Airs composed in the gapped and diatonic quinque-
grade scale of D, includes this air.　" A great many Irish melodies,"
he writes, " have been composed in this key, and are so very peculiar
and different from our modern music, that they have not yet found
their way among modern musicians." . . . as specimens he names
Cáilin a stór, Drimin dun og, and Sláinté Righ Philib or " a health
to King Philip."　Sullivan, "Introduction to O'Curry's ' Manners
and Customs,'" Vol. I., 1873.

[1] The Irish name " Spáilpin fánach," the " Roving Spalpeen,"
designates one of the flock of migratory labourers, once so com-

Nor on days of fairs rove up and down,
  Nor join the merry-making.
There mounted farmers came in throng
  To seek to hire me over,—
Now I'm hired, and my journey's long,
  The journey of the Rover.

I've found, what Rovers often do,
  I trod my health down fairly ;
That wandering o'er the dawning dew
  Will gather fever early.
No more shall flail swing o'er my head,
  Nor my hand a spade-shaft cover,
But the colours of France will float, instead,
  And a pike stand by the Rover.

When to Callan once, with hook in hand,
  I'd go for early shearing,
Or to Dublin town,—a welcome grand
  Met the Rover gay appearing.
And soon with savings home I'd go
  And my mother's field delve over,
But no more—no more this land shall know
  My name as the merry Rover.

Five hundred farewells, Fatherland !
  My loved and lovely Island,—

mon, when tillage was more used in Ireland.   The bard was one of
those who had been dispossessed in the Penal times ; he joined the
roving Bohemian band, but soon put aside the sickle for the sword.

And to Culach boys, they'd better stand
 Her guards by glen and highland.
But now that I am poor and lone,
 A wand'rer,—not in clover—
It makes my very heart's core moan
 I ever lived a Rover.

In pleasant Kerry lives a girl,
 A girl whom I love dearly,
Her cheek's a rose, her brow's a pearl,
 And her blue eyes beam so clearly!
Her long fair locks fall curling down
 O'er a breast untouched by lover—
More dear than dames with a hundred pound'
 Is she unto the Rover.

Ah, once, indeed, my own men drove
 My cattle in no small way,
With cows, with sheep, with calves, they'd move,
 With horses, too, to Galway.
Christ willed I'd lose each horse and cow
 And my health but half recover—
It breaks my heart for *her* sake now
 I'm only a sorry Rover.

But when once the French come o'er the main,
 With stout camps in the valley,
With Buck O'Grady back again
 And poor true Taig O'Dally—

The royal barracks shall fall away,
The yeomen we'll chase over,
And the Gaelic clan shall bear the sway—
'Tis the strong hope of the Rover.

SONG OF THE DEAD INSURGENT. 1798.

MICHAEL ÓG O'LONGAIN.[1]

On Whit Monday morning,
The Goblin-foes begin,
They come, with scoff and scorning,
And fill the vale with din.
We flash the fire before us,
We smite around in chorus,
We raise the druid-mist o'er us
And let the sunshine in !

[1] The bard was a member of a respectable intellectual family. His grandfather was agent to the Knight of Glyn (Limerick), but when the Knight's brother, by conforming, got possession of the estate, O'Longain refused to serve him. He settled near Carrignavar, in Cork county. As he took part in the Insurrection of 1798, with which his district sympathized, he narrowly escaped death. He was an Irish scholar, as were his son, Michael óg, and his grandson, who was scribe to the Royal Irish Academy. There is poetry in the conception of a dead combatant sending from his Wexford grave a message to his native South. History should take interest in the statement as regards the number of Ulster and Connacht allies who went to battle in Wexford. The fact that Munster did not join generally in the Insurrection of 1798 has not been understood by

From Ulster come two thousand
  True heroes to the fray,
Like hosts in Connacht rouse and
  Advance with courage gay.
Our rest was short and scanty,
We gave them battles twenty,
And saw the dead in plenty,
  At dark'ning close of day.

Take Munster home my greeting,
  O Comrade, kind and good !
And say we faced the meeting
  And armies strong withstood.
Say, children now are cheerless,
That maidens, once so peerless,
With true men, frank and fearless,
  Are lying in their blood.

My woe on Munster's slumbers,
  When we rose out to fight,
And fronted tyrant numbers
  With weapons keen and bright.

writers.   Its quiescence was the result, not of loyalty to the Irish
Parliament or Government, then in the hands of a cabal, but of its
Jacobite and anti-Jacobin principles.   Many families had kinsmen in
the " La Brigade irlandaise," and were royalists; the Reign of
Terror, with its massacres, did not win them and drove many of their
kindred home.   In Ulster and Leinster such intimate relations with
the Continent did not exist, and republican enthusiasm spread.

But now that all is over,
And fierce foes o'er us hover,
Tell Leinster true, I love her
   Who kept the flame alight!

O youth, if 'mid the Living,
   They question of that day,
And ask you how I've striven
   And where I passed away—
Then say to each beholder,
That no man battled bolder,—
Though I, forgotten, moulder,
   Beneath the mountain clay.

THE SLIGHT RED STEED.

A.D. 1798.

I SLEPT when,—O wonder!
   Dread sounds precede,
Thro' south-clouds in thunder
   Flashed Knight and Steed!
"Ho, bard, dost thou slumber—
   Or hast thou life?
Rouse, rouse thee—our number—
   Is armed for strife!"

I sprang, pale, affrighted,
  In visioned dream,
All voiceless, benighted,
  I some time seem ;
The sweat-drops rolled under
  By terror freed,
And my Soul leaped in wonder
  On the Slight Red Steed.

Soon, thousands of warriors
  We stood among,
In a lios [1]—armed barriers
  'Gainst grief and wrong.
Then queried I, sudden,
  That brave, bright band :
" Shall the Gael aye be trodden
  In their Fathers' Land ? "

These tidings of glory
  Were told to me,
By my hand, 'twas a story
  Of rapturous glee.
The spells of Clan London
  Shall henceforth fail,
And their power be undone
  Before the Gael.

                [1] Fairy Fort.

What a joy to our sireland,—
  What heart's delight—
When Freedom to Ireland
  Comes through the night—
Like sunshine adorning
  The dew-white mead,
Through clouds of the morning,
  On the Slight Red Steed !

THE GAY AND GALLANT GAEL.

CONCOBAR O' RIORDAIN.

WHEN the gay and gallant Gael were alive in the Land
The lays were lightning flashes, the lore a blazing brand ;
Brave and bright-eyed princes met bards with honour
    grand—
When the gay and gallant Gael were alive in the Land !

Full gracious were the chieftains, the champion men of
    might,
The scatt'ring shatt'ring Spears of Fame, the Shields of
    Valour bright !
Most modest, mild, and mirthful, each beauteous maiden
    bland,
When the gay and gallant Gael were alive in the Land !

Ah, did our fathers live the life, those peerless knights of
  yore,
The Sire of all the Munster land—the dauntless Eogan
  Mór,
Mac Airt, Mac Cuinn or that high host, the fearless
  Finnian band—
They would drive like shiv'ring sheep the gaunt Gall
  from the Land.

O, did they live the life again, those hero-hosts so gay,
Who fought with Conn the Hundred Fights, with Eogan
  urged the fray,
Or had we here Turgesius's foes—the Gall would shun
  the strand,
And the gay and gallant Gael be alive in the Land !

XII. — EIGHTEENTH CENTURY:
SONGS OF THE EMOTIONS, ETC.

CEANN DUV DILIS.

AUTHOR UNKNOWN.

BLACK head dearest, dearest, dearest!
Lay thy hand, dearest! my hand above;
Small mouth of honey, thyme-scented, sunny—
No heart that lives could refuse thee love!

The maids of the vale in their sorrow are sighing,
Their long tresses flying all loose in the wind,
That I for the sake of my Darling am dying,
And grieving and leaving those who are kind.

Black head dearest, dearest, dearest!
Lay thy head, dearest! my heart above;
Small mouth of honey, thyme-scented, sunny—
No heart that lives could refuse thee love!

---

[1] Pronounced Kan doov deelish. No date was assigned to this poem by Hardiman: it (and possibly others) may belong to the sixteenth or seventeenth centuries. Miss Dora Sigerson (now Mrs. Clement King Shorter) has a true Irish poem with this title ("Poems," Elliot Stock, 1894).

THE DARK GIRL OF THE GLEN.[1]

AUTHOR UNKNOWN.

O HAVE you seen, or have you heard, the darling of all
　delight?
In glens of gloom, I wander lone, without rest in the day
　or night.
Her quiet eyes distress me, they trouble the heart in me—
My blessing go before her still, wherever on earth she be !

What songs have sung thy slender shape, the curve of
　thy graceful brow !
Thy small sweet mouth that never, I think, could wound
　by deceiving vow,
Thy hand more bright and soft than silk, or down of the
　birds above—
I'm vexed and fretted whenever I think I'd part with the
　girl I love.

So sharp the pang, I faint, I flee, when her presence I do
　behold,
Her glowing cheek, her pearly teeth, her flowing tresses
　of gold,
More bright that sight than Deirdré's self, who lowered
　King Conor's pride,
More fair than blue-eyed Blanaid, for whom thousands of
　heroes died.

[1] Original in Miss Brooke's "Reliques of Irish Poetry," 1819.

O, flow'r of Maids, forsake me not for glitter of worldly
    gain,
Unsung, unpraised, unprized it is, but by flattery's noisy
    train—
Whilst I would sing brave Irish songs, when harvest nights
    grow cold,
And tell the tale of Fianna chiefs and the warrior Kings
    of old !

THE BARD AND MISFORTUNE.

WILLIAM FITZGERALD.

THE BARD.

PASS on, Misfortune, much you weary me,
Stay not on straw, nor such discomfort dree ;
Go forth—silk couches wait you now, and see !
What dainty dishes, where red wines run free.

MISFORTUNE.

Not I, my Cousin, hence I will not flee,
I've arrows still unsped,—my poet's fee :
I'll guide the gray rain through your low roof-tree,
And here are thorns of sickness still for thee.

A FAR FAREWELL.

AUTHOR UNKNOWN.

'TIS mad to leap the lofty wall and strain a gallant steed,
When close beside is the flow'ry fence to vault across at
    need,   .
O bitter the bright red berries that high on the Rowan
    grow,—
But fresh and sweet the fruit we meet on the fragrant
    plant below.

Farewell, farewell a thousand times to the green town of
    the trees,
Farewell to every homestead there from o'er the surging
    seas ;—
Ah, many a wild and watery way, and many a ridge of
    foam
Keep far apart my lonely heart and the maid I love at
    home.

I move 'mid men but, always, their voices faint away,
And my mind awakes and I hear again the words her dear
    lips say ;
Her sparkling glance, her glowing cheek, her lovely form
    I see—
As flowers that grow, like flakes of snow, on the black
    and leafless tree.

If you go from me, Vuirneen, safe may you depart!
Within my bosom I feel it, you've killed my very heart—
No arm can swim, no boat can row, nor bark can mariner
    guide
O'er the waves of that woeful Ocean that our two lives divide.

LAMENT FOR O'CAROLAN THE MINSTREL.[1]

By Mac Aib, 1738.

My grief, my wounding, my anguish,
  My sickness long,
Thy sweet harp-chords now languish
  Without touch or song.
Who hence shall make music, vying
  'Mid chiefs, for aye,—
Since thou, O my friend, art lying
  Cold in the clay.

---

[1] O'Carolan was born at Nobber, Meath, in 1670; he lived for a
time in Leitrim, died and was buried at Kilronan, Fermanagh, in
1738. This elegy by a brother bard, Mac Aib (now Mac Cabe)
shows how greatly he was esteemed and loved by those who knew
him. Four notable things he did : (1) He composed many exquisite
airs; (2) adapting words to these, he made a revolution in Irish verse-
methods; (3) his vivacious and inspiriting minstrelsy cheered the
heart of his nation throughout the Penal Régime, and largely con-
tributed to give gaiety a place in the Irish character; (4) his genius,
delighting all classes, made him an honoured guest amongst the
Williamites as amongst the Jacobites, softened animosities, and
helped to fuse them into one people. He had one failing : at a time
when all were convivial, he was convivial; in the case of stupid

I rise, I behold, every morning
   A land woe-smit;
Till black is the west, in mourning
   On hills I sit.
O Saviour, comfort me pleading,—
   My life's grown dim,
My eyes have become two bleeding
   Founts after him.

Thy life was a poem noble,
   My king-friend, proud:
I go sleepless all night with trouble—
   My mind one cloud,
Through my heart's core pains are flying
   Of piercing woe,
For Toralach O'Carolan, lying
   Lifeless and low.

St. Francis, St. Dominic, listen,
   St. Clare, and all
Ye host of the saints, who glisten
   On heaven's high wall:
Give welcome to Toralach's spirit
   Your ramparts among,
And the voice of his harp ye shall hear it
   With glorious song!

persons, who have endowed the world with nothing, this failing is
passed over; in the case of any man whose genius has made him a
benefactor, it affords a welcome theme for censure to that respectable
class—the men of no genius.

THE DELLS OF ORRERIE.

SEAN CLARACH MAC DONNELL.

Air: "A Feather-bed and Bedsticks."

THE drowsy dawn
  Half oped his eye,
A red ray shone
  Across the sky;
And o'er dim lawn
  The sun rose high
    In chariot bright and golden!

I wandered then,
  From sorrow free,
O'er dale and fen
  Of Orrerie,
Through pleasant glen
  And greenwood lea,
    'Mid mossy trunks and olden.

Not far or wide
  Had been my way,
Till lo! I spied
  The graceful fay—
Of maids the pride
  With heart so gay
    And showers of curling tresses!

Quick leaped I o'er
  The bramble screen,
And bowed before
  Her beauteous mien,
And prayed full sore
  From her, my queen,
    A thousand sweet caresses.

Thus sighed my pray'r :
  "O radiant sprite !
O, branch most fair
  Of beauty bright !
'Twill cause despair
  As black as night
    If pleasantly you flee not--

"Come seek some glade
  Beside the sea,
From every shade
  Of sorrow free,
Or, peerless maid,
  A stór mo chree ! [1]
    In life I'll shortly be not."

"O minstrel, pause—
  Fair youth, beware !
For I must cause
  That black despair

[1] O treasure of my heart.

Though ne'er there was
A suit more fair—
'Tis all lost time and labour !

" For sure you know
That God above,
Who made earth grow
With grass and grove,
Said long ago :
' Thou shalt not love
The wed wife of your neighbour !' "

MAIRE NI MILLEÓIN.[1]

Author Unknown.

" Will you come where golden gorse I mow,
Mo Mauria ni Milleóin ? "
" To bind for you I'll gladly go,
My Share of Life, my own ! "
" To chapel, too, I would repair
Though not to aid my soul in prayer,
But just to gaze with rapture, where
You stand, *Mo buachil baun !* [2]

[1] Máire ni Milleóin, pronounced Mauria nee Milone : in the vocative Mauria is softened to Vauria, hence in the ballad it becomes O Vauria.

[2] My white or fair youth.

"Will you rove the garden glades with me ;
　O Flower of Maids, alone ?"
"What wondrous scenes therein to see,
　My Share of Life, my own ?"
"The apples from green boughs to strike,
To watch the trout leap from the lake,
And caress a pretty colleen, like
　Mo Mauria ni Milleóin !"

"Will you seek with me the dim church aisle,
　O Mauria ni Milleóin ?"
"What pleasant scenes to see, the while
　My Share of Life, my own ?"
"We'd list the chanting voice and pray'r
Of foreign pastor preaching there,
And we'd finish the marriage with my fair
　White Flower of Maids alone !"

She sought the dim church aisle with me,
　My Share of Life, so fair !
She sought the dim church aisle with me,—
　O grief ! O burning care !
I plunged my glitt'ring, keen-edged blade
In the bosom of that loving maid,
Till gushed her heart's blood, warm and red,
　Upon the cold ground there !

"Alas, what deed is this you do,
　My Share of Life, mo stór [1]
What woeful deed is this you do—
　O youth whom I adore!
Ah, spare your child and me, my love,
And the seven lands of Earth I'll rove,
Ere cause of care to you I prove
　For ever—ever more!"

I bore her to the mountain peak,
　The Flower of Maids, so lone!
I bore her to the mountain bleak,
　My thousand loves! mo vrón! [2]
I cast my coat around her there
And, 'mid the murky mists of air,
I fled, with bleeding feet and bare,
　From Mauria ni Milleóin!

THE SWEET LITTLE CUCKOO.

Author Unknown.

'Tis in the night I suffer woe,
Within my heart the shadows go,
Since I fell in love with my fair foe—
　The faultless, high-bred maiden.

[1] My treasure.　　　[2] My grief.

O God, that fate, in an hour of ruth,
Would bear us both to the Land of Youth,
Then days of delight would dawn in sooth !
Friends and foes should stay behind,
Suitors and sorrows go in the wind,
    And some cold isle be laid in.

The voice of birds from blossomed tree
Should give us musical minstrelsie,
How sweet that these should neighbours be
    With gladness every morrow.
For now I am worn with weary pain,
A full long year I've borne in vain,
My heart's hot fire still burns amain.
O Lord of life, look down, I pray,
Or soon I must lie in the quiet clay,
    My head brought low with sorrow.

My aged sire, my sister dear,
In woe they walk, they live in fear ;
My strength is going, the end draws near—
    'Tis gone, the manly bearing ;
Through the sinless cause—my Love snow-white ;
More fair her brow than silver bright,
Her very glance would fill with light
The darkest dell of the misty South,
And sweeter a kiss from her little mouth
    Than all the honey of Erinn !

MY WISHES.

PATRICK O'HELIDE.[1]

COULD I give to my wishes relief
  And shape for my lifetime a lease,
I would be like the happy old chief,
  In alliance with no one but—peace.
I would make of my acre or two
  My kingdom and never seek pelf,
And large I'd consider it, too,
  And loyal 'twould be to myself.

My subject, the farm, would grow fat
  With share of the finest of grain,
Which no wetness nor wind should come at
  Save in welcoming seasons of rain.
My castlekin still would be gay
  And full of all kinds of delight;
And sweet would the song be, by day,
  And pleasant the book towards night.

My cot would be airy to view,
  In a nook by the wood and the well,
Where, on waking, each dawning of dew,
  I'd hear the sweet bird-music swell.

· This name is now usually written O'Hely or O'Healy.

The many-flowered grassy-edged stream
  Would hum through bright fruit and new corn,
And would glitter and glimmer and gleam
  With trout dancing up to the morn.

To cap all my pleasure and pride,
  And the comfort of youth to complete,
I'd choose me a winsome young bride,
  Sweet-tempered and comely and neat.
Her age should be nineteen, the best,
  My own should be just twenty-four,
And the heart would leap up in my breast
  To see our babe smile at the door.

THE CLUSTER OF CURLS.

WILLIAM INGLIS.[1]

Air : " Róis geal dub."

No sweet hope, no gladness
  Comes ever to me,
But deep woe and sadness
  Wherever I be,

---

[1] William Inglis (wrongly English) was born at Newcastle, Limerick, taught contraband classics for a time, and wrote some beautiful Gaelic songs. He relinquished song-writing on becoming an Augustinian friar, but made an exception of one humorous satire. He died in 1778 in Cork, and was buried in St. John's Churchyard.

O sistreen[1] of tresses
    That sweep to the dew
Who caused my distresses
    Don't keep me in rue.

How fine in its splendour
    Thy hair flowing down!
Thine eyebrows so slender
    Were formed not to frown.
I pine heavy-hearted
    In pain, night and day,
From the Curl-cluster parted
    By fate in the way.

O, brown head of beauty!
    Thou'st conquered my heart;
I'm mournful and moody
    Whenever we part.
A Vuirnin! I sue thee
    For heaven above,—
Thou hast sped the wound thro' me,
    Then save me, my love!

O bright as the berry's
    The cheek of my love,
As foam by the ferry's
    Her white brow above.

----

[1] Sistreen : Irish diminutive of sister.

The voice of the maiden 's
    The harp's melody,
Its musical cadence
    Has caused death to me.

I travel the mountain
    All weary and worn,
My heart is a fountain
    Of tears, for her scorn.
As I rove, when I ponder
    My love and my woe,
I ramble, I wander,
    I stray to and fro.

O dearest, O fairest,
    O Love of my breast !
'Mid the noblest and rarest
    Thy sires were the best.
I'm wasting in anguish,
    All pleasures have flown ;
For thy sake I languish,
    For thee I make moan.

Through country, through city,
    Each day of my days,
Without hope or pity
    I move in a maze.

I see maidens rarest,
  And still see but thee,
Who art fair o'er the fairest
  And dearest to me.

THE FLOWER OF LOVE.

By William Inglis, 1740.

There's a maiden fair to see,
A fair maid known to me,
    With tresses bright,
    With looks of light,
All gladsome grace is she.

The harp gives sweetest notes
When her voice of music floats,
    My woe, my loss !
    I may not cross
With her the brine of boats.

There's a stately maiden seen
Of all brave youths the queen—
    The Star of Love—
    The Sun above—
The golden blithe báibin ! [1]

[1] Pronounced baubeen, affectionate diminutive, "little baby."

Her heart 's a spotless shrine
Of noble gifts divine.
    My loss, my woe !
    'Twere joy to go
With her beyond the brine.

Her curling golden hair,
That flows to feet so fair,
    Floats out to please
    The laughing breeze,
And all our hearts ensnare,

With voice of tender ruth,
She reads the Bible's truth :
    Where'er I rove
    May Christ's sweet love
Keep ward around her youth.

The crimson berry's glow
Is on her cheek of snow :
    What joy, what pride,
    To win that bride,
The Luck of Life below !

But now on the green brine
Of barques is floating mine,
    And I must leave
    My love to grieve,
My Flower of Love to pine.

DOREEN LE POER.[1]

ANDRIAS MAC CUIRTIN, 1737.

'TIS woe-smit I've been,
And mournful my mien,
   Through true love,
   For you, Love,
My soft, stately queen.

None deems it disgrace
To pine for that face,—
   The fairest,
   The rarest,
Of Adam's whole race.

Thy small teeth to me
Seem pearls of Tralee,
   Thy white breast
   The bright breast
Of swan on the sea.

No hand this may know
Nor thy neck of snow—

---

[1] A poem of praise, made by the bard in honour of a young lady
—a specimen of the *Vers de Société* and Madrigals which helped to
grace and sweeten society under the Penal Code.

Their gladness
Brings sadness,
And causes my woe.

I start, I awake
Ere birds in the brake,
  Lest never
  I'd ever
Win worth for her sake.

I grieve, I repine
The maid is not mine,
  With palace,
  In valleys,
And walls jewelled fine.

The world will not meet
Such beauty to greet—
  Glance tender
  In splendour,
And mouth music-sweet.

How lovely her mien—
The kind, gentle queen !
  The berry
  On merry
Bright white cheek is seen.

How peerless her grace !
How priceless each tress !
   All Munster
   Can't once stir
When seen her sweet face !

THE RED FELLOW'S WIFE.[1]

Author Unknown.

You're welcome, my love !
   Of girls the fairest young girl !
Beauteous above
   Deirdré, tho' bright as a pearl ;
The country I'd fill
   With conquering clamour and strife,
And come to you still—
   A slave to the Red Fellow's wife !

Love, whiter your neck
   Than swan that floats on the sea,
And redder your cheek
   Than roses that blush on the tree.
O sweeter by far
   Thy mouth than soft song of cuckoo ;
Thy long tresses are
   More fine than the silk glossy new.

[1] A very popular ballad, in Gaelic, throughout Ireland, South and North.

X

O peerless young maid,
　With beauty beaming all o'er,
Whate'er may be said—
　Whoe'er may desire or deplore—
In vain were I dumb,
　They all know what ruins my life,—
My heart-wound has come
　From love of the Red Fellow's wife.

For ever and aye
　I'd warrant to ward you from ill,
Your faithfullest stay
　If fate did not fetter your will—
The tribute of Troy
　I'd give with merriment rife,
If only my joy
　Were never the Red Fellow's wife.

O bloom-maid, I breathe
　A thousand of blessings to thee,
I'm wounded to death,
　And die every minute from thee.
My heart, could it speak,
　Would tell how deep went the knife;
Why should it not break?—
　My one love's the Red Fellow's wife.

If yonder, I lay
　In prison fettered and fast,

All chains on the clay
  And manacles over me cast—
As swan to the sea
  I'd fly to that gloomiest life,
In hope you should be
  No longer the Red Fellow's wife.

THE BELOVED GAELIC.

WILLIAM O'LIONAIN.

NEVER was heard a strain so soft—
A speech so noble—so flood-like oft,
Yet bright and sweet as a cooing rill,
Never weak, but all beauteous still.

Never sang Homer, old and grand,
Nor brilliant Ovid, gay and bland,
In language more liquid—a cascade that ne'er
Meets earth, a music that's floating in air !

Than melodious tones of golden chords,
Than ethereal voices of tuneful birds,
Its flowing sounds more joy impart,
And its noble song o'ercomes the heart !

FAIRY MARY BARRY.

AUTHOR UNKNOWN.[1]

O FAIRY Mary Barry, I tarry down-hearted,
Unknown to kith or kin, health and wealth have departed.
When I'm going to my bed, or I wake in the morning,
My thought is still of you and your cold, cruel scorning.

O fairy Mary Barry, take counsel, my bright love,
Send away the stranger from out of your sight, love ;
For all his fine airs there's more truth in me, love,
Then come to me, mochree![2] since our parents agree, love !

I thought I could coax you with promise and kisses,
I thought I could coax you with vows and caresses,
I thought I could coax you ere yellowed the barley—
You've left me to the New Year with sore sorrow early !

'Tis delight unto the earth when your little feet press it,—
'Tis delight unto the earth when your sweet singings bless
  it,—
'Tis delight unto the earth when you lie, love, upon it—
But, O his high delight who your heart, love, has won it !

I could wander through the streets hand-in-hand with my
  true love,
I would sail the salt seas with no fortune but you, love ;

---

[1] A Munster song.   [2] My heart.

My nearest and my dearest I'd leave them for ever—
You'd raise me from death if you said "We'll not sever."

I gave you, and I gave you, I gave you my whole love,
On the Festival of Mary, my poor heart you stole, love;
With your soft gray eyes like dew-drops on corn newly
    springing,[1]
With the music of your red lips, like sweet starlings
    singing!

I'd toast you, and I'd toast you, I'd toast you right gladly,
And if I were on ship-board, I'd toast you less sadly,
If I were your sweetheart!—through Erinn so wide, love,
None could see (here's your bright health!) so happy a
    bride, love!

LOVE'S LAST APPEAL.

Air : " Caislean ui Neill." [2]

O DARLING and true love,
  In early summer, if you come with me
'Mid dim glens of dew, love,
  Or where the bright sun shineth free—

---

[1] See Appendix : "Green Eyes."
[2] Pronounced Caushlan-o-Nail; this air is given in Bunting's
"Irish Music," p. 15, edition 1797. The words are not fashioned
for form's sake, but are the earnest utterance of a breaking heart.

Calves, kine, sheep the whitest
For your fortune I'd not take that day,
But my hand beneath your white waist
And sweet lonely converse with you for aye !

My garden is wasted,
Dear Love, have you no regret?
Fruits fall now untasted,
The grass and the boughs have met.
I list not the clearest
Soft harp, nor the birds' sweet low wail,
Since from me fled my dearest
Curled Cooliun to Cáislean O'Neill.

I'll leave not life's battle
Till conquered be fortune's fell harms,
Till I've won sheep and cattle,
And my darling again in my arms :
The spare meals of Lent-time
I'll quit not on high days of feast—
Sweet, swift were the spent-time
I'd spend with my head on his breast.

Farewell last even !
Ah, would it were back now to me,
With the fair youth of Heaven
Who caressed me awhile on his knee !
I'll say what bereft me
Of joy—but let no one know,—

My own white Love has left me
O Mary, O God! what a woe!

Sickness and sorrow
Are too much around my heart,
The wan tears each morrow ,
To my eyes ever and ever start,
For love and love only
Of him who has left me nigh dead—
I cannot live lonely
If the dark mountain maid he should wed.

The people say ever
That many a man loves me dear,
But never—O never
Could I love whilst he is not heie :
I'd wander far rather
Nine days, nine nights, nine weeks and ten,
And sloe-berries gather
Near my Love's house, to see him again !

You promised me purely
You'd love me while green grasses grew,
You promised me, surely,
One Home between me, Love, and you.
My woe on that even
When I gave up my heart unto thee,
O black, O bitter grieving—
The World's between you, Love, and me !

SHAUN O'DEE.

PIERS FITZGERALD.

I NE'ER believed the story,
   Prophetic bard! you sung,
How Vulcan, swart and hoary,
   Won Venus fair and young,—
Till I saw the Pearl of Whiteness
   By kindred forced to be,
In her robe of snowy brightness
   The bride of Shaun O'Dee!

Nor thought the Spirit holy
   A bridal would allow,
Where Mammon spurs them solely
   To crown her drooping brow.
"The richest weds the rarest"—[1]
   That truth, alas, I see,
Since the sunny pearl and fairest
   Is bride to Shaun O'Dee.

Were I like most, ere morrow,
   A dire revenge I'd take,
And in his grief and sorrow
   My burning anguish slake:

[1] "Mopso Nisa datur" is the quotation in the original.

For gloom o'erclouds my lightness,
O woe's my heart to see
That form of snowy whiteness
Embraced by Shaun O'Dee.

A RULE OF LIFE.

AUTHOR UNKNOWN.

I TRADUCE no man,—my honour to none confide ;
If I am traduced, I feel no stain abide.
When men sit merry, none merrier is than I,
Who in diff'ring minds still find some common tie.

THE CAOINÉ[1] OF THE CHILDREN.

FÉILIM MAC CARTHY.

I'LL sing their caoiné, if I can—
My faultless four, my heart's dear clan ;
Since o'er all men I'm lorn to-day,
I'll sing their caoiné mournfully.

---

[1] Pronounced keené, a death-song, equivalent to the Scots' "coronach." Despoiled of his land by confiscation, Féilim McCarthy, a scion of the McCarthys Mór, took refuge amongst the mountains, where he built a shieling. During his absence seeking food, the house fell, in a storm, killing his four children. The poem has the ancient instinct of form, reserve in diction, with intense feeling.

Frail my life-stay evermore,
Death my heart has wounded sore ;
I am alone in all the land,
No kindred now shall near me stand.

Since I must tell, thus left behind,
The cause of tears, with darkened mind,
My head is sick to-night from woe,
My voice, too, faint and trembling low.

Not so sad the young bride's heart,
Or husband's when their loved depart ;
Like bird, nest-ruined, is my lot,
Wailing the young that they live not.

Or like to swans, the waves among,
When singing their unwilling song,—
As death comes nigh them and more nigh,
Singing their dirge with piteous cry.

I'll sing each day until my death,
A lay which never sweetness hath;
Since I am worn, and weak and drear,
I'll sing their dirge—my children dear.

My grief ! in clay lies Callachan;
By Cormac's side, my sweet-voiced son :
Anna and Mary, too, my own
White Loves, beneath the same gray stone.

My children four, without a stain—
Few the gifts they did not gain,
My bleeding heart-wound this, for aye,
To wail them all, within one day.

The noble boughs of Eber Mór,
Erinn's prosperous King of yore,
Are gone from me, in youth and bloom
Unchanged, in beauty, to the tomb.

Theirs no kin of craven brood,
From Scythian rulers flowed their blood;
Miled's[1] offspring, near and far,
Their kindred brave in truth ye are.

The Spaniard-kings of sharp blue spears
To these were kin, and these their peers;
To them were England's kings allied,
In other times, when that gave pride.

Sweet their cries whene'er I'd come,
Gaily running to greet me home,—
Who now shall kiss or welcome me,
Since they, in one grave, buried be?

Unless I looked to Christ—His thorns,
His anguish, cross, and cruel scorns—
I'd swiftly join them in the clay
Or it would wrench my mind away.

---

[1] Latinized "Milesius."

On seeing Lazarus lie low,
Christ mourned for him in pain and woe;
With weeping tears His eyes grew dim,—
Yet He was far from kin to him.

Tis right that I in gloom should weep,
And lifelong pine in anguish deep,
After my lost loved children four.—
The Virgin Mother sorrowed sore.

Mary did not refrain from tears,
Her bleeding heart was rent with spears,—
When He was crucified and scorned.
I shame not mourning when *she* mourned.

For I have lost my kin most near,
I am robbed of all most dear,
In the narrow house of pain I lie,
Thrice racked with woeful misery.

In hushed midnight of heavy sleep,
Ah, plundered heart! ah, ruin deep!
My stainless four, I lost them all
In one brief moment tragical.

How oft I thought, when gray age frowned,
My children dear would gird me round;
Not that they to death would go
And leave me here in helpless woe.

To me my children's love was due,—
(I gave my whole heart unto you)
Since I, too, was more aged than they,—
'Twas meet respect to me they'd pay.

Yet woe is me ! they've left my side,
Close by my heart they did not bide,
Nor let me first the dim way pass,
Because that I have sinned.   Alas !

Small my care for sport or rime,
I'm very lone this little time ;—
Not sweet to me is harp or "rann," [1]
I wander like a witless man.

Gone my aspect, gone my strength,
I am broken down at length ;
Death's face alone I care to see,
Since all my friends are gone from me.

In hushed midnight of heavy sleeping,
When I am watching, sobbing, weeping,
My children glide before my woe,
Seeking that I should with them go.

I see them in the night-time ever,
From me in no place do they sever ;
At home, abroad, still near are they,
Till I go with them to the clay.

[1] Song.

Sweet to them that visit made !
Dear to me each sunbright Shade !
Full soon I'll follow on their way
Through God's most blesséd will, I pray.

Woe is me, her sorrow's pall,
Who high affection gave to all,—
Whose heart gave life and love to each,
Woe is me her plaining speech !

Woe is me, her hands now weak
With smiting her white palms so meek :
Wet her eyes at noon, and broken
Her true heart with grief unspoken.

I wonder not at her despair,
She has lost life's light most fair.
She, o'er all of Erinn's daughters,
Has seen the ruin of dark slaughters.

O Glen, which saw this ruin sore,
And wrecked all joy for evermore,
God's malison fall on thee, dread,
In eric [1] for my darlings dead.

Glen-an-áir, the Slaughter-Glen,
Be hence thy name amongst all men ;
Venom-treason thou'st done to me—
And now Accurséd shalt thou be !

[1] Blood-fine, or vengeance.

May'st thou ne'er see sun, nor noon,
May'st thou ne'er see star, nor moon,
For that thou'st seen a deed of tears
Which makes me old before my years.

May never eye behold in thee
Flower, nor grass, nor leafy tree,—
But dire decay deform thee, ever,
By blackened banks and moaning river

DOWN BY THE STRAND.

CHRISTOPHER CONWAY.[1]

Air: " Since Celia's my foe."

DOWN by the strand
Lives a young maiden, bland,
    The fairest,
    The rarest,—
The Flower of the Land.

She's a bough of perfume
With ever-bright bloom.

---

[1] Christopher Conway, of Tigh-na-hala (House of the Swan) on the River Laune (Killorglin Parish, Kerry), composed this song in praise of Ellen, daughter of Mac Carthy Mór, his wife. The Conways of Kerry were of noble Welsh descent.

'Tis my glory,
Her story
And deeds to illume.

Dames I behold,
The offspring of gold,
All shining,
And pining,
In jewelry cold :

My heart nevermore
Could seek them, mo stór !
With thee, love,
I'd flee, love,
To Italy's shore !

THE FICKLE FAIR.

Author Unknown.

When cease the ducks upon the lake to go,
When cease the swans to sail in plumes of snow,
When cease the hounds to gnaw the bones, we know
Deceit will cease in woman's heart to grow.

A FAIR FOE.

WILLIAM McCOITER.

THERE's a shade on my soul,
  And my heart is in dole
From pearly day dawning till soft even air,
    With love for the white
    Fresh Flower of Delight,—
With love for the Maid of the fair-flowing hair.

  Her mind is a dove,
  And the wit of my love
Is more supple and swift than a bird on the wing :
    More sweet is her mouth
    Than wine of the South,
Or all the hill honey that Greek poets sing.

  To the dew-drops below
  Her golden curls flow,
See, the flame of the berry her smooth cheek upon !
    In each little ear,
    That no picture could peer,
There sparkles a jewel as bright as the sun.

Y

Over earth far and wide
Could I choose me a bride,
And wed a rich daughter of royalty's line;
Through life she could be
But a sorrow to me—
For the Flower of the World has this poor heart of mine!

AN EPIGRAM.

AUTHOR UNKNOWN.

HE whose paddocks are showing fat herds of kine,
He whose harvests o'erflowing fill granaries fine,
Sees no kinsmen, when going, if poor they pine,—
All are out of his knowing who do not dine!

FAREWELL TO THE MERRY MONGER.[1]

SEAN O TUAMA.

FAREWELL, until death, to thy brightness and thy mirth,
Farewell from our priests, from the nobles of the Earth,

---

[1] *I.e.* the Mangaire Sugach, a name by which Andrias Mac Craith was usually known. His life, in some respects, resembled that of Burns. Having written a "Farewell to the Maig," when leaving, these verses were composed in reply: they, like others, indicate that a taste for literary composition was then common in Ireland.

Farewell from the Fair, farewell to thee from all,
May it shield thee and shift thy pain's gloomy pall.

My want—my woe—my bitter grief and sorrow !—
That the gentlest, the gayest, most generous of sages,
The singer of sweet song—now the chill tempest rages,
    Should wander forlorn, night and morrow.

Mac Craith, 'tis to sing of thy merits I have sought,
Thou Master of Learning, thou Thinker of bright thought,
The darling of damsels, the bard of sunny brow,
True scion of Dalcassia's deedful race art thou.

Nigh green Maig river, 'tis woeful now to stand
And list the lament of the dwellers in the land,
Of the people, the priests, of the lordly and the low,
And see maidens mourn and tears in silence flow.

'Tis cause, sure, for gloom and for heaviness of heart,
A man should have left us, a faithful friend should part,
A bard of true poet-mind, generous of soul,
Should wander the peaks in dreariness and dole.

Ah, great is my grief that a mist should overcloud
The frank fiery mind of which the land was proud,
That woman should lure to darkness and disgrace
One who boasts poet-gifts and noble Irish race.

And yet, this has been since the earth was in its youth,
Lo, Paris of Troy to testify this truth,—
And Ajax, and Jason, for cause wellnigh the same
To battle and to die in foreign lands ye came.

And Aengus[1] and David—'twere weariness to mind
Of all who found fate for the sake of womankind,
Then wail not for aye thy falling from above,
Since mightier than thou bore the penalty of Love.

May hardship avoid thee, O dearest to my heart,
Be welcomes and gladness and feasts where'er thou art,
Be thy sky ever clear and thy spirit ever gay,
And my Blessing thy Shield against ev'ry ill for aye.

THE VISIT OF DEATH.

AUTHOR UNKNOWN.

O YOUTH, so loved and faithless !
    You've covered me with grief,
You mind not my heart breaking
    Nor care to give relief.
How great shall be your shaming
If you save me not from blaming,
Who swore upon the Manual
    To leave me not in grief.

[1] Doubtless, Aeneas.

Death will come to seek you
  A short half hour ere day,
And for each guileful action
  He'll make you strictly pay.
In the small room, lying lonely,
The white shroud round you only,
How gladly you'd do penance
  If then you found a way !

I was a happy maiden,
  With gladness in my voice;
You brought the sorrow with you—
  No more can I rejoice.
And now, since you're forsaking,
And your path from me are taking,
If I die through your heart-breaking
  How black will seem your choice !

I'd manage all your household
  With skilful hand so well,
Your hose, and shirt, and raiment
  Would be fairest in the dell.
If care or cloud hung o'er you
To youth I would restore you—
O wed me, and the Glory
  Of God shall with us dwell !

I had once no lack of clothing,
  Of food, or dwelling place,

I earned good fame and found it
　　Among my kindred race :
Nor could Gall or Gael[1] upbraid me
Till your false voice—it betray'd me.
But the Envoy I send with you
　　Is the Most High King of Grace !

My love ! my heart's own neighbour !
　　How deep to-night my woe,
How dark I'll be to-morrow
　　When you from me will go !
You've broke death's wall before me,
The grave's cold breath blows o'er me,
Yet take one kiss, my Darling !
　　Before you leave me, so.

A COMPLIMENT.

Author Unknown.

Had I for ink the ocean,
　　And Earth for paper white,
Did ev'ry wing in motion
　　Give me its quills to write,
Were my reward the rarest—
　　All Europe's sovran might—
Thy virtues, O my Fairest !
　　I never could indite.

[1] Stranger or native, friend or foe.

BIRDS ON A BOUGH.

Air: " *There was a Maid in Bedlam.*"

How pleasant for the small birds
    To waken in the grove,
And, close upon the same bough,
    To whisper to their love.
Not thus, alas, our fortune—
    My very heart's delight !
'Tis far apart each morning
    We waken to the light.

She 's fairer than the lily,
    Such beauty there is none :
She 's sweeter than the violin,
    More lightsome than the sun ;
But better than all beauty
    Her noble heart and free,—
O God, who art in heaven,
    Remove this pain from me !

LOVELY LOCH LEIN.[1]

THOUGH often I'd rove, through grove, and valley, and
    mount,
From Shannon to Rath, each path, by fort and by fount,
I saw not elsewhere so fair and so beauteous a scene
As the little white town, the crown of the lovely Loch
    Lein.

How sweet in its grace, that place with fruit ever fair,
The trees white with flowers and showers of scent on the
    air :
Waters and boats, where notes of melody pour
From Ross Castle tower, the bower of dames we adore !

What damosels fair ! 'tis there is gaiety found,
Red wine on the board, a hoard of dainties around ;
High chase of the deer, the cheer, and winding of horn,
With thrush's sweet song among the branches at morn !

I've wandered brown Beare, from there to Erne in the
    North—
I've watched, in the west, the best of its beauty and
    worth—
But afar or anear, the peer I never have seen
Of the fairy-fond place, whose grace is the lovely Loch
    Lein.

[1] The name of the lake at Killarney.

THE VICTOR MAIDEN.

Patrick O'Conor.

Air: " Cashel of Munster."

My heart is o'erladen with sorrow and strife—
The love of a maiden has wounded my life ;
Astray among strangers afar I have been,
But the peer of that dear one I never have seen.

Her beauty so rare is—to love her is best !
The snow not so fair is ; how swan-like her breast !
Her words' tuneful measure all music 's above—
It wounds me with pleasure the voice of my Love !

Her curls in their clusters are rippled and rolled,
The sheen of their lustre 's like billowy gold ;
So radiant her glances I faint with delight,—
For beauty entrances and great is love's might.

How pure is her brow and how fair her cheek glows
With the whiteness of snow and a blush of the rose !
Her breast is a bower of blossoming joy—
More beauteous that flower than was Helen of Troy.

Her soft taper fingers are skilful as fair,
How graceful she lingers o'er broideries rare ;

As swiftly she sketches from lake and from land,
How featly she fetches each bird at command.

Though long, proud, and stately, from women afar,
'Mid chiefs gay and great lay my revel and war,
To this victor I yield me to serve as love's slave,
For fight cannot shield me, and flight cannot save !

AXIOMS.

Author Unknown.

No Lazy Wealth can think with Hunger's mind,
Yet Lazy always leaves a lack behind :
No love of woman woos decrepit Age,
And Death waits not for Beauty's equipage.

AN ELEGY.

A.D. 1782.

In Abbey ground,[1] by the wild western sea,
The true Knight rests, safe-shielded, Stone, by thee.
Here oft the Tiarna led the galloping band—
Now his home-coming saddens all the land.

[1] This lament is a superior specimen of the elegiac Irish style.
It will be noticed that the concluding words of each stanza are
repeated at the beginning of the next, and that those which ter-

The land held high his generous renown
From Beare to Diarra, from Lee to Liffey brown,
From Galway west to southernmost Cape Clear,
Kilkenny to Loch Cé—afar, anear.

Anear, afar, how mournful maids and men,
And every eye is wet by hill and glen;
The Suir o'erflowed, methought, the hills rent wide,
The Skellig,[1] shrieking, said "A Man has died!"

A Man has died. In grief all darkens o'er,
From Scarriff's Bay, from Deen, and far Timore
To the last sunset isle, no sail I see;
Valentia mourns with tears wept bitterly.

O bitterly cry Ards and Coom the keene,
And Ballinskelligs, where no lack hath been

minate the poem are identical with its opening words. This is the
classic form. The Elegy has been held in esteem and is still recited.
I have several versions taken from oral recitations, and Dr. Douglas
Hyde kindly brought under my notice a written transcript (made in
1832), kept in the Royal Irish Academy. This gives the author's
name as Tadg Rua O'Sullivan, whilst local tradition (which supplied
more accurate versions) ascribes it to Diarmad O'Shea, who lived in
the last century. The subject of the elegy was Francis Sigerson,
whose ancestors were lords of the manor of Ballinskelligs before the
Cromwellian confiscations. It is most interesting to meet with such
a Gaelic dirge, and to find that Irish rivers, mountains, seas, and
people lamented so deeply the descendant of a Norseman.

[1] The Skellig Isles, off the south-west coast of Kerry, one of
which belonged, with Ballinskelligs, Coom, Ards, etc., to the
subject of this Elegy.

Of sea-borne wine and welcomes as to home—
The Giver greeting all who chose to come.

Who chose to come of that glad hall were free,
With meat, brown ale, and honey from the bee—
Through Christ's sweet will, he surely shall have rest,
Francis, whose welcome cheered the poorest guest.

Guest, void of all, with want his only friend,
Found shield and succour, kindness to the end,
Linens and woollens where the tall looms stand,
Gifts hid in gifts and red wine in his hand.

O handsome Hawk, who tower'd the country o'er !
Top-spray of all who sprang from Segerson More !
And pure thy mother's blood, Clann Connell's old,—
Thou dashing chief—thou joyous hand with gold.

Clean gold with poverty well shared alway,
O head of Counsel still,—the people's stay ;
'Tis my belief from Skellig west, to Cove
No heart alive could match thy heart of love.

Love thy life's rule, from life's dawn till its night,
How many a wrong that rule humane made right,
How many a grief it chased and bitter moan—
Now the Church grieves for thee, here, lying lone.

Lone here and dead.   'Tis this makes heav'n dark,
From Rath to Ruachty, o'er mountain, sea, and bark :

What his hand gathered for the Lamb he gave,
The lofty, faultless Tree, our princely chieftain brave.

White chief of mankind, true Cavalier all o'er,
None e'er repelling, never closing door,
Gloom-sad the Gael, because our strength is low,
Eclipsed our souls, and wails the Voice of Woe.

Woe o'er Iveragh's woods and waters wide—
My wound! the steadfast generous man who died;
Not hard the way to ope with papal keys,
Lord, grant the Peace-maker thy perfect peace.

Peace to give peace where he may not return
To heal our hurt, to light the eyes that mourn;
Shield of our hearts, our strength in sorrow found,—
My grief, my woe!—the Chief laid low, in Abbey ground.

LOVE'S SUNSHINE.

AUTHOR UNKNOWN.[1]

O LOVE, and O Treasure, art sick or in sorrow?
    I've pined for thy coming, all lonely:

[1] Hardiman's "Minstrelsy" (abridged). The last two lines of the first stanza anticipated, and may have suggested, the central thought in Tennyson's lines:

> "Shine out, little head, running over with curls,
>   To the flowers and be their sun."

Gone is all pleasure,—by night and by morrow,
    I mourn for thee, ever and only.
That thou couldst distress me, who fain would caress thee,
    Is surely the sorrowful wonder ;
Arise, O bright Sun ! give the light of thy morning
    And my clouds it will scatter asunder.

Alas, and alas !—'tis my heart is dying,
    To have ever been born must still grieve me ;
My wand'ring mind is around thee flying—
    My Hope, and my Life, do not leave me !
Come, Wayward and Froward ;—come now, toward
    The home that ere now should have seen us ;
Come, Dearest and Rarest !—and Love true and fairest
    Shall ever abide there between us !

"ORO MOR, O MOREEN."[1]

IMITATED FROM THE IRISH.

DAINTY maid is Mary,
    When she goes a-marketing ;
Dainty in her dairy,
    Setting every heart to sing.

---

[1] In Petrie's " Ancient Music," p. 120, an Irish song is given with this chorus, but it is addressed to a young man, and the chorus is evidently adopted from a previous song,—which is here invented in imitation of the Irish. This seems to be its history : a playful satire was addressed to a maiden, and she answered it by a similar address,

Oro, Mor, O Moreen !
Oro, Mor, art coming now ?
Oro Mor, O Moreen
O Coolin óir, art coming now ? [1]

She was saying, and saying,
  Saying she would surely come ;
But her ruffles went a-straying :
  That is why she stayed at home.
    Oro Mor, O Moreen,
    Oro Mor, art coming now ?
    Oro Mor, O Moreen,
    O Coolin óir ! art coming now ?

She was saying, and saying,
  Promising she'd come away ;
But the brindled bat was baying :
  That is why she had to stay.
    Oro Mor, O Moreen,
    Oro Mor, art coming now ?
    Oro Mor, O Moreen,
    O Coolin óir ! art coming now ?

where the fisher youth is represented as excusing his delays because his shirt was not smoothed, his socks were not darned, a mountain rock fell upon him ; it concludes by wishing wreck to his coracle if he should not come on the appointed day.

[1] Mor is the name of a female, and Moreen (*rectè* Moirin) is its diminutive, Coolin (Cuilin) óir means "Chevelure of gold." In pronunciation, in the vocative, the "m" is softened to "w" and the "c" to "h" thus : "oro wór o wóreen"—"O hoolin óre."

She was saying, and saying,
　Promising she'd swiftly come;
But the moon had gone a-maying:
　That is why she stayed at home !
　　　Oro Mor, O Moreen,
　　　Oro Mor, art coming now?
　　　Oro Mor, O Moreen
　　　O Coolin óir ! art coming now?

YOU REMEMBER THAT EVENING.[1]

You remember that evening
　At my window still staying,
Bare-headed and gloveless
　For love, long delaying :
I stretch'd my hand to you,
　You clasp'd it, caressing ;
And we kept in soft converse
　Till the lark sang his blessing.

You remember that evening
　We spent both together,
'Neath the red-berried Rowan
　In still snowy weather.

[1] A peasant ballad. The Irish words, noted by O'Curry, are given in Petrie's " Ancient Music of Ireland," Vol. I., p. 142.

Your white throat was singing,
　　Your head on my shoulder—
Ne'er thought I, that evening,
　　That love could grow colder.

My heart in you !—darling !
　　Come soon to me, hither,
When my household are sleeping,
　　To whisper together :
My two hands shall clasp you,
　　While my story is given,
How your soft and sweet converse
　　Took my prospect of Heaven.

THE SHEPHERD'S PET.

AUTHOR UNKNOWN.[1]

I WISH the shepherd's pet were mine,
I wish the shepherd's pet were mine,
I wish the shepherd's pet were mine—
　　His snowy lamb, no other.
　　　And O I'm calling, calling you,
　　　Love, my heart is all in you,
　　　And O I'm calling, calling you,
　　　　The white pet of your mother.

---

[1] A simple peasant song, taken from the singing of a blind man,
in Clare ; quoted in Petrie's " Ancient Music of Ireland," Vol. I.,
p. 43, whose first three lines are here given.

I wish I had a herd of kine,
I wish I had a herd of kine,
I wish I had a herd of kine
  And Mollie from her mother !
    And O I'm calling, calling you,
    Love, my heart is all in you,
    And O I'm calling, calling you,
      The bright pet of your mother !

MY SUMMER.

AUTHOR UNKNOWN.

SHE 's the White Flower of the Berry,
She 's the Bright Bloom of the Cherry,
She 's the fairest, noblest Maiden
  That ever saw the day :

She 's my pulse, my love, my pleasure,
She 's the Apple's sweet bloom-treasure,
She 's Summer 'mid the storm-time
  'Tween Christmas and the May !

A WISH.

I WOULD the Apple-bloom I were,
  Or the little daisy only,
Or red rose in the garden, where
  Thou'rt wont to wander lonely

In hope some day thy eyes would stay
And of my flow'rets choose some,
To bear in thy bright hand away
Or wear in thy sweet bosom.

LOVE'S DESPAIR.

DIARMAD O'CURNAIN.[1]

I AM desolate,
Bereft by bitter fate;
No cure beneath the skies can save me,
No cure on sea or strand,
Nor in any human hand—
But hers, this paining wound who gave me.

I know not night from day,
Nor thrush from cuckoo gray,
Nor cloud from the sun that shines above thee—
Nor freezing cold from heat,
Nor friend—if friend I meet—
I but know—heart's love!—I love thee.

---

[1] O'Curnain was born in Cork in 1740, and died in Modeligo, Waterford, in the first quarter of the present century. He was a tall, handsome young farmer. He travelled to Cork to purchase wedding presents for his betrothed, but was met on his way home by the news that she had married a wealthy suitor. He flung all his presents into the fire, and, from the shock, lost his reason, which he never recovered. He was known to several persons recently alive.

Love that my Life began,
Love, that will close life's span,
Love that grows ever by love-giving :
Love, from the first to last,
Love, till all life be passed,
Love that loves on after living !

This love I gave to thee,
For pain love has given me,
Love that can fail or falter never—
But, spite of earth above,
Guards thee, my Flower of love,
Thou Marvel-maid of life for ever.

Bear all things evidence,
Thou art my very sense,
My past, my present, and my morrow !
All else on earth is crossed,
All in the world is lost—
Lost all—but the great love-gift of sorrow.

My life not life, but death ;
My voice not voice—a breath ;
No sleep, no quiet—thinking ever
On thy fair phantom face,
Queen eyes and royal grace,
Lost loveliness that leaves me never.

I pray thee grant but this,—
From thy dear mouth one kiss,
That the pang of death-despair pass over :
Or bid make ready nigh
The place where I shall lie,
For aye, thy leal and silent lover.

XIII.—FOLK-SONGS, LULLABIES, OCCUPATION-CHANTS, AND MARINER'S SONG.

IRISH LULLABY.

Author Unknown.

I'LL put you, myself, my baby, to slumber,
Not as 'tis done by the clownish number,—
A yellow blanket and coarse sheet bringing,
But in golden cradle that softly swinging
  To and fro, lu la lo,
  To and fro, my bonnie baby!
  To and fro, lu la lo,
  To and fro, my own sweet baby!

I'll put you, myself, my baby, to slumber,
On sunniest day of the pleasant summer,
Your golden cradle on smooth lawn laying,
'Neath murmuring boughs that the birds are swaying
  To and fro, lu la lo,
  To and fro, my bonnie baby!
  To and fro, lu la lo,
  To and fro, my own sweet baby!

Slumber, my babe! may the sweet sleep woo you,
And from your slumbers may health come to you—
May all diseases now flee and fear you,
May sickness and sorrow never come near you!

> To and fro, lu la lo,
> To and fro, my bonnie baby!
> To and fro, lu la lo,
> To and fro, my own sweet baby!

Slumber, my babe! may the sweet sleep woo you,
And from your slumbers may health come to you,
May bright dreams come, and come no other,
And I be never a sonless mother!

> To and fro, lu la lo,
> To and fro, my bonnie baby!
> To and fro, lu la lo,
> To and fro, my own sweet baby!

FAIRY LULLABY.

O WOMAN, washing by the river!
  Hush-a-by, babe not mine,
My woeful wail wilt pity never?
  Hush-a-by, babe not mine.
A year this day, I was snatched for ever,
  Hush-a-by, babe not mine,
To the green hill fort where thorn trees shiver,
  Hush-a-by, babe not mine.

Shoheen, shoheen, shoheen, shoheen,
   Sho-hu-lo, sho-hu-lo,
Shoheen, shoheen, shoheen, shoheen,
   'Tis not thou my baby O !

'Tis there the fairy court is holden,
  Hush-a-by, babe not mine,
And there is new ale, there is olden,
  Hush-a-by, babe not mine,
And there are combs of honey golden,
  Hush-a-by, babe not mine,
And there lie men in bonds enfolden,
  Hush-a-by, babe not mine.
               Shoheen, etc.

How many there, of fairest faces !
  Hush-a-by, babe not mine,
Bright-eyed boys, with manly graces !
  Hush-a-by, babe not mine,
Gold-haired girls with curling tresses !
  Hush-a-by, babe not mine,
—There, mothers nurse with sad caresses.
  Hush-a-by, babe not mine.
               Shoheen, etc.

Ah, bid my husband haste to-morrow,
  Hush-a-by, babe not mine,
A waxen taper he shall borrow,
  Hush-a-by, babe not mine,

A black knife bring to cross my sorrow,
　　Hush-a-by, babe not mine,
And stab their first steed coming thoro',
　　Hush-a-by, babe not mine.
　　　　　　　Shoheen, etc.

Say, pluck the herb where gate-thorns quiver,
　　Hush-a-by, babe not mine,
And wish a wish that God deliver,
　　Hush-a-by, babe not mine,
If he come not then—he need come never,
　　Hush-a-by, babe not mine.
For they'll make me Fairy Queen for ever!
　　Hush-a-by, babe not mine!
　　　　Shoheen, shoheen, shoheen, shoheen,
　　　　　Sho-hu-lo, sho-hu-lo,
　　　　Shoheen, shoheen, shoheen, shoheen,
　　　　　'Tis not thou my baby O!

"BABE WILL BE UNEASY."

Citruag O'Daigenain.[1]

And O bo, my baby bright!
Do you know a woman's way?
'Tis I, myself, that learned it right
Whatsoe'er she seem to say.

[1] O'Kearney Irish MSS., Royal Irish Academy.

Is she sick, or is she slow,
Is her soft heart sinking low,
If dad don't kiss the nurse, I know
                 Babe will be uneasy !
If wine of wines you bring to her,
                 Babe will be uneasy !
Give all the birds that sing to her,
Fruits from Roe to Ring to her,
The country of a king to her,
Unless a kiss you bring to her,
                 Babe will be uneasy !
If Limerick you gave to her,
                 Babe will be uneasy !
And Cork so bright and brave to her,
                 Babe will be uneasy !
Gems that monarchs crave, to her,
Give gold that fills a cave to her,
If no caress you gave to her,
                 Babe will be uneasy !
Wine were want and miss to her,
                 Babe will be uneasy !
Norway's flock no bliss to her,
                 Babe will be uneasy ?
Gold a hate and hiss to her,
                 Babe will be uneasy !
Unless you give a kiss to her,
                 Babe will be uneasy !

SMITH'S SONG.

IMITATED FROM THE IRISH.

DING dong didero,
    Blow big bellows,
Ding dong didero,
    Black coal yellows,
Ding dong didero,
    Blue steel mellows,
Ding dong didero,
    Strike !—good fellows.

Up with the hammers,
    Down with the sledges,
Hark to the clamours,
    Pound now the edges,
Work it and watch it,
    Round, flat, or square O,
Spade, hook, or hatchet—
    Sword for a hero.

Ding dong didero,
    Ding dong dero,
Spade for a labourer,
    Sword for a hero,

Hammer it, stout smith,
　　Rightly, lightly,
Hammer it, hammer it,
　　Hammer at it brightly.

PLOUGHMAN'S RIME.

PLOUGHMAN.

" HASTE, and hurry, and speed,
The beldame's sluggard steed,
Leap up, Tom, take heed
　　And see if our dinner is near."

THIRDMAN.

" 'Tis a sowing,"
　　　　" Haste, and hurry, and speed."
" 'Tis a growing,"
　　　　" Haste, and hurry, and speed."
" 'Tis a-mowing."
　　　　" Haste, and hurry, and speed."
" Home 'tis going."
　　　　" Haste, and hurry, and speed."
" Fire 's a-blowing,"
　　　　" Haste, and hurry, and speed."
" Cook 's a-glowing."
　　　　" Haste, and hurry, and speed."
" Here, 'tis showing ! "

PLOUGHMAN.

"Cheer, and cherish, in deed,
The good wife's gay young steed,
Off with bridle, forth with feed—
    Now that our dinner is here."

SPINNERS' SONG.

"LOOREEN, o loora, loora, laura [1]
Run by the river, and find me my lover."

"Looreen, o looreen, loora, laura,
'Tis Flann O'Keeffe I'll fetch for you over."

"Looreen, o loora, loora, laura,
His cattle are plenty in meadows of clover."

"Looreen, o loora, loora, laura,
Run by the river and find me my lover."

"Looreen, o loora, loora, laura,
'Tis Cormac Fada I'll fetch for you over."

"Looreen, o loora, loora, laura,
His head is in Dublin, his heels are in Dover."

[1] Luirin o lurtha, lurtha, lartha.   See Appendix.

MALLO LÉRO.

SPINNERS' SONG.

"MALLO léro is im bo néro
I wandered the wood, when dews were pearly,
Mallo léro is im bo bán."

"Mallo léro is im bo néro
For Conn O'Carrol you roved so early
Mallo léro is im bo bán."

"Mallo léro is im bo néro
With withy waist set him ploughing barely
Mallo léro is im bo bán."

"Mallo léro is im bo néro
You mannerless maid, he'd match you fairly,
Mallo léro is im bo bán."

"Mallo léro is im bo néro
Nay, find me the man I love so rarely
Mallo léro is im bo bán."

"Mallo léro is im bo néro
Take and be happy with Tom O'Harely
Mallo léro is im bo bán."

" Mallo léro is im bo néro,
I welcome, I take, I hail him fairly,
Mallo léro is im bo bán."

" Mallo léro is im bo néro
Then ne'er may you part, or late or early
Mallo léro is im bo bán."

ORO, O DARLING FAIR.

SPINNERS' SONG.

" ORO, O darling fair ! and ioro O Fairness fair !
Who 's the young maid to be wed upon Shrove-tide there ?
Oro, O darling fair ! O lamb and O love !

" Oro, O darling fair ! and ioro O Fairness fair !
Maid to be married I hear is sweet Annie Clare,
Oro, O darling fair ! O land, and O love."

" Oro, O darling fair ! and ioro O Fairness fair !
Who 's the glad youth upon whom fell this happy air ?
Oro, O darling fair ! O lamb, and O love."

" Oro, O darling fair ! and ioro O Fairness fair !
Florence O'Driscoll they say has the luck so rare,
Oro, O darling fair ! O lamb, and O love !"

"Oro, O darling fair! and ioro O Fairness fair!
What is the outfit they give to the wedded pair?
Oro, O darling fair! O lamb, and O love!"

" Oro, O darling fair! and ioro O Fairness fair!
Feathers the finest that ever had bird in air,
Linen the whitest that ever the spindle bare,
Quilting of silk that is softest beyond compare,
Candlesticks golden, graceful and carved with care,
Red and white pieces in pocket to spend and spare,
Plenty on board with gay guests to gladly share,—
Victory I wish them, that Joy may be ever there!
Oro, O darling fair! O lamb, and O love!"

THE MARINER'S HYMN.

AUTHOR UNKNOWN.

BARK, bravest in battle of billow and breeze!
True tower in the tempest, dry deck in the seas!
When flash the wild waters, in mountains of might!
You leap through the breakers with bounds of delight!

The high, bright tide! the high, bright tide!
Queen of my heart, my joy, my pride!
My beautiful bark on the high, bright tide!

A A

With robes from the Indies I've dighted my fair,
How swells her white bosom against the blue air!
Right buoyant the craft below, shapely the sail,
And, O God! but to see her rise out of the gale!

On the high, bright tide! the high, bright tide!
Queen of my heart, my joy, my pride!
My beautiful bark on the high, bright tide!

"Gray Deelan, who stand with unchangeable brow,
Behold how the surges race off from her prow,
Behold, and give judgment if ever you've seen
Bark on the waters to peer with my queen."

On the high, bright tide! the high, bright tide!
Queen of my heart, my joy, my pride!
My beautiful bark on the high, bright tide!

Then answered gray Deelan: "Since first I withstood
The roar-rush of ocean's tumultuous flood,
By night and day watch I, but never could mark
From seaward or shoreward, a bark like thy bark!"

On the high, bright tide! the high, bright tide!
Queen of my heart, my joy, my pride!
My beautiful bark on the high, bright tide!

"Lord of the heavens!" the mariners pray,
"Give succour, give shelter, keep, keep her away,
She cleaves the blue billows, she comes like a flash,
And through us and o'er us she'll instantly dash"—

On the high, bright tide! the high, bright tide!
Queen of my heart, my joy, my pride!
My beautiful bark on the high, bright tide!

XIV.—PARAPHRASES FROM THE GAELIC.

THE KING'S LAY.[1]

I.

THE Hill of all Supremacy was void
Of rule supreme.   For seven years, no King
Had entered there, nor thence gone forth in state,
With chief and bard and royal equipage,
To make procession through the Land of Erinn,
And all was ill.   There crept a faint gray mist
Across the fair face of the Island then,
And darkness came on many hearts, and slow
Forebodings grew, and petty enmities
Were omens of a mighty wrath to come.
Peace was no more, although the Isle was still
And all her shoreward seas and curvéd bays
Unvexed by sharp prows from the snowy North.
Fate hung in air, as hangs a towering hawk
O'er silenced woods.   Whereat the Land was moved

---

[1] Paraphrased from a passage in the "Sick-bed of Cuchulainn and only Jealousy of Emer," Atlantis, Vol. I.   See Appendix.

As by one thought, to cast away the cause,
Not loving thus to see fair Tara void,
Discrowned, and desolate, her glory gone;
Not loving that the Kingship of the Land
Should be without a King to judge supreme,
And make procession through the Land of Erinn,
Redressing wrongs and making good the Right,
Ruling the kings and settling all dispute,
Welding more closely the white bond of love
That linked in one the Great Five Chieftainries.
So all the scattered chiefs arose and sped
Their gathering chariots to the Hill of Kings,
Whose bright-browed fortress glances o'er the green
And tremulous sea of branches, like a moon
New-risen.

      The clangour ceased; they entered, still,
The Court of Niafer, by mystic rite
To find what man should rule the royal fort.
Lo, in their midst, the Chiefs of all the Druids
Came; in their midst a stripling stood, new robed
In vesture white that fell in myriad folds.
Then him Four Druids gave to eat the heart
Divided, of the spotless, snow-white bull;
And when he ate, they made deep slumber drown
His form inert, and, glimm'ring round, pronounced
The magic charm that wrought the Dream of Truth.
Silent they stood awhile, and all repressed
The anxious throbbing of their hurried hearts.
Listless in sleep he lay till, suddenly,

Lifting his right hand slowly toward the North,
He murmured words that died within his throat :
His arm returning fell across his heart.
And yet a little time and, suddenly,
Half-rising up, with eager-bending brow,
Stretching his hand unto the North, he spake
With accent now assured, and full : "Behold !"
And then, at once, upstarting to his feet,
He made low rev'rence to the Unseen Man
And cried aloud : "All hail, my lord the King !
All hail, O noble hero, crimson-flecked,
Sitting beside the Mournful Chieftain there
In fair Emania : thou, in all great deeds,
His worthy pupil, peer, and truest friend !"
This when they heard, the Chiefs sent forth a Chief
Who, journeying through the long glades of the woods,
And fording mighty rivers in his way,
Came swift to fair Emania in the North.
   Then, sending round his glances he beheld
Eastward, the palace of the Crimson Branch,
And on his left he saw the Speckled Mansion
Solemn and still, and in the sun, before
The great White Palace of the Royal Branch
And hosts of knights were swarming round its door
Passing and re-passing, for all Ulad
Had gathered here to greet their King, and watch
The mournful sickness in the Speckled House.
The herald Chieftain smote upon a door
In the great Palace of the Royal Branch,

And he was led before the King, who naught
Would hear, till feasts were spread, and humming chords
From lines of lofty harps had wiled away
The irksome burthen of long journeying :—
For such was aye the custom of the Realm.
Three days had passed ; he stood before the King,
And showed to him the weighty charge he bore.
King Concobar of Ulad answering him,
Replied : " There is with us a noble, free,
And high-descended hero, crimson-flecked,
Sitting beside a Mournful Chieftain here
In fair Emania, and in all great deeds
His worthy pupil, peer, and truest friend."
    Then forth they fared : the King, the Envoy-Chief
And all the Council from the Royal Branch
Unto the Speckled Mansion in the West ;
And entering soft they saw Cuchulainn lie
Upon his couch of sad decline, and there
Stood over him to solace and to speed
The heavy hours of mournfulness away
Our noble Lugai of the Crimson Hand.
    When he had heard the Envoy, Lugai spake
With rising anger as at insult done
And all the nobleness of ardent youth :
" Even for Tara's self, I will not leave
This couch of sickness where Cuchulainn lies.
Doleful his room of darkness would become
Were I afar, but not so sad and lone
As the darked chamber of my heart, while he

Lay all forsaken by his pupil here."

But then Cuchulainn, rising slow and weak,
Above his couch of sad decline, stood tall
And grand once more; and on his Lugai's head
He laid his hand, so strong,—and now so worn:
"Thou now hast given thee a charge, my son,
Beside which private bonds must seem as naught;—
Go forth!—and from thy glory there will come
New life into my heart, and I will live
In sorrow less, that I may see thee rule
According to the best weal of thy Land,
And see thy Land grow happy under thee,
And see thy praises in the greater deeds
That, following thee, all Erinn shall perform!"

He then, recalling from the Past the things
He ever taught, and to show forth the ways
That most become a King, did speak this Lay:

II.

"In the Time—
In the red Time of Battles,—
When the foeman advances,
   With a myriad of glaives
And a myriad of lances,
   When slaves
Shrink back from the terrible chime
Which the War-harp outrattles
   Whose chords

Are the jubilant Warriors' swords—
   Be thou
  The Torch of the Brave :
    Not timid, oppressed, or unready
  In woe or affright,
  But Man in his might,
Clear-glancing, and fearless, and steady,
  Ready the foeman to smite,
Ready the friend and the foeman to save,
  Calm and intrepid of brow,—
    Even as now.

   " In peace or in war
    Dwell not afar
From the voice of thy people, nor hide
Thy heart in the purple of pride ;
  Bend down thine ear,
Let the doors to thy mansion be wide,
  Let the pathway be clear
  So that all thou shalt hear,
And the injured shall come to thy side.
  Never be passionate,
  Never precipitate ;
  Never intoxicate
With that which of evils is worst,
  Which deadens the health
  Of Mind, and makes Earth
Seem a wilderness drear and accurst,

If it yield but a dearth
To him, who thus lusteth, of Wealth.

" In all of thy regal processions,
In the mansions of welcoming kings,
   Show thou the example
How little the lofty mind clings
To feasting and mead ;—and a sample
   Of temperance also be thou
      Whenever a stranger
   Come 'mid thy possessions,
      Shield him from danger,
   And guard him from wrong ;
Let courtesy sit in thy heart and thy brow,
   Let him be gladdened, but thou
      Hast duties, so wield them—
See that the feasts be not many nor long :
   In such there is danger,
   In such there is wrong,
From ills of each kind thou must shield him.

" Let not thy path lie among
Men who are plotters of guile,
   Men who are doers of wrong.
      If any
A tract of the lands of thine Isle
Have got them by fraud or by wile,
   By lie, or by might,
      Though many

A year may have rolled on its way,
And the hair of their youth have grown gray,—
   Let them not rest !
Let not the Wrong be as Right !
Call witnesses quickly together,
Ask the historians whether
     Their scrolls can declare
  The descendants of him,—the true heir,
Him whom their guile dispossess'd ;
   Seek the clear truth
Recalling the past into life.
     Lo, then
    Having found,
  'Mid their fraudulent actions, the Right—
Arise, without slowness or ruth,
  Arise, in thy sternness and might,
   And gather thy men,
And drive them, with vigorous strife
  With sword and with javelin, afar,
  And for ever and ever debar
   Their return to the ground.

   " Be sparing of words,
Be calm and not loud in thy speech ;
   Loving to think—
Knowing 'tis easier to cross o'er the fords
  When the flood is not flush with the brink,
   And the waters are clear
  And the currents not loud, are but low—

Knowing 'tis easier to reach
The Truth which abideth beyond
    The River of Words,
In the still bark of Thought, when slow
    Is the rush of that River.
        Thus be thou ever,
            And wear
In thy dutiful bosom, a fond
    Respect for the Good, who are old ;
        Even forbear
To mock or deride those who never
Have earned the regard of the Bold,
    Of the Good, and the True,
But whom Age bringeth grieving, and rue,
    Deep woe and despair.

        " My son !
Be thou kindly disposed towards all ;—
        Thinking evil of none,
Till their deeds show their sorrowful fall ;
        Do evil to none,
From those who offend thee demand
Not things over bitter to bear.
        Be gentle, be merciful, and
            Open of hand.
If thou hast wronged any, by chance,
    Be not shamed, but declare
Thine error, and yield him his share.

Set forth all the righteous laws
   That the Isle may advance,
Knowing the truth of its cause.
      Hearken
And follow the words of the Wise,
Remember the rules of thy Fathers,
Let the knowledge of Age be a star to thine eyes
  When shadows surround thee, and darken
    The goal which thou seekest.
    Be firmest, but meekest;
      So striving that ever
    The great bond which gathers
Thy girdle of free friends may never
    Slacken, nor sunder, nor sever.

"Bear with them, bear for them, endure
    Much that their circle increase
    In purity, honour, and peace.
      With thy foes
Be strong, word-keeping, and sure.
Be courteous, nor taunt with their woes
    Those who have suffered defeat.
Let the taunts of thine enemies pass—
Let thy captives abuse and defame—
    Their tattle
May writhe like snakes to thy feet,
But weaker than withering grass
    In the flame.
Thou shalt be nobler, and scorn

Their tauntings or threats to return
In peace or in battle.

"Spend not thy time
In riotous waste,
Nor lean to the contrary crime,
Hoard not thy wealth, and
Alienate never thy land.
Give answering calm, without haste ;
And bear,
With thy wrath all unmoved,
To hearken thy conduct reproved
And thy Counsellors blame thee,
And thy deeds, if they were
Not such as became thee.

"Sacrifice naught
Of thy truth to the wishes of man ;
Nor even in thought
Let men's wickedness fan
The fire of thine anger to hate
Lest thou do even them
An injustice, through loathing
Their former misdeed,
And discover it, late.
Take care and good heed
For Truth is a king's diadem,
And Justice his clothing.

Release not thy capture
But with bond of security given,
Lest, when his fetters are riven,
　　Wrath and not rapture
　　Should run through his veins,
And, knowing thy force and thy land,
He should come with a ravaging band
To be venged for captivity's stains.

　　" Let not thy heart
Sink into slumber and sloth,
Lest thou shouldst shrink from thy duty,
　　Lest thou be loth
　　To act the true part,
And thy glory depart
And the Will, and the Power, and the Beauty
　　Which exist in the might
　　To repress and redress
　　The Evil and Wrong—
To bring kindness and mercy to light
And uphold the fair Banner of Right
　　With the hand of the Strong.

　　" Ask not a favour
　　Again, if refused thee at first;
For the mind becomes mean,
　　If the heart be a craver;
And a subtle Enslaver,
　　A Torturer vilest and worst.

Is the Yearning obscene,
　　The immodest Desire,
　For that which belongs to another,
Whom the soul grows to hate, and not love as a brother ;
　　And will fall from its higher
　　Emotions and cease to aspire,
　And smoulder 'mid passions accurst.

　　　" Do not compete,
　　　Being zealous,
　　With thy subjects in action or feat,
　　　Lest thou be jealous ;
And wish not their glory, but that they should meet
　　With sorrow, o'erthrow, and defeat.
　　　Nor forget that a King
　　　Whom his people elect
Should be stainless of heart and blameless of mind,
　　Of courage and honour unfleckt,—
　Loving his clans with a loving refined ;
Should joy in their gladness, grieve in their grief,
　　Toil to give light to their blind,
　　Toil till true happiness sing
　In the homes of the Rich and the Poor,—
　　　A Palace of Purity,
　　　A Wall of Security,
　　　He alone, be thou sure,
Is truly their King, and their Prince, and their Chief.

THE BLESSING OF DUBLIN.[1]

CHILL and dead
  Lies the King of Dublin's son:
At his head
    Sits gray Alpin, stern and still,
    Neither eat nor drink he will,
    Till the Earth have had her fill,
        And Valhall be won.

Patrick came,
  Lauding loud of holier things,
Flashed the flame
    From the Viking eyes : "Can He,
    Maker of all things, make *be*
    That which is no more for me ?
        Thy King of Kings !

"Speak the word,
  Let the sovran deed be done,
Then, thy Lord

---

[1] Paraphrased from a passage in *Leabar na g-Ceart*, "The Book of Rights." This work is supposed to have been written by Cuan O'Lochain, Chief Legislator of Erinn, after Clontarf, and the death of Brian Boruma. The passage is referred in this book to St. Benean (sometimes made Benignus), St. Patrick's disciple. If he were the author, it proves the antiquity and good repute of the Norse settlement ; if, on the other hand, Cuan O'Lochain be the

Lord of mine is—Lord of all—
Each a liegeman at his call,
Bows in battle, horns in hall,
    For him—my son !"

Patrick prayed,
    Moving as the sun moves round ;
Naught dismayed,
    King and jarls thrice followed him,
    Heard, with understanding dim,
    Of the mystic murmured hymn,
      The strange weird sound.

Then great dread
    Fell upon them, and behold !
Stood the Dead
    In their midst, erect, with gaze
    Fixed on them, in mute amaze,
    Lit with red returning rays,
      The visage cold.

Said the king,
    Standing with his war-men nigh,

author, then it is even more valuable. For it is a testimony, borne
after the battle of Clontarf, by the most eminent Gael of Erinn, to
the high estimation in which the Norse-Irish of Dublin were held by
the contemporary Gael.   They are shown to the nation at large as
enjoying the fruits of the blessing of the Apostle of Erinn, in eleven
special gifts.   This of itself would condemn the partisan views of
some rude moderns, who appear to be impartially ignorant of the
opinions of St. Patrick, St. Benean, and Cuan O'Lochain.

"For this thing
    We are vassals to thy Lord,
    Followers fast by field and fiord,
    True at trysting, staunch at sword,
        Sea, shore, or sky !

"I pronounce
    Tribute to this King of thine :
Each an ounce
    Weighed aright of ruddy gold
    Ev'ry year shall be thrice told,
    From the Northman's Dublin hold,
        At Macha's shrine." [1]

Patrick raised
    His right hand in benediction,
"God be praised !
    If the toll be paid each year,
    Not the world need Dublin fear :
Else, three times the Gaelic spear
        Shall bring affliction.

"Gifts eleven,
    Guerdons, in return shall fall,
From high Heaven :
    Goodly wives the wives shall be,
    The men live manful and die free,

---

[1] Ard-Macha, the height of Macha, now Ardmagh, the primatial see of Ireland.

Beauty still the maidens' fee
    Of the pure proud Gall.

"Feats of swimming
    Mark the youth, sea-loved, sea-strong ;
Bright horns brimming,
    Welcome all to bounteous board,
    Gift of war-triumphant sword,
    Gift of trophies, many a hoard,
        Make its glory long.

"Champions brave,
    Gallant kings to bear the crown
On land and wave,
    Gift of commerce from all parts,
    Gift of ever-widening marts,—
    Gift in church of reverent hearts,
        Bless stout Dublin town.

"Through the haze
    Whence, in long succeeding lines,
Come our days—
    I behold ascending spires :
    When to Darkness all retires,
    One of Erinn's last Three Fires,
        The Fire of Dublin shines.

"Tara proud
    Over woods upstanding airy,
Not thus crowd

Gracious gifts around thy name,
From Tara here this day I came,
Great its mighty monarch's fame,—
    My curse on Laeré!"

Patrick spoke :
    Benean, I, have shaped this lay,
With measured stroke
    In the right-resounding rime,
    That his words in every clime
    Should re-echo through all Time
    Till the Judgment Day.

APPENDIX.

THOUGH it is now common to apply the epithet "Celtic" to the old inhabitants of Ireland, I have preferred to write of them as the "Ancient Irish," that being a term less exclusive and more exact. Some English historians have given currency to the strange fallacy that the Angle and Saxon colonists extinguished the Britons, whom the Roman legions could not annihilate. They overlook the fact that the policy of invaders was usually to retain the natives as their vassals. In Ireland a similar fallacy obtains. The Milesian invaders are now generally supposed to have superseded completely the former owners of the island. This is essentially a modern fancy, founded on ignorance; for the elder Irish historians—often Milesians themselves—not only admit but emphasize the fact that the population of the country was composed of different races.

The island, according to them, was in the possession of a northern Scandinavian colony—the Tuata Dé Dananns, —when a southern race, the Milesians, coming from Spain, invaded the country. The Fomorians, a northern people also, occasionally harried the coasts and effected temporary settlements. There were some minor colonists of inferior importance.

Mac Firbis (A.D. 1650), in his book of the "Genealogies of the Colonies of Erinn," includes the lines of the Fomorians, the Lochlanns (Norsemen), and the "Sax-Normans," so far as these connect with Ireland. He quotes from an ancient writer these characteristics of the great earlier colonists:

"Everyone who is fair-haired, vengeful, large, and every plunderer, the professors of musical and entertaining performances : who are adepts in all druidical and magical arts ; they are the descendants of the Tuata Dé Dananns in Erinn."

He also mentions that the greater part of their nobles (or higher classes) were full of learning and druidism. All old accounts agree that they were pre-eminently skilled in the arts and sciences, including medicine.

"Everyone who is white (of skin), brown (of hair), bold, honourable, daring, prosperous, bountiful in the bestowal of property, wealth, and rings, and who is not afraid of battle or combat; they are the descendants of the sons of Milesius, in Erinn." [They had bards, harpers, and learned men, but their predominant character was that of a militant race.]

Lastly : "Everyone who is black-haired, who is a tattler, guileful, tale-telling, noisy, contemptible ; every wretched, mean, strolling, unsteady, harsh, and inhospitable person ; every slave, every mean thief, every churl, everyone who loves not to listen to music and entertainment, the disturbers of every council and of every assembly, and the promoters of discord among people, these are the descendants of the Firbolgs, of the Gailiuns, of Liogairné, and of the Domnanns, in Erinn. The descendants of the Firbolgs are the most numerous of these."

The Irish have always held a firm belief in the influence of heredity, but Mac Firbis judiciously notes that the intermixture of races must be taken into account.

Nevertheless, it is remarkable that the mysticism which some now assign to the Celts, Gaels, Scots, or Milesians, was ascribed by this very people to its predecessors, the Tuata Dé Dananns. The latter formed a world of Faery for the Celts.

AMERGIN'S LAYS (pp. 93-95).

According to the historical legend, Ireland was invaded from the south, in the year of the world 3500, by Milesius and his followers. They found the isle in the possession of a fair and highly gifted race, the Dé Dananns.

It is related that when the Milesians landed, a conference took place with the kings of the island: these offered, if the Milesians withdrew for three days, they would decide upon one of three courses, namely: retire, submit, or fight. Amergin (brother to Miled, or Milesius), a bard, druid, and judge, was chosen as arbiter. He decided that the island belonged of right to the Dé Dananns, and that his kindred should withdraw over nine green waves.

If then they could land again and conquer, the island should belong to them by the right of battle. Accepting this judgment they set out from Inver-scene (Kenmare Bay), over nine green waves, to sea. The Druids and poets of Erinn by their incantations raised so violent a storm that the vessels were driven westward and separated. "This is a Druidic wind," said Donn, son of Milesius. "It is," replied Amergin, "if it does not blow above the masthead." Then Aranan, Donn's youngest brother and helmsman, went aloft and discovered that the upper air was calm. "It was treacherous of our soothsayers," exclaimed Donn, "not to have prevented this Druidic wind." "There was no treason," replied Amergin. Thereupon Amergin stood up and chanted his "Incantation." This strange poem is unquestionably very ancient, and pre-Christian, but of course its exact date is uncertain. It is composed in "Conaclon," the end word of one line rimes to the first word of the line following, and indeed the rime is sometimes secured by repeating the word. Alliteration of two initials is also sought and usually obtained. These characters can be seen in the following specimen :

> Ailim iath n *ereann,*
> *Ermac* muir m*otach,*
> M*otach* sliab s*reatach*
> S*reatach* coill ciotach.

These characters are of exceeding interest, since they prove that the rime-sense was well developed in the very ancient Irish. Amergin's "Song of Triumph," composed when he landed, differs much in metre, being irregular, and appears to dispense with rime, so that it might pass as the first example of blank verse. Even alliteration seems rather avoided than desired in the shorter lines, though permitted in the longer. It seems to me, however, that Amergin may have intended a mode of rime altogether overlooked, which I would call "entrance-rime,"—each of the shorter lines begins with the verb "am" (I am), and the repetition of this accented word sufficed.

This triumph song has been called the "Mystery of Amergin," in the "Lyra Celtica" of Dr. and Mrs. Sharp; some, with Dr. D'Arbois Jubainville and my friend Dr. Douglas Hyde, see a pantheistic spirit in it. That is possible, of course; still I think it open to another interpretation. This archaic poem is glossed by old Irish writers in the Books of Leacan and Ballymote, and by the O'Clerys. Professor Connellan gives these glosses with his translation. They have it that Amergin declares he is the wind at sea, in subtle action; the billow, in overwhelming power; the roar of ocean, in terrific approach; a bird of prey on a rock, in cunning or keen vigilance; a sun ray, for clearness; a salmon in a river (known to it) for swiftness; and a lake on a plain for extent, or magic greatness.

This view is supported by the fact that, in later but still ancient bardic verses, enigmatic metaphors were much affected, and needed explanation by the author. Amergin might have written " I am the sun after leaving the stars," and left us in doubt; but when Dallan so describes a king, the bard himself explains: "'Thou sun after leaving its stars,' that is when the sun has left its stars, this is the time its figure is best, and not better is its countenance than thine." My contention is conclusively proved by the existence of another poem, identical in form and structure, in which Cuchulainn (in the "Battle of Ros-na-ree") makes his vaunting song, like Amergin. He uses similar expressions, as "I am a fire avenging floods," "I am a fierce flaming lion," with others which are unmistakably personal vaunts—not pantheistic, but pan-egoistic.

THE FIRST ELEGY (p. 96).

O'Reilly, in his work on Ancient Irish Writers, says that though the language of this poem does not seem so old as that of Amergin, it is undoubtedly of "great antiquity." Lugai, son of Ith, was nephew to Milesius, whose daughter he married. He was therefore a contemporary of Amergin: his words may have been modified by copyists. His poem presents a most noteworthy instance of remarkable riming skill:

> Suideam sund uas an tra*cht*
> Ainbteach fua*cht*
> Crit for mo d*ed* adbal e*cht*
> E*c* dom rua*cht*
> Aisneidim duib atbad b*ean*
> Brogais bla*d*
> Fail a hainm, fris niad nea*m*
> Os grian gla*n*

Adbal **eg, ecc** dom r*uacht*
Cruaid rom cla*id*,
Nocht a *fir*, ar ro s*il*,
Siu ro su*id*.[1]

This short poem shows parallelism, alliteration, vowel rime, and consonant rime (*e.g.*, fuacht, ruacht), I have endeavoured to reproduce the peculiarities exactly in English.

The short peculiar rhythm may be intended to remind one of the rocking of a boat.

THE FATE OF THE SONS OF USNACH [2] (pp. 107-111).

This is the first of "The Three Sorrows of Story." Though now presented as a heroic romance, interspersed with poems, it appears to me probable that this romance form covers, and partly conceals, a more ancient drama. If this be so, then it is a mistake to search for an Epic in what was really a Tragedy.

Let us see how this idea will work out.

First we have the Prologue, in which a short account of the genesis of the drama is related.

King Concobar of Ulster was feasting at his Storysayer's house, when the wife of the latter bore a child, hereafter known as Deirdré (Alarm). The king's Druid declared

---

[1] This is quoted from "Transactions of the Ossianic Society," Vol. V. (though I have omitted h's, as too confusing; my versions of these archaic pieces are founded on translations of Connellan (3) and O'Curry (1), but some passages were not clear to these scholars.

[2] "Proceedings of the Gaelic Society," Dublin, 1812.

her fateful of evil; the nobles decided she should die, but Concobar ordered that she be bred apart, as his betrothed. In the lone fort she grew up with her nurse Lebarcam and her tutor only. On a day, she saw a raven drink of a pool of blood in the snow. "Would I had a youth with those hues," she said, "raven-hued his hair, blood-hued his cheek, snow-hued his skin." Lebarcam secretly brought Naisi, of the king's household, to her nursling, and they fled to Alba (Scotland) with his two brothers, and a company of warriors. The Alban king gave them quarters; but seeing Deirdré's beauty, claimed her: Naisi defeated him, and took possession of a region by the western sea. The champions of Erinn lament his exile and hard fortune.

Now comes the drama itself. The tale at the slightest touch falls into five acts. The great passions of Love, Jealousy, and Revenge, accompanied by Treachery and War, tread the stage; whilst a mystic over-world is shadowed forth in Deirdré's visionary warnings, and the Druid's potent spell. It may be thus arranged:

Act I.

Scene I.—King Concobar presides in the Royal Banquet-Hall of Emania, amidst the nobles, bards, musicians, historians, and heralds of his realm. When song, music, story, and pedigree have ended, the king, raising his voice, questions if any saw hall more fair, and if aught be lacking. They cry out in praise and negation. But he: "There is a lack: the Three Torches of Gaelic Valour are absent. Envoys shall go for them." All hail his clemency. One of three champions—Conall, Cuchulainn, or Fergus—must be Naisi's guarantor. Concobar takes each apart, and asks what he would do if Usnach's Sons were slain. Conall and Cuchulainn declare they would slay all who harmed them; —Fergus that he would spare the king alone. Fergus is chosen, and sent with his two sons, pledged, however, to speed his wards to Emania when they land, be it day or night.

Scene II.—The Exiles are in their hunting booth of woven boughs, at Loch Etive, in Alba. Naisi and Deirdré sit, playing chess. A sound comes over the water: " That is the call of a man of Erinn," says Naisi, raising his head. Deirdré twice dissuades him, pressing the game. At the third call Naisi orders his brother, Ardan, to meet the envoys. Then Deirdré, confessing she knew the sound, tells her first premonition. She had had a dream that three ravens came with honey in their beaks, who flew away with drops of their blood instead.

Scene III.—Ardan enters with the three envoys, Fergus and his sons, Fair Illan and Red Buiné. After cordial greetings news is asked of Erinn, and Fergus tells how they come with sweetest news, Concobar's sanction for their return, under Fergus's guarantee. Deirdré dissuades them: their sway is greater in Alba than Concobar's in Erinn. But Fergus pleads: "Better is one's country than all things else, for 'tis unpleasing, however great be the power and prosperity, if we see not our native land each day." "True," said Naisi, "dearer is Erinn than Alba to me, though greater my sway in Alba." The guarantee of Fergus secures his trust.

Scene IV.—Their bark has left the shore, and Deirdré looking back at the receding mountains sings her sad, sweet lay of Farewell, recalling all the happiness that filled the glens, when the four dwelt there together.

ACT II.

Scene I.—They land on the northern shore of Erinn. Chief Barach welcomes them to his mansion, with great display of feeling, thrice kissing each of his guests. Then he bids Fergus to a banquet. Now Fergus was pledged to speed his wards at once to Emania, but it was one of his bonds as a knight not to refuse such an invitation. He reddened with wrath and vexation, and divining the plot of Concobar's vassal, vehemently reproaches Barach. But the latter holds him to his bond.

Scene II.—Fergus lays the matter before the Sons of Usnach, for whom he is bond—a tacit appeal. But Deirdré cries out: "Forsake the feast; forsake not the Sons of Usnach." Fergus pleads that he sends his sons with them. Naisi haughtily remarks that "this was much for him, but they were wont to be their own defence." They depart, leaving Fergus to his suffering.

Scene III.—Journeying through forests and wilds, Deirdré suggests that they retire to the isle of Rathlin till the feast be over : Naisi refuses to retire. The sons of Fergus recall his potent guarantee and their presence. Then Deirdré, having fallen again into visioned sleep, relates that she had seen Fair Illan beheaded, and Red Buiné unhurt, and foretells the latter's treachery.

Scene IV.—They stand at last upon the Height of Willows, overlooking fair Emania. Deirdré points to the Cloud of Blood which hangs above the fateful city, and implores Naisi to pass it by and go to Cuchulainn in Dundelgan, returning to Emania when Fergus should be free. Naisi would not deign to show sign of fear, and then Deirdré sang her last lay of warning, in which she tenderly reminded him how he and she had never differed in the old days. " Take it for an omen of treachery," she says, " if Concobar receive us not in his mansion amongst his nobles, but send us to the Red Branch Mansion."

ACT III.

Scene I.—King Concobar is banqueting amongst his nobles once more. They hear knocking without, at the gate of Emania. The king gives orders that if the Sons of Usnach come they shall be entertained in the Red Branch Mansion. Then, after a time, Concobar calls for one to go and report if Deirdré be still beautiful as before. Her nurse Lebarcam accepts the mission.

Scene II.—Naisi and Deirdré are also, once again, seated at the chess table. Lebarcam enters and embraces them in delight and anguish. She warns them of the deathless jealousy, enmity, and treachery of the king, bidding to close and barricade the Red Branch House, and keep keen watch. She sings her song of sorrow.

Scene III.—Lebarcam returns to the monarch's hall, with the good news that the Sons of Usnach are so mighty that with them he could now conquer Erinn, and the ill tidings that Deirdré's beauty had passed away. This lulls Concobar's jealousy; but after a time he called for another spy. None offering he reminds Trendorn that Naisi had killed his father. Trendorn goes out, and afterwards returns wounded. He had found the mansion barred and closed, save one forgotten casement. He looked in. Deirdré turning, saw his face, and he hers; she spoke to Naisi, who flung a chessman which smote him through the eye. "He who made that cast," said Concobar, "would conquer a kingdom if his life were left him. What of Deirdré?" "Deirdré is the most beautiful woman alive," says the spy. Then the king's jealous rage bursts bounds: he commands an instant attack on the Red Branch, and the banquet is broken up in disorder.

Act IV.

Scene I.—Inside the hall of the Red Branch. Three fierce shouts are heard without; and the flash of torches gleams through the casement slits. Naisi challenges the assailants: "Who come?" "Concobar and Ulster," is the answer. Naisi resumes chess-playing, leaving the

matter to his guarantors. Illan calls the king to respect
the guarantee of Fergus. The wrathful monarch demands
revenge on those who bore off his bride. Deirdré bitterly
denounces the treason of Fergus. " If he have betrayed
thee, so shall not I," cried Red Buiné. He rushes forth.
The crash of arms is heard from Buiné's victor-raid.
Then a pause. Deirdré, looking out from her place of
espial, reports that Buiné and Concobar are parleying.
She hears their words : the king has offered their champion
lands and dignities. He accepts. "Fit son of a false
father," she cries.

Scene II.—Fair Illan dons his arms : "While lives
this small straight sword in my hand I will not betray
you," he says. He rushes forth, shouts of terror are
heard, and Illan returns triumphant to where Naisi and
Ainlé are seated playing chess. Forth again he goes,
with a lighted torch in his left hand, and clears a space
around the house, littering it with dead.

Scene III.—"Where is Fiacra, my son?" cries Conco-
bar : Fiacra appears, and the king commands him to
encounter Illan, his equal in age. " He bears his father's
arms : take thou mine—Ocean my shield, ·my victor-
darts, my green glaive." The young champions meet in
fierce battle. Illan drives down Fiacra beneath the
shield. Then a strange weird hollow sound arises—
the roar of Concobar's shield for its bearer's peril.
From afar the three Great Waves of Erinn answer
roaring back. Called by them to save his king, as he
thought, Conall comes rushing to the field, and smites

Illan from behind. They speak, and Conall learns the dread truth. "By my hand of valour," exclaims Conall, "Concobar shall take his son dead in vengeance for his treason." He strikes off Fiacra's head, and flees. Then Illan, flinging his arms into the house he had protected, bids Naisi defend himself, and dies.

ACT V.

Scene I.—The flare of flames shows the Ultonians advancing to fire the house. Ainlé strides forth, makes his battle raid, and drives them off. Next Ardan goes forth and returns in triumph. Lastly Naisi—then Concobar gives the "Battle of the Morning;" the Ultonians flee before the outrush of the Three Champions and their men, who remain victorious.

Scene II.—Concobar appeals to Catbad, his Druid. He urges that all Ultonians will be destroyed, unless his magic power impede it, and pledges his hero-word that harm shall not befall the Sons of Usnach if they submit. The Druid, hearing this, exerts his science, and the Sons of Usnach feel as though surrounded by "a viscid sea of whelming waves," and the earth seems to vanish beneath them.

Scene III.—The Three Champions strive for a time. Their weapons at last fall from their hands. Then the Ultonians approach and make them captive. Concobar commands that they be killed. None obeys the order, till a Norse prince, whose father and brother Naisi had killed, consents. Each of the younger brothers asks to be slain first : Naisi demands that they all be beheaded together by the keen sword of Manannan. It is done. Three shouts of heavy lamentation arise from the Ultonians.

Scene IV.—Deirdré stands alone, all distraught, her golden tresses dishevelled and torn. She recites aloud the heroic feats, great adventures, and deeds of friendship of her beloved Naisi, and of his faithful brethren. The glory of past happiness is evoked, and she sings their death-song in tearless anguish. "After this lay, Deirdré flung herself upon Naisi in the grave, and died forthwith." The Ultonians raise their cam (tomb) and inscribe their names in Ogham.

Scene V.—Solitary on a rock, the dread figure of the deceived Druid appears, amid a weird mist of enchantment. He stretches forth his hands over Emania, and utters the terrible malediction against the royal city, its false king, and the Ultonians, so that the city shall be burned to the ground by Fergus, that nor Concobar nor his race shall rule in it for ever, and that wailing and anguish shall not cease in Ulster, by day or by night, till that generation perish.

From this outline, it will be seen how naturally the tale resolves itself into a Tragedy. There is manifestly dramatic purpose shown in repeating the opening royal banquet-scene, followed by the peaceful chess-scene of Act I., under contrasting circumstances in Act III. The characters are well sustained, and the heroine is kept prominent. It is difficult to suppose its characters were never impersonated by male and female actors—declaiming their different parts. The lays were sung, accompanied by music. If we remember that the Gael are dramatic even in conversation, and that masquerading parties (with deer-skin masks) used to visit Anglo-Irish quarters, such as Charlemont, the probability becomes almost a certainty. This piece may, therefore, be the first Tragedy, outside of the classic languages, in the literature of Europe.

FAND AND CUCHULAINN [1] (pp. 97-101).

The ancient tale entitled "The Sick Bed of Cuchulainn and the only Jealousy of Emer" was cited by O'Curry as a specimen of the Irish language, as old and as pure as that of Cormac's Glossary, which dates from the ninth century. Its tone and its theme are more ancient still, and clearly date from pre-Christian times. The following summary will suffice to explain the poems quoted in this work.

The Ultonians were wont to hold a Fair at the feast of Summer's end (November 1st), on the plain of Muirteimné (now in Louth). Once, at this time, there came upon the lake two lovely birds linked together with gold.

---

[1] "The Sick Bed of Cuchulainn and the only Jealousy of Emer." From "The Yellow Book of Slane." "Atlantis," Vols. I., II. Edited and translated by Professor O'Curry, 1858.

Cuchulainn sought to obtain them for his beloved, but his casts, hitherto unerring, now failed; and turning away, depressed, he leaned against a rock and slept. It seemed to him that two women drew near: one in green, one in five-fold crimson. Each in turn smiled on him and smote him with a horse-switch, until he felt near death. When night came he stood up and spoke in his sleep, bidding his friends take him to the Speckled Palace of Emania; but he could neither answer their questions nor converse. He remained in this state till another Summer-end approached, his friends keeping watch and ward about his Couch of Decline. One day an envoy came, who claimed his protection, and addressed him. In a lay, he bade Cuchulainn know that the daughters of Aed Abrat could heal him, that Fand[1] desired to become his bride, and that Liban would come, at Summer-end, to guide him to the Happy Land. Before leaving he gave his name, Aengus, son of Aed Abrat.

When he departed Cuchulainn arose, drew his hand across his eyes, spoke, and went forth to the rock where he had slept. There he beheld the green-clad woman approach again: she was Liban, and she invited him to the Fairy Abode in Magh Mell—the Plain of Happiness, where lived her husband Labraid, "quick hand at sword," amid beautiful women and learned men, in a mansion upheld by columns of silver and of crystal. In guerdon for Cuchulainn's help in battle for one day, he would give

---

[1] Fand had been the bride of the Sea-god Manannan, who had forsaken her.

him Fand. Cuchulainn declined to go, on the invitation
of a woman, but allowed his charioteer Laeg to go with
her. These fared away past the Plain of Races and the
Tree of Triumphs, and the fair-green of Emain, until they
arrived at the assembly-place of the Forests, where Aed
Abrat and his daughters were. Laeg returned with a
message from Fand,[1] imploring the champion to come as
the battle would begin that day. Laeg sang the beauties
of their palace, with its splendid kings, coloured couches,
swift steeds, strange crimson and silver trees, fountain,
ever-flowing mead-vats, and above all, yellow-haired Fand,
fairer than all the women of Erinn. Were Laeg's all
Erinn, and the kingship of the Happy Hills, he would
give them, to abide there for ever. Others were beautiful,
but she took hosts out of their senses. Then Cuchulainn
went forth to Fairy Land, encountered the enemy with
Labraid, and, coming in triumph from the battle was
welcomed by Fand and her maidens, with the lay:
" Splendid stands the Charioteer." Cuchulainn abode
there a month; on leaving, it was agreed that Fand
should come wherever he wished. She came to Ibar
(now Newry). They were playing chess here, when Fand
perceived Cuchulainn's mortal bride, Emer, with fifty
maidens, deckt with gold, but armed with green knives
who came to slay her. Cuchulainn took Fand into his

---

[1] " Fand now was the daughter of Aed Abrat ; 'aed' is fire—the
fire of the eye is the pupil. 'Fand' then is the name of the 'tear'
which passes over it. It was for her purity she was so named and
for her beauty ; for there was naught else in being comparable to her.'

chariot for protection, and avoided Emer. After debate, Emer said: "I shall not refuse the woman, if thou followest her. But, indeed, everything red is beautiful, everything new is bright, everything high is lovely, everything common is bitter, everything we are without is prized, everything known is neglected, till all knowledge is known. Thou youth," said she, "we were at one time in dignity with thee, and we would be so again, if it were pleasing to thee." And she was overcome with grief. "Thou art pleasing to me," said he, "and thou shalt be pleasing as long as I live."

Then Fand, broken-hearted, exclaimed: "Let me be repudiated." "It were fitter to repudiate me," said Emer. "Not so," said Fand, "it is I who shall be repudiated, and I have long been in peril of it." She fell into great grief and depression, and spoke her "Farewell to Cuchulainn."

Now Manannan had become aware of Fand's danger and he sped thither from the east. "He was in their presence, and no one perceived him but Fand alone." The sight of him filled her with terror. She thought the Spirit-spouse, who had abandoned her, now came to increase her humiliation, but he had magnanimously come to protect her. She sang her lost estate. "Even if to-day he were nobly constant, my mind loves not jealousy: affection is a subtle thing. It makes its way, without labour."[1] Manannan saluted her, and bade her

---

[1] Cf. "Love will venture in, where it daurna well be seen."—
BURNS.

choose between them. She avowed her preference for
Cuchulainn, but he had forsaken her, and so she would
return with Manannan who had no queen.[1] Cuchulainn
(to whom Manannan was invisible) asked Laeg what had
happened, and when it was made clear to him, he ran
distraught, without food or drink, among the mountains,
and so remained for long.

At last the Druids spoke their incantations over him,
and laid hold of his limbs until he had recovered a little
of his senses. "He then besought them for a drink.
The Druids gave him a drink of forgetfulness. The
moment he drank the drink he did not remember Fand,
and all the things he had done." Emer also, being in
no better state, was given draughts of oblivion; whilst
Manannan shook his cloak between Fand and Cuchulainn
so that they should never meet again.

Appended to this legend, there is a concluding state-
ment, seemingly added by some Christian copyist. It
explains that "the demoniac power was great before the
Faith, and such was its greatness, that the demons used
to corporeally tempt the people, and show them delights
and secrets, as of how they would be in immortality."

There are passages here, as in other ancient Gaelic
legends, of interest to the physiological psychologist.
Unwittingly, the writers have enumerated many signs of
extreme nervous excitability in Cuchulainn, such as the

---

[1] The sudden presence of Manannan, invisible to all the actors in
this piece, except Fand, suggests the source from which sprites in
modern plays and pantomimes have come.

distortion of his face in battle, his convulsive leaps, his long inexplicable debility, into which he was thrown by strokes of wands, and from which he rouses suddenly. Symptoms similar, in many respects, are found in cases of "induced lethargy," or hypnotic trance. It is remarkable, also, that when aroused, Cuchulainn seeks a certain place (as if "suggested") and there beholds a vision of Fand. The Druids, by their incantations, seemed to possess the power of inducing hypnosis.

Descriptions such as those given, though exaggerated, were founded on observed facts, and are quite in harmony with our knowledge of neurotic exaltation in Celtic races.

COPPER AND BRONZE BOATS.

A curious anticipation of modern inventions is found in this passage in "The Sick-bed of Cuchulainn : "

"They saw the little copper ship upon the lake before them. They then went into the ship, and they went into the island."—*Atlantis*, Vol. IV., p. 381.

Now the extant Irish manuscript from which this is translated was compiled by a grandson of Conn of the poor, an Ulster noble, who died in the year 1031. It is therefore certain that the Irish had conceived the idea of metal ships at a time long anterior to their recent invention. They may also have reduced this idea to practice, for their riveted cauldrons in the Royal Irish Academy's Museum show great skill, and quite lately the model of a small gold ship was found. For mention of a bronze boat, see p. 184.

THE KING'S LAY [1] (pp. 357-369).

This paraphrase is founded on an episode in the tale of " The Sick-bed of Cuchulainn," and supplies a strangely remarkable example of induced hypnosis amongst the ancient Irish. Thus runs the story :

There had been no sovereign over Erinn for seven years, and four of its five realms met, in the year of the world 5167, at Tara, to select one who should be king. " They deemed it an evil that the Hill of Supremacy and Lordship of Erinn, that is Tara, should be without the rule of king upon it, and they deemed it an evil that the tribes should be without a king's government to judge their houses." They would not take the Ultonians into their council.

In order to discover a suitable person, they prepared a bull-feast, thus : " a white bull was killed, and one man eat enough of his flesh and of his broth ; and a Charm of Truth was pronounced on him by four Druids ; and he saw in a dream the shape of the man who should be made king there, and his form, and his description, and the sort of work that he was engaged in. The man screamed out of his sleep, and described what he saw to the kings, namely, a young noble strong man, with two red streaks around him, and he sitting over the pillow of a man in a decline, in Emania, the royal capital of the Ultonians." The Druids were thus able to produce what modern medicine has recently recognized as hypnosis.

[1] " The Sick-bed of Cuchulainn," etc.

When the envoy arrives and identifies Lugai, Cuchulainn orally instructs him in the duties of a king. The original is printed as prose, by O'Curry, but is (I think) in irregular "Rosg," composed of brief injunctions, beginning thus in O'Curry's translation: "You shall not be a terrified man in a furious slavish fierce battle. You shall not be flighty inaccessible haughty. You shall not be intractable proud precipitate passionate. You shall not be bent down by the intoxication of much wealth."

These injunctions are rendered into English verse, in a very free paraphrase.

THE FATE OF THE CHILDREN OF LIR (pp. 140-143).

This, the second "Sorrow of Story," concerns the gifted Dé Danann people. The tale relates that, after their defeat at Tailltin by the Milesian invaders (A.D. 3500), they held a general assembly, where their nobles chose Bove the Red as king. Lir withdrew in wrath, but after a time espoused Bove's daughter, Aev, and submitted. Twice she bore him twins (one of whom, Fionnuala, was a girl), then she died. Lir survived through the love he bore his children, and espoused his dead wife's sister, Aifa. For a time she loved them also, then sickened with jealousy, plotted their death, and, failing in that design, changed them by druidic power into swans, dooming them to abide for a long period on Loch Derryvara, in Meath ; for a second period on the current of the Moyle (now the Mull) of Cantire, and for a third period on the sea of Erris (Mayo). They should never recover human forms until the Tonsured (St. Patrick) came to Erinn. When Bove the king, a mighty Druid, heard of the crime he transformed Aifa into what she most hated, a demon of the air. It was ordered that henceforth no swan should be killed in Erinn, and even still, as O'Curry wrote, it is considered that an ill fate follows their killing.

The prose narrative is interspersed by lays, in which Fionnuala describes, and laments their fate. The most pathetic are those given in this volume, in which she contrasts their bitter exile on the Moyle with the former delights of home ; and where, when the term of banishment is over, coming back joyful to their native city, she tells how they find it empty, desolate, overgrown with weeds and forests.

The end of their doom came with the coming of Christianity. On a day, the brothers heard a strange sound, and were greatly alarmed, but Fionnuala bade them rejoice, in a little lay :

> ".Hark, the cleric's bell now rings,
> Rise, and raise aloft your wings ;
> Thank the True God for that voice
> Listen, grateful, and rejoice.

> " Right it is that he should reign
> Who shall part you from your pain ;
> Part you from rude rock pillows
> And part you from rough billows.

> " Hence, I rede you now give ear,
> Gentle Children of King Lir !
> Let us faith in heaven sing
> While the cleric's bell doth ring."

This old romantic tale has supplied themes to Moore, Dr. Todhunter, Dr. Douglas Hyde, Mrs. Katharine Tynan-Hinkson, and some others.

FATE OF THE CHILDREN OF TUIRENN[1] (p. 189).

In this, the third of "The Sorrows of Story," the visible and the invisible, the historical and the mythical are mingled. This summary will suffice:

Nuad of the Silver Hand was sovereign of the fair and skilful Dé Dananns. At this time the Fomorians, another section of the ancient Northmen, levied tribute on the Dé Dananns, which was paid each year at the Hill of Usna, which was also named Balor's Hill (in Westmeath), where the five parts of Erinn met. The king had called an assembly. Soon they beheld an army advance, whose chief was radiant as the sun at setting. This was Lugh the Long-handed, chief of the Fairy Cavalcade, a friend of the Dé Dananns. When the grim Fomorian tax gatherers appeared, Lugh fell upon them and slew all but nine, whom he spared to go as envoys to Lochlann (*i.e.* Norway), where their king Balor ruled —who was Lugh's grandsire.

Balor, on hearing the tidings, sped his son Breas with ships and men, who promised to bring the head of Lugh, the Ioldanach (craft master) to Berbe.[2] Then the Fo-

---

[1] "Atlantis," Vol. IV. Text edited and translated by Professor O'Curry.

[2] This may be intended for Bergen.

morian king, following Breas to the port, made a mighty
menace :

"Give battle to the Ioldanach and cut off his head,"
he said, "and tie that island which is called Erinn to the
stern of your ships and your good barques, and let the
dense verging water take its place, and set it upon the
north side of Lochlann (Norway), and not one of the
Dé Danann people will follow it there till doom."

Breas landed at Easdara (now Ballysadare, Sligo) and
took the spoil of West Connacht.   One morning he cried
out amazed at seeing the sunrise in the west—but it was
the radiance from the face of Lugh, who led the Fairy
Cavalcade against him.   Lugh saluted and parleyed,
being of half Dé Danann, half Fomorian blood; but
Breas, refusing restitution, was defeated.

Now Lugh's father had been slain in a blood-feud by
the Children of Tuirenn.   The earth gave evidence
against them.   Then in expiation of their offence, they
were condemned, with the sanction of the Dé Dananns,
to perform nine tasks of exceeding difficulty, the first
being to obtain apples from the Hesperides.   Their
doom was a prolonged torture.   The tale is chiefly con-
cerned with their wonderful and perilous adventures.
After many dangers and disappointments, wounded to
death, they accomplished their last task and returned to
Erinn.   This ship approached its shores, having suffered
on the weary seas, and Brian, the strongest, cried out:
"I see Benn Edair, Tuirenn's fort, and Tara of the
Kings!"   "We were full of health could we see them,"

exclaimed another, "and for thine honour's love, raise our heads on thy breast that we may see Erinn from us, and then—come life or death, we care not, after that."

They reached their country and their fort, wounded to death, and their father bore to Tara the result of their last victorious effort. All their tasks were done, but they were dying, and their father implored Lugh to give him one of their spoils—a magic skin, which should cover and cure them. Lugh, remembering his own father's fate, remorselessly refused their father's prayer. Then Brian was borne into his presence, bleeding, in order to beseech that his younger brothers at least might be saved. Lugh pitilessly replied that for earth's expanse in gold he would not yield the skin, because of their deed.

Then Brian returned and lay down between his brothers, and they died together. Tuirenn spoke their dirge, and, falling upon the breasts of his sons, his soul went forth from him. They were buried in one grave.

DIVER'S DRESS IN THE TUIRENN TALE.

Besides the strange parallel in Balor's speech to a passage in John Bright's, there is a curious anticipation of the diving dress (invented about 1825!) in the following:

"And then Brian put on his water dress, with a transparency of *gloine* (of crystal or glass) upon his head; and he made a water-leap, and it is said that he was for a fortnight walking in the salt water seeking the Isle of Fianchairé."—*Atlantis*, Vol. IV., p. 219.

LAYS OF FINN AND THE FIANNA: OSSIANIC POEMS
(pp. 115-135).

A long and acrid contest has been waged between some of the Gael of Erinn and of Alba in relation to this poetry. The cause of the war lay in the strategy of Macpherson, who, in order to exalt the Ossianic poetry which he professed to translate, depreciated certain later Irish Ossianic lays. He also, indeed, bore ardent testimony to the beauty of Irish love poetry, and the skill of the Irish bards; but this was passed over. When it was ascertained that Macpherson had no original for his pretended translation, the reaction against him made men forget that the poor Highland tutor, who could combine Gaelic fragments into a work so remarkable as his "Ossian," must have been a man of genius.

O'Curry cannot assign any certain date to the poems attributed to Fionn (or Finn) and Oisin (or Ossian). He remarks, however, that some of these compositions are contained in the "Book of Leinster," which was compiled in the early part of the twelfth century, "and certainly from much more ancient books."

Mr. W. F. Skene, in his introduction to the Dean of Lismore's Book, states that the oldest poem of this character in MSS. preserved in the Highlands is found prior to the year 1500. Mr. Skene thinks that Ossianic poetry passed through three stages: 1st. There were pure poems common to Ireland and Scotland (and some to the Isle of Man and to Wales); 2nd. Some of the archaic forgotten verses were replaced by a prose narrative; 3rd. "The third class of Ossianic poems belongs principally to that period when, during the sway of the Lords of the Isles, Irish influence was so much felt on the language and literature of the Highlands, and when the Highland bards and Seannachies were trained in bardic schools presided over by Irish bards of eminence."

Though I believe, with Mr. Skene, that in many cases a later prose romance enshrines archaic poems, I also believe that, in some cases, as in "The Fate of the Children of Usnach," there was another order of composition. Here we had the story presented in dramatic form, with ancient lays introdued to be sung, just as some of Shakespeare's dramas include older English ballads.

The most impressive fact in connection with these ancient poems is their immense vitality. Thus Hector Mac Lean, the Bard of Islay, in a preface to the "Ultonian Hero-Ballads"[1] says: "These ballads have for many centuries been sung and rehearsed in the Highlands. There have been many who could sing 'Fraoch' till very lately in Islay. A few years ago Angus Mac Eachern often sang and rehearsed 'Conlaoch,' and many other old Gaelic poems, but there are few left now in Islay who can sing old Gaelic ballads or rehearse old Gaelic poems."

"In Ireland," O'Curry writes, "I have heard my father

[1] "Ultonian Hero-Ballads: collected in the Highlands and Western Isles of Scotland," by Hector Mac Lean. Glasgow: Sinclair, 1892. The Mac Leans claim descent from the Irish Fitzgeralds, as the Mac Leods from the last Norse king of Man.

sing these Ossianic poems, and remember distinctly the air and the manner of their singing." Previous to this there had been a teacher, named O'Brien, "who spent much of his time in my father's house," O'Curry adds, "and who was the best singer of Oisin's poems that his contemporaries had ever heard. He had a rich and powerful voice; and often, on a calm summer day, he would go with a party into a boat on the lower Shannon, at my native place, where the river is eight miles wide; and having rowed to the middle of the river, they used to lie on their oars . . . on which occasions O'Brien was always prepared to sing his choicest pieces, among which were no greater favourites than Oisin's poems. So powerful was the singer's voice that it often reached the shores at either side of the boat, in Clare and Kerry, and often called the labouring men and women from the neighbouring fields at both sides down to the water's edge to enjoy the strains of the music."

How noble and astonishing would such statements seem if they related to the peasantry of other countries. If the Venetian boatmen were heard singing Dante from their gondolas, the Norman peasants the Romance of Roland, the Spanish the lays of the Cid Campeador, the German the Nibelungenlied, the Norse the Eddas— if the English peasants assembled to sing the verse of Chaucer, Layamon's "Brut," or the "Battle of Brunanburh," there would be just and general praise, with wise and generous encouragement. A different policy directed the extinction of the intellectual inheritance of the Gael, because pigmy prejudice ruled where large intelligence would have guided.

DIRGE FOR CAEL, BY CRÉDÉ, OR GELGEIS (p. 126).

When the great battle of Ventry Harbour, famed in Irish romance, was over Crédé and other gentle and simple women of Erinn went over the shoreward region seeking the bodies of their husbands on the field of slaughter. Whilst still searching, Crédé observed a heron risking her own life to defend her two younglings against a fierce fox. "No wonder I should love my gentle comrade," she said, "when a bird is in such anguish over its birds." Then she heard the stag on the mountain over the bay, belling lamentably from pass to pass, for his dead hind. They had dwelt in the forest nine years together, and now, for nineteen days, he had touched neither grass nor water, mourning her loss. "No shame for me to find death through grief for Cael," said Crédé, "when the stag is shortening his life for a hind." Then she met Fergus on the battle-field, and asked had he tidings of Cael for her. "I have," answered Fergus, "for he and the chief of the household of the King of the World (the invader) have drowned each other." "Little the need for me to bewail Cael and the Clanna Baiscné, for the birds and the billows do strongly bewail them." She sang his death-song, and when it was ended, the soul of Crédé parted from her body for grief of Cael, the son of Crimtann. Her grave was made over Ventry, a stone was raised above her tomb, and her funeral games were celebrated.

This account of the poem is summarized from the translation given by Professor Kuno Meyer,[1] who states that the Bodleian manuscript from which it was taken dates from the fourteenth century, and was written out for the Lady Saiv O'Maillé.

One episode in the romance is peculiarly chivalric and pathetic. When the news spread that Erinn had been invaded, the aged king of Ulster lamented his inability to march against them. His only son, Goll, a boy of thirteen, offered to go, but was forbidden on account of his years, and confined. He, however, could not bear to remain aloof, and, taking arms from Emania, he and his twelve foster-brothers escaped to the battle-field. The twelve youths fell in the fight, and Goll, seized with grief and battle-fury, slew the hostile champion, but lost his senses. His madness has been taken as the theme of a powerful poem by Mr. W. B. Yeats.

St. Columbanus: An Epoch-making Poem (p. 36).

In the evolution of European verse, one poem, the epistle of St. Columbanus to Fedolius, deserves a most prominent place. It has been mentioned with praise because of its singular classic form and grace and ethical

---

[1] Meyer, "Anecdota Oxon." Oxford: Clarendon Press, 1885. Another version is given in "Sylva Gadelica," by Mr. Standish Hayes O'Grady, in which the heroine is identified as Crédé.

interest by several writers. None has discovered that it is the first Latin poem (not being a hymn) which presents a perfect system of vowel or asonant rime. This poem, copied and circulated by his great monastic Schools of Annegray, Luxueil, and Bobbio, by that of his famous disciple St. Gall, and by the Irish professors of the School of Charlemagne, and of the Palace, must have exercised a controlling influence over the emerging literatures of Europe. Not less important than its asonance is the fact that it introduces into Latin verse the use of returning words, or burthens, with variations, which supply the vital germs of the rondeau and the ballade. It is also very curious that St. Columbanus describes how to construct his poem, just as Voiture told how to make a rondeau and La Fontaine a ballade. The Gaelic precursor of the rondeau is seen in St. Columba's short poem, "The Fall of the Book-Satchels." St. Columbanus died in 615, and, in a few hexameters accompanying this light Adonic verse, he makes a touching allusion to his debility and age. He died soon after.

To appreciate the harmonious riming, the vowels should be pronounced in the Continental manner : we must also remember that the Irish (and the Spaniards after them) recognize rime between the "slender" vowels, i, e (and here æ), and amongst the broad vowels, a, o, u. Now, in this poem, the dissyllabic rimes are so chosen as to produce the fullest effect and variety. Thus we find, (1) a slender and a broad vowel end-rime (*quæso, versu*); then, (2) a broad and a slender (*—ali, nobis*); next, two broad vowels (—*orum*, *parua*); and lastly (4) two slender vowels (—*enter*, *redde*). Again, these rimes are varied in distribution, so that sometimes they alternate, sometimes several of the same kind are grouped together —an early suggestion of *la poésie libre*.

This discovery seems of such importance to the history of European literature that I quote the poem in full, ranging the lines according to their asonant rimes.

EPISTOLA COLUMBANI AD FEDOLIUM.[1]

Accipe, quæso,
    Nunc bipedali
Condita uersu
    Carminulorum
    Munera parua :
    Tuque frequenter
    Mutua nobis
    Obsequiorum
Debita redde.
Nam uelut æstu,
    Flantibus Austris,
    Arida gaudent
Imbribus arua
Sic tua nostras
Missa frequenter
    Lætificabit
Pagina mentes.

    Non ego posco

    Nunc perituræ
    Munera gazæ :
    Non quod auarus
Semper egendo
    Congregat aurum :
Quod sapientum
Lumina cæcat
    Et uelut ignis
        Flamma perurit
    Improba corda.
    Sæpe nefanda
    Crimina multis
    Suggerit auri
Dira cupido,
E quibus ista
    Nunc tibi pauca
Tempore prisco
Gesta retexam.
    Extitit ingens

---

[1] Ex. MSS. bibliothecæ monasterii S. Galli, anno 1604 a M. Goldasto et Henr. Canisio edita. In Veterum Epistolarum Hibernicarum Sylloge. Usserius, 1632.

Causa malorum
Aurea pellis.
   Corruit auri
Munere paruo
Cœna Dearum ;
Ac tribus illis
Maxima lis est
Orta Deabus.
   Hinc populavit
Trojugenarum
Ditia regna
Dorica pubes.

Juraque legum
Fasque fidesque
Rumpitur auro.
Impia quippe
Pygmalionis
Regis ob aurum
Gesta leguntur.
Sic Polydorum
Hospes auarus
Incitus auro
Fraude necauit.
Fœmina sæpe
Perdit ob aurum
Casta pudorem.
Non Jouis auri
Fluxit in imbre :
Sed quod adulter
Obtulit aurum
Aureus ille
Fingitur imber.
Amphiaraum
Prodidit auro
Perfida conjunx.
Hectoris heros
Uendidit auro
Corpus Achilles

Et reserari
Munere certo
Nigra feruntur
Limina Ditis.
   Nunc ego possem
Plura referre
Ni breuitatis
Causa uetaret.
Hæc tibi, Frater
Inclyte, parua
Litterularum
Munera mittens,
Suggero uanas
Linquere curas.

Desine, quæso,
Nunc animosos
Pascere pingui
Farre caballos :
   Lucraque lucris
Accumulando,
   Desine nummis
Addere nummos.
Ut quid iniquis
   Consociaris,
   Munera quarum
Crebra receptas ?
Odit iniqui
Munera Christus.
Hæc sapienti
Despicienda,
Qui fugitiuæ
   Atque caducæ
Cernere debet
Tempora uitæ.
   Sufficet autem
Ista loquaci
Nunc cecinisse
Carmina uersu.

Nam nova forsan
Esse videtur
Ista legenti
Formula uersus.
Sed tamen illa
Trojugenarum
Inclyta uates
Nomina Sappho,
Uersibus istis
Dulce solebat
Edere carmen.
Si tibi cura
Forte uolenti
Carmina tali
Condere uersu,
Semper et unus
Ordine certo
Dactylus istic
Incipiat pes :
Inde sequenti
Parte trochæus
Proximus illi
Rite locetur.

Sæpe duabus
Claudere longis
Ultima versus
Iure licebit.
Tu modo, Frater
Alme Fedoli,
Nectare nobis
Dulcior omni,
Floridiora
Doctiloquorum
Carmina linquens,
Frivola nostra
Suscipe lætus..
Sic tibi Christus
Arbiter orbis
Omnipotentis
Unica proles,
Dulcia uitæ
Guadia reddat :
Qui sine fine,
Nomine Patris
Cuncta gubernans
Regnat in æuum.

SEDULIUS: BARDIC POEM IN LATIN (p. 38).

Whilst the great bard, Sedulius, in the fifth century, gave in his "Carmen Paschale" the first Christian epic, another Sedulius, in the ninth century, obtained distinction in lighter verse, as well as in prose. Appearing at the time it did, the graceful poetry of the later Sedulius must have greatly influenced the nascent literatures of Europe. Preserving the Latin metrical forms, he infused into the structure of his verse the subtle and profuse Irish rime, a fact which has passed unnoticed by his learned editor, Herr Duemmler.[1]

Sedulius's poem, " The Contest of the Rose and the Lily "—which should have been translated by Moore, so kindred in spirit, is given here. In the first two stanzas I have marked the bardic alliteration and other rimes :

DE ROSÆ LILIIQUE CERTAMINE,

SEDULIUS CECINIT.

POETA.

Ciclica quadri*fidis* curre*b*ant tempora m*etis*,
uernabat uar*io* tellus decorataque p*eplo*,
lacteo cum ros*eis* certabant lilia s*ertis*,
cum rosa sic cro*cc*o sermo*nes* prompserat *ore* :

ROSA.

Purpura dat regnum, fit purpura gloria regni,
regibus ingrato uilescunt alba col*ore*,
albida pallescunt misero marcentia uultu,
puniceus color est toto uenerabilis o*rbe*.

LILIUM.

Me decus auricomum telluris pulcher Apollo
diliget ac niueo faciem uestiuit honore ;
quid, rosa, tanta refers pudibundo perlita fuco
conscia delicti, uultus tibi nonne rubescit.

---

[1] " Sedulii Scotti Carmina Quadraginta ex Codice Bruxellensi " edidit Ernestus Duemmler. Halis Saxonum, 1858. Herr Duemmler gives forty poems selected from the Brussels Codex which contains eighty-seven. This codex dates from the twelfth century. He states that Sedulius left Ireland between 840 and 860 ; that he was probably Abbot of St. Lambert's Monastery, Liége. He was a friend of Guntharius, Archbishop of Cologne, of Haddo, Abbot of Fulda, and mentions five fellow Irish priests, Fergus, Marcus, Benchellus, Dermoth, and Blandus.

Rosa.

Sum soror Auroræ diuis cognata supernis
et me Phebus amat, rutili sum nuntia Phebi.
Lucifer ante meum hilarescit currere uultum
ast mihi uirginei decoris rubet alma uenustas.

Lilium.

Talia cur tumidis eructas uerba loquelis,
quæ tibi dant meritas æterno uulnere penas?
nam diadema tui spinis terebratur acutis,
eheu! quam miserum laniant spineta rosetum!

Rosa.

Ut quid deliras uerbis, occata uenustas,
quæ tu probra refers plenia sunt omnia laude,
conditor omnicreans spina me sepsit acuta,
muniit et roseos præclaro tegmine uultus.

Lilium.

Aureoli decoris mihi uertex comitur almus
nec sum spinigera crudelis septa corona,
profluitat niueis dulci lac ubere mammis,
sic holerum dominam me dicunt esse beatam.

Poeta.

Tunc Uer florigera iuuenis pausabat in herba,
olli tegmen erat pictum uiridantibus herbis,
ipsius ad patulas redolebant balsama nares
floripotensque caput sertis redimibat honoris.

Uer.

Pignora cara mei, cur uos contenditis? inquit,
gnoscite uos geminas tellure parente sorores,
num fas germanas lites agitare superbas?
o rosa pulchra, tace tua gloria claret in orbe,
regia sed nitidis dominentur lilia sceptris.
hinc decus et species uestrum uos laudet in æuum,
forma pudiciciae nostris rosa gliscat in hortis
splendida Phebeo uos lilia crescite uultu,

tu rosa martiribus rutilam das stemmate palmani,
lilia uirgineas turbas decorate stolatas.

POETA.

Et tunc Uer genitor geminis dans oscula pacis
concordat dulces patrio de more puellas.
lilia tunc croceæ dant oscula data sorori
illa sed huic ludens spinetis ore momordit.
lilia uernigenæ ludum risere puellæ
ambroseo bibulum potant et lacte rosetum.
at rosa puniceus calathis fert xenia flores
ac niueam largo germanam ditat honore.

VISION POEMS (p. 39).

In the last century many popular ballads, largely
Jacobite, were constructed on a common model, though
differing in metre. The bard slept, when, suddenly,
there came to him a beautiful maiden, more radiant than
the sun, who comforted him in sorrow, and foretold a
brilliant future for his country. I have found a poem in
Latin elegiac verse, dating from the ninth century, con-
structed in the same manner.[1] So that this Gaelic model
(for the author of the Latin was one of the monks of
St. Gall's) dates back a thousand years. The type seems
to have disappeared for ages and to have been inde-
pendently revived. This is the opening of the Latin
poem, where the vision is Wisdom :

"Umbrifera quadam nocte de pectore somnum
Carpebam fessis luminibusque meis,
Auricomæ quedam tunc fulgens forma puellæ
Clarior enituit sole rubente mihi.

---

[1] In "Reliquie Celtiche : il manoscritto irlandese di San Gallo,"
Constantino Nigra. Firenze, Torino, Roma, 1872.

Illa puro nimis tangens a vertice celum
  Florida tellura dum graditetur ea,
Lumina contulerat radientia fronte superna
  Quis uidet etheria rura mareque simul.
Ubera lactifero referebat pectore bina
  His pascit modicos quos jubet atque rudes.
Sic exorsa sua verba pulcherrima virgo
  Cum gelidus sudor fuderat ossa mea :
Quid miser ut trepidus non sum fallentis imago
  Sed permissu deo uera referre sinor,
Cognita gravigenis sic sum ueneranda latinis
  Utrisque merito signaque dupla veho
Inde Sophia vocor grece Sapientia rome,"[1] etc.

Queen Gormlai's Lament (p. 179).

Perhaps the most pathetic and picturesque figure in
Irish history is that of Queen Gormlai, who lived in the
early part of the tenth century. Daughter of Flann Siona,
King of Ireland, she was, according to an old writer, "a
very fair, vertuous, and learned damosell." She was first
married to Cormac, King of Munster, but he became an
ecclesiastic, renounced the marriage, and restored the
princess with her dowry to her father. From motives of
policy, she was forced to accept King Cearball of Leinster,
and her father and husband, with united forces, made
war upon Munster, defeated, killed, and beheaded its
king-bishop Cormac, in 903. Cearball was wounded,
and Gormlai watched over his sick-bed. Seated one
day at the foot of his couch, she ventured to regret the

---

[1] There are some interlinear emendations which I omit.

mutilation of the dead king-bishop; on which Cearball, in a rage, thrusting forth his foot, threw her upon the floor, in presence of her attendants. She at once left his court, because of this outrage, and sought refuge with her father; but Flann, instead of avenging the insult, sent her back to his ally. Her kinsman, the Prince of Ulster, Niall Glunduv, however, took rapid action, for, gathering the northern clans, he marched to Leinster, offered his protection, and secured her a separation and royal maintenance. Cearball also released her from her spousal vows; but she declined to accept the hand of Niall, and resided with her father. Next year Cearball was killed in battle by the Norse-Irish of Dublin, and then her marriage with Niall was celebrated. Then came a time of prosperity and splendour, when life was full of happiness. Her husband succeeded as Over-king of Ireland. In 917 he planned a great assault upon Dublin, and, confident of triumph, called all comers to share the spoils. The Irish-Norse met him outside their city, at Kilmasog, near Rathfarnham. The cleric who had refused him a horse to leave the battle-field, administered the last sacraments. Queen Gormlai's elder brother was killed there, her younger brother succeeded and reigned for a time. Then the sovereign power passed away from her father's and her husband's houses.

By King Niall, says the old chronicler, "she had issue a son, who was drownded, upon whose death she made many pittiful and learned ditties in Irish." But, "after all which royal marriages she begged from door to door, forsaken of all her friends and allies, and glad to be relieved by her inferiors."

After wanderings, many and sorrowful, she at last received the injury which ultimately proved her death-wound. It came to her in a manner sad and touching as anything poet ever imagined. Having one night taken refuge in an humble hut, she went to sleep on a rude couch. Then: "She dreamed that she saw King Neale Glunduffe, whereupon she got up and sate in her bed to behold him; whom he for anger would forsake, and leave the chamber; and as he was departing in that angry motion (as she thought), she gave a snatch after him, thinking to have taken him by the mantle, to keep him with her, and fell upon one of the bed-sticks of her bed, that it pierced her breast even to the very heart, which received no cure until she died thereof."

During the fatal progress of this "long and grievous wound," she composed some of her "learned and pittiful ditties." That of which a translation is given has surely the very spirit of poetry, and lovers of literature owe gratitude to the Dean of Lismore for its preservation.

Irish Music in Legends (p. 126, etc.).

The ancient Irish were as devoted to music as to literature, and excelled in both. Giraldus Cambrensis, who accompanied King Henry II. to Ireland, and wrote an account of the country, describes the Irish as more skilled in music than any other nation. Two strange legends, translated by O'Curry, may be quoted to show what power was assigned to music in their old imaginative literature.

The "Cruit," or harp, is the first musical instrument mentioned. This reference is found in an ancient historical romance, which professes to describe a battle that was fought, sixteen hundred years before the Christian era, between the Tuata Dé Dananns, and the Viking Fomorians. The Fomorians, defeated at Moy Tuiré (Sligo), retired, taking as their captive the harper of the Dagda—a great chief and druid of their foes. Dagda, the King, and the Champion of the Dé Dananns followed ; and, when the invaders sate at food, the three heroes entered the door of the banqueting house. They saw the harp hanging mute upon the wall, for the music was spell-bound in it, so that it gave answer to none who essayed its chords, till the Dagda evoked it. Thus he spoke : "Come, Murmur of the Apple Tree ; come, Hive of Melody ; come, Summer ; come, Winter, from the mouths of harps, and hollows and pipes." Then the harp sprang from the wall and rushed through the banquet hall, killing nine foemen in its way, till it came to the Dagda. He clasped it, and played the Three Masterpieces of Music—he played the *Goltrai* (plaintive music), until the Fomorian women wept tears ; then he played the *Gentrai* (mirthful music), until their women and young warriors broke into laughter ; lastly he played the *Suantrai* (slumberous music), until the whole host fell asleep. Then the three champions retired safely from the midst of their enemies, who had been eager to slay them.

The second story is stranger and wilder still, though the date assigned to the subject—the Battle of the Hill of Almain (now Allen, Kildare),—is later, A.D. 718. The Over-king, Fergal, who lived at Aileach (near Derry) invaded Leinster to exact the Borumean tribute; he brought with him Donnbo, the most accomplished youth in the world, as regards singing, telling royal stories, mounting spears, and equipping steeds. When the monarch had pitched his tent at Almain, he sent to his minstrel Donnbo, and bade him make melody then, as they would give battle in the morning. Donnbo declared that he was unable that night, "but wherever thou art to-morrow night, I shall make melody for thee. Let the king's fool[1] amuse thee this night." The battle was fought, the Northern army defeated, and both minstrel and monarch were slain—the former in defence of his king.

That night, whilst the Leinster chiefs were feasting and relating their exploits, Murcad, the king's son, challenged any Champion to go forth to the battle-field, and return with a token. A Champion of Munster accepted, donned his arms, and went far into the darkness. At last, upon the battle-field, he came to the place where King Fergal's

---

[1] It is curious that motley was the fool's garb, as in Shakespeare's time in England. The rules regarding colours of dress given in the Book of Ballimote are these: "Mottled to fools, blue to women, crimson to all kings, green and black to noble laymen, white to pious priests."

body lay. Then, in the night-silence, he heard Something near, in the air above him, which said (for he heard the words): "Here is a command to you from the King of the Seven Heavens. Make melody for your lord to-night: though to-night ye be all, pipers, trumpeters, and harpers, fallen on the field. Let nor fear nor feebleness hinder ye from performing for Fergal." Then the Warrior heard arise the music of singers, and trumpeters, and pipers, and harpers—a great variety of music he heard, and better heard he never, before or after. And he heard in a cluster of rushes near him a *Dord Fiansa* (a strange strain)—the sweetest of all the world's music. The Warrior went towards it. "Come not nigh me," said the head. "I quest who thou art?" said the Warrior. "I am the Head of Donnbo; I was bound in bond to sing to the king this night: do not thou interrupt." "Where is the body of Fergal?" "'Tis the body that shineth beyond thee, yonder," said the Head. "I ask, shall I take thee also, for thee I would prefer," said the Warrior. "I would that nothing should take me but Christ, God's Son: give me Christ's guarantee thou wilt bring me back to my body," said the Head. "I will bring thee," said the Warrior. Then he returned to the banquet at Condail,[1] with the Head, and found Leinster drinking. "Hast brought a token with thee?" asked Murcad. "I have brought the Head of Donnbo," replied the Warrior. "Place it on yonder post," said Murcad. Then all the assembly knew it to be the Head

[1] Now Old Connal, Co. Kildare.

of Donnbo, and they all exclaimed: "Alas, for thee, O Donnbo, fair was thy countenance! Make melody for us to-night as thou'st made it for thy lord." He turned his face towards the wall of the house, that it might be in darkness, and he raised his *Dord Fiansa* on high, and it was sweeter than all music on the surface of the earth, so that all the assembly were wailing and sorrowing, through the mournfulness and tenderness of the melody."[1]

MUSIC IN THE IRISH-NORSE KINGDOM (p. 185).

The generosity of the Norse-Irish to the bards, which is extolled in the Irish Viking lay, extended to the minstrels. This is manifest from the following historical fact. About the year 1100, the Welsh, already distinguished in music, had their musical canon regulated by Irish harpers. Now, Griffith ap Conan[2] appealed for these instructors to King Olaf (or Aulaf), son of King Sitric, of Dublin. The Norse-Irish king, acceding to his request sent a number of eminent harpers, the chief of whom, Olar Gerdawwr, bore a Norse-Irish name as did each of the company, with the exception of Mathuloch Gwyddell—the Gael.

Irish airs were carried northward, and the late eminent Swedish harper, H. Sjöden, gave examples of several which have survived, with some variations—the "Cruiskeen lán" being one.

[1] O'Curry, "Manners and Customs," Vol. III., p. 311; translation slightly modified.

[2] "Welsh Archæology," Vol. III.

EARL GERALD THE POET (p. 208).

Here we have an excellent example of the fascination which Irish literature threw over high-natured invaders. The southern branch of the Fitz Geralds took the name of Fitz Maurice (from Maurice Fitz Gerald). The first Earl of Desmond (South Munster) obtained his title in 1329, and had some literary taste as an enemy called him "the rhymer," and suffered for it. Gerald, the fourth Earl, married a daughter of the Earl of Ormond, and became Lord Justice of Ireland in 1367. He was, therefore, a Palesman of the Pale. But his large and cultured mind passed the frontiers, and obtained a knowledge and a mastery of the language and literature of the ancient nation. In the Annals of the Four Masters, the note of his death bears tribute to his qualities : " Gearoitt, Earl of Desmond, a pleasant and courteous man, surpassed all the foreigners of Erinn and a multitude of the Gael in the knowledge and science of the Irish language, in poetry, and history, as well as in other learning." The Annals of Clonmacnóis give more detail, in the old translator's words : " The Lord Garett, Earle of Desmond, a noble-man of wonderful bountie, mirth, cheerfulness in conversation, charitable in his deeds, easy of access, a witty and ingenious composer of Irish poetry, and a learned and profound chronicler, and, in fine, one of the English nobilitie that had Irish learning and professors thereof in greatest reverence of all the English of Ireland, died penitently, after the receipt of the Sacraments of the Holy Church." He also composed some Norman poetry.

The specimen of his Irish poems which has been translated in this volume, as an example of the work of a bard of the Galls (or Foreigners) of Erinn, was obtained from the Dean of Lismore's Book (Edinburgh, 1862). This is a selection from the " Gaelic Commonplace Book " of James McGregor, Dean of Lismore, in the Perthshire Highlands, wherein James and Duncan, his brother, committed to writing, in phonetic form, 307 Gaelic poems. Many of these are by Irish bards, of which eight are Earl Gerald's. It was fortunate for Irish literature, that these fine old Highlanders rescued so many lays, which might otherwise have been lost. That Perth should retain what had disappeared from Kerry is one of those strange things which are occasionally found in connection with Irish literature.

But the Norman noble, the English King's Lord Justice and Earl, was not only an Irish bard. He was absorbed completely into the Irish nation, which ever absorbed and assimilated all worthy invaders, and he was promoted into the mythology of the Gael ! O'Donovan says : " Tradition still vividly remembers this Garrett : it is said that his spirit appears once in seven years on Lough Gur, where he had a castle." Hardiman gives the legend more fully, though he attaches it to the Great Earl, whose estates of 800,000 acres Elizabeth confiscated : " He is supposed," writes Hardiman, " by the country people, even to this day, to be bound to an enchanted pillar in Lough Gur, a lake nine miles south of Limerick. They report that, at the end of every seven years he may be seen riding on the lake, on an enchanted charger, and that, when his horse's shoes, which are of silver, are worn out, he will return to life and destroy the enemies of Ireland."

GREEN EYES, GRAY EYES (p. 309).

The Greek poets mention, at least, two colours in speaking of eyes : θεα κυάνῶπις and γλαυκῶπις, blue-eyed and green-eyed. But the latter epithet denotes a pale green, like the sea's tint, at times. The Latin poets use *niger*, black, and *cœruleus*, sea-green, or dark blue. In Gaelic there are two words representing green, one is *glas* meaning both the sea (archaic) and the colour : the other is *uaitne*. Both are used to describe the eyes in poems of praise.

I believe *glas* is employed to describe that colour seen in " Irish gray eyes "—" the grayest of all things blue, the bluest of all things gray." This belief is founded on the comparison of such eyes to sparkling dew. In " Fairy Mary Barry " the maiden's eyes are like dew on springing corn,—hence it may have a tint of green ; but in other verses dew alone is the term of comparison. Thus we have :

> " Do rioga rosg úr
> Is glaise ná drúcd."

> "Thy royal young eyes
> More gray than dew."

again :

> " A súile as glaise deallrad
> Ná 'n drúcd air maidin t-samraid."

> " Her eyes more grayly radiant
> Than dew on morning of summer."

But the second word for green, *uaitne*, is also used, without such reference, *e.g.*:

> "A stoirin an roisg uaitne."
>
> "O little treasure of the green eyes."

In this case the bard probably refers to a dark, velvety green which is sometimes noticeable in southern Irish eyes.

English poets do not venture to sing of green eyes, except as associated with jealousy. But Dante describes Beatrice's eyes as emeralds, and Longfellow quotes the commentator Lami, who wrote: "Erano i suoi occhi d'un turchino verdiccio, simile a quel del mare." "Her eyes were of a greenish hue, similar to that of the sea." In "The Spanish Gipsy" the poet quotes references to green eyes from Bohl de Faber:

> "Ay, ojuelos verdes
> *   *   *   *
> Tengo confianza
> De mis ojos verdes."

This characteristic may yield some support to the Milesian claim of Spanish ancestry.

EIVLEEN A RUIN (p. 237).

Professor Blackie in 1867 directed attention to the cultivation of the ancient Celtic language in Ireland. He rebuked the learned men of Ireland and of Britain for their shameless neglect of a noble and historic tongue which had attracted the attention and merited the earnest work of the best philologists of the Continent. "Welshmen of every class," he said, "cultivate their language with assiduity. Some of the brilliant names in English literature are of Welshmen ; but, being profound English scholars, they are not the less profound Cymric." Having referred to the abundant products of the press in Wales, he proceeded : "When the Cambri-Briton leaves his barrens for fat and fertile England, or when he crosses the Atlantic to build himself a home on the St. Lawrence or the Mississippi, he carries his language with him, and clings to it with the same tenacity that he strives for wealth. Such feelings are the sureties of National Life. Yet we venture," he added, " to ask for a Welsh parallel to ' Eibhlin a Ruin.' "

> " Is breaga na Bénus tu,
> Is ailne na réultan tu,
> Mo Helen gan béim is tu
>   A Eibhlin a Ruin.
> Mo rós, mo lil, mo caer is tu,
> Mo stór a bfuil 's an tsaegal so tu,
> Run mo croide is mo cleib is tu
>   A Eibhlin a Ruin."

> " More beauteous than Venus, far,
> More fair than the midnight star,
> My Helen unstained you are,
>   Eivleen a Ruin.
> My red rose, my lily white,
> My treasure on earth so bright,
> Darling ! my heart's delight,
>   Eivleen a Ruin ! "

" The horrible materialism that asks ' where will Irish carry you when you cast loose from Dublin quays measures everything by money value or mechanical utility, and contemptuously scouts every measure but its own."

THE MORNING POWER OF FAIRIES (pp. 239, 249, etc.).

The dawning hour seems the most favourable to spirit manifestations. This may be observed in the "Dawning of the Day," and in other poems. The belief in also well shown in an ancient legend, quoted by O'Curry:

Of a morning, Conn of the Hundred Battles fared at sunrise to the ramparts of the Royal Fort at Tara, accompanied by his three Druids, and his three bards; for he was wont daily to repair thither to watch the firmament, so that no hostile aerial beings should descend upon Erinn, unknown to him. While standing in his wonted place, this morning, Conn trod upon a stone, and immediately it shrieked beneath his feet, so that it could be heard all over Tara and throughout all Bregia. His Druids, after many days, discovered and told him on the same spot that this was the Lia Fail—the Stone of Fail (whence Innis-fail)—the number of its shrieks told the number of kings of his race who should succeed him on the throne.

Conn stood musing on the revelation, when suddenly a mist arose and inclosed them in such darkness, that they could not see each other. Then, in the deep silence, they heard the tramp of a Cavalier approach, and thrice a spear was cast rapidly towards them, coming each time closer. The Druid cried aloud in protest: "it is a viola-

tion of the sacred person of a King to cast at Conn in
Tara." The Cavalier disclosed himself, saluted the King,
and invited all to his mansion. There, on a noble plain,
they entered a royal court, and beheld a beautiful princess.
Before her was a silver vat full of red ale, a golden ladle,
and a golden cup. The Cavalier, assuming the seat at
the head of the table, bade all his guests be seated. The
princess presented Conn with the bare ribs of a giant ox
and giant boar, and the vessels of gold and silver   Then,
filling the cup from the ladle, she asked the Knight (who
was one who had returned from the Dead) to whom she
should give the cup. He answered "To Conn:" the
question was then repeated time after time, and the
Phantom-Prince named all the kings in succession who
should after Conn inherit the sovereignty of Tara.

FAIRY WINDS.

"The Irish held the belief," wrote O'Kearney, "that
the Red Wind of the Hills as they called the blasting
wind, against the influence of which they had a potent
charm, was caused by the rapid evolution of the fairies
through the air, while engaged in their battles."

Again: "There was another species of blast which
was supposed to destroy fruit and cereal crops as well as
having power to injure man and beast: this was caused
by the ashes of the Dead deposited in foreign countries,
returning on the breeze of summer to settle in the ancestral
place of burial, and whatever object came in contact with

this dust, in the course of its transit, suffered more or less injury."

It is surprising to find an ancient legend which so closely anticipates a recent medical theory touching the causation of Russian influenza by emanations from Chinese corpses.

FAIRY LULLABY (p. 344).

The tune to which these words are sung, is, says Petrie, a beautiful and a very ancient example of the *Suantraide* (or Slumber-music)—one of the three classes of music said to have been brought to Erinn by the Tuata Dé Dananns. He points out its strong affinity with the lullaby tunes of Hindostan and of Persia. Professor O'Curry referring to the Irish words, observes: "The preceding rare and remarkable poem contains more of authentic fairy fact and doctrine than, with some few exceptions, has been ever before published in Ireland. The incident here narrated was believed, at all times, to be of frequent occurrence. It was for the last sixteen hundred years at least, and is still as firmly believed as any fact in the history of this country that the Tuata Dé Dananns, after their overthrow by the Milesians, went to reside in their hills and ancient forts, or in their dwellings in lakes and rivers—that they were in possession of a mortal immortality—and that they had the power to carry off from this visible world, men and women in a living state but sometimes under the semblance of death. The

persons taken off were generally beautiful infants, wanted
for those in the hills who have no children, fine young
women before marriage, often on the day of marriage, for
the young men of the hills who had been invisibly feasting
on their growing beauties, perhaps from childhood;
young men for the languishing damsels of fairyland; fresh
well-looking nurses for their nurseries. The usual mode
of abduction was by throwing the object into a sudden
fit or trance, and substituting an old man or woman or
sickly child. Seemingly," he continues, "there was no
exchange. Sometimes apparent death and actual burial
took place, but people divined the invisible action. In
other cases, the person was whipt off the brink of a river,
lake, or the sea, by a gust of wind and was apparently
drowned and lost, but he had only been taken down
to some noble mansion and plain, over which the water
was but a transparent atmosphere." They could also
inflict punishment, and debility of body and mind on
objects of their hatred and jealousy; so, strong men were
stricken by the power of fairy women who were unable to
take them away.

The poem is supposedly sung by a mother who was
borne away to nurse a fairy's babe; she was snatched off
her palfrey and now, from within the ramparts of a fairy-
fort (or old rath) she sees a woman washing at a stream.
To her she appeals, whilst assiduously hushing the
fairy-babe to sleep. She relates her story, and reveals
how she may be delivered, whilst at the close of every
stanza she sings the lullaby more loudly to avert suspicion

from within the fort. Her husband was to bring a black-hafted skian, or knife; with this he should stab the first horse of the fairy cavalcade—(once a second stab undid the deed)—when passing out through the gate of the fort, on the morrow. Then the magic veil would fall, and she would become visible. The herbs at the gate, when pulled, prevented re-capture. She implored quick relief, for "fairy captives are redeemable within a year and a day, but after that they are lost for ever." Professor O'Curry gives some striking instances of the intense belief in fairy influences which came under his notice amongst Protestant and Catholic peasants in 1812 and 1818 in Clare. The most remarkable case, however, was that which gave cause for judicial interference in Tipperary, in the year 1895, when a respectable young farmer believed his wife had fallen a victim to the fairies, and kept night-watch by a fairy-fort or rath, duly prepared to deliver her after maltreating the supposed changeling.

Lullaby (p. 343).

Petrie considers the tune to which these words go as a beautiful nurse-tune of remote antiquity. He adds that the affinity with Eastern melody is not confined to the nurse-tunes of Ireland, but that it is "found in the ancient funeral *caoines* (dirges), as well as in the ploughman's tunes and other airs of occupation—airs simple indeed in construction, but always touching in expression;—and I cannot but consider it as an evidence of the early antiquity of such melodies in Ireland, and as an ethnological fact of much historical interest, not hitherto attended to."

Dr. Joyce wrote in reference to the verses: "These songs so far as I could learn, were many of them very similar in ideas, expression, and general character. The child was very generally soothed to sleep with the promise of a golden cradle, rocked by the wind on a fine sunny day, under the shade of trees, a combination of circumstances in perfect keeping with the poetical character of the Irish peasantry. The verses were always followed by the burthen 'Sho-heen sho' etc. and when sung by a good voice, the whole melody and song must have had a powerfully soothing effect." [1]

SMITH'S SONG (p. 348).

"'The Smith's Song,'" Petrie remarks, "has very evidently been suggested—like Handel's 'Harmonious Blacksmith'—by the measured time and varied notes of his hammers striking upon the anvil; and its melody is therefore one of much interest as an ancient example of imitative music." O'Curry considers song and tune to be of great antiquity. He has always heard them sung by women to soothe and pacify a cross or crying child, without intending to put it to sleep; the nurse sang it with a swaying motion, to and fro, and from side to side, or marking the measure by rising on heel and toe alternately. It was also sung as a boy's play, where

[1] "Ancient Music of Ireland," p. 46.

each player took the name of a hammer, hand-sledge, and big sledge, whilst one sitting in a chair served as the anvil. The Irish words, given in the preceding pages, are taken from O'Daly's (not O'Curry's) version, and the English words are, in part, a substitution for the imperfect Irish original.

SPINNERS' SONGS (pp. 350-353).

The Gaels set their work to music. From the number of song-tunes of occupation extant, Petrie says, it seems certain there was no kind of labour to which song was not wedded. Bunting, speaking of Spinners' Song, or Luinnioch, describes it as a peculiar species of chaunt, having a well-marked time, and a frequently recurring chorus, or catchword. It is sung at merry-makings and assemblages of the young women, when they meet at 'spinnings" or "quiltings," and is accompanied by extemporaneous verses of which each singer successively furnishes a line, "the intervention of the chorus, after each line, gives time for the preparation of the succeeding one by the next singer." "The airs themselves have all the appearance of antiquity."

Professor O'Curry observes that it has been and was, when he wrote, the custom of peasant girls, when engaged in preparing wool or flax, to assemble. Sometimes the daughters of the house, and some helpers, sometimes the girls of two or three neighbouring families formed the group. They sang whilst they worked. Now, each sang in turn a popular song; again, and more frequently, two sang alternately extemporaneous verses to peculiar airs, reserved for this kind of song. One girl starts the song by saying she had wandered in the wood ; her comrade supplies a motive, and with quiet irony suggests a name which she knows will be rejected, whilst she affects to commend its owner. The jest goes on, until a favourite is found, when a benison is pronounced. Then the rôles are reversed, and the comrade, beginning, gives an opportunity to the other to compliment and quiz, in her turn, "and thus, the song, the wit, and the fun go on, among the girls, two at a time, until they have all played their parts, to their own great pleasure, as well as to the pleasure or displeasure of the group of young men, who are present—generally at night work—according as they find themselves accepted or rejected by their laughing tormentors."[1]

Such amusements speak of quick wit and intelligence among the peasant-girls who could improvise so readily in their native language.

PLOUGHMAN'S RIME (p. 349).

Dr. Petrie says : "Amongst the numerous classes of melodies which a people so music-loving as the Irish invented to lighten the labour and beguile the hours devoted to their various occupations, there is perhaps no one of higher interest and certainly no one that I have

---

[1] O'Curry, in Petrie's "Ancient Music of Ireland," p. 84. Dublin: Gill, 1855.

listened to with a deeper emotion than that class of simple, wild and solemn strains which the ploughman whistles in the field, to soothe or excite the spirit of the toiling animals he guides. The accompanying songs of the birds are scarcely so pregnant with sentiment, so touching to a sensitive human soul: and it would be difficult, if not impossible, for a mind not closed to the sense of beauty, to hear such strains without feeling a glow of admiration for the character of a people amongst whom, whatever may have been the faults engendered by untoward circumstances, the primæval susceptibility to the impressions of melody was yet, despite of all destructive influences, so generally retained, and which susceptibility has preserved to us so many indigenous airs, which in their fitness for the purposes for which they were employed, no mere intellectual art could rival."

The " Fead an Oirim," or " Whistle of the Ploughman " should be heard in the quiet twilight glen, in order that its strange sweet pathos may be fully felt. Both Bunting and Petrie agree that such airs belong to the most ancient class ; the latter believes them to have come with the race who introduced the plough. That period was remote, as plough-coulters and sochs of stone are mentioned. The air, to which the ploughman's rime is attached, is peculiar in so far that words are sung with it. This and the words were supplied by Professor O'Curry. He states that, even in his own youth, it was customary to plough with four or six horses. Three men were engaged, one, the ploughman, held the handles, another, "the driver," guided the horses, whilst the "third man," with a forked stick, pressed upon the beam. To the first half of the air they sang "hóbó, hóbobobó" to encourage the horses; to the second half the words given. The ploughman led off by addressing the driver, the third man responded at the close; all merrily repeated the last lines, as a chorus, in unison."

"Sirim dom hilluag mo saethir
A lenmain alt cen dichill
Cin neimnitnecht nacrad
Ocus atrab nid richjth."

BOOK OF DIMNA, A.D. 620.

"Would I might have as wages,
For work these pages given,
Freedom from critic's scorning
And morning peace in heaven."

TRANSLATION, 1897.

CHISWICK PRESS:—CHARLES WHITTINGHAM AND CO.
TOOKS COURT, CHANCERY LANE, LONDON.

www.ingramcontent.com/pod-product-compliance
Lightning Source LLC
Chambersburg PA
CBHW022009110726
47901CB00006B/1454